D0394480

RIDING

HIGH

How I Kissed
SoulCycle Goodbye,
Co-Founded FLYWHEEL,
and Built the Life
I Always Wanted

Ruth Zukerman

St. Martin's Press
New York

This is a work of nonfiction. However, the author has changed the identi-
fying characteristics of certain individuals and the dialogue has been reconstructed to the best of the author's recollection.

RIDING HIGH. Copyright © 2018 by Ruth Zukerman. All rights reserved.
Printed in the United States of America. For information, address St.
Martin's Press, 175 Fifth Avenue, New York, N.Y. 10010.

www.stmartins.com

Library of Congress Cataloging-in-Publication Data

Names: Zukerman, Ruth, author.
Title: Riding high : how I kissed Soulcycle goodbye, co-founded Flywheel,
    and built the life I always wanted / Ruth Zukerman.
Description: First edition. | New York : St. Martin's Press, 2018.
Identifiers: LCCN 2017023622| ISBN 9781250127587 (hardcover) |
    ISBN 9781250149718 (ebook)
Subjects: LCSH: Zukerman, Ruth. | Physical fitness centers—United
    States. | Businesswomen—United States—Biography. | Spinning
    (Trademark)
Classification: LCC GV429.A2 Z85 2017 | DDC 796.06/9—dc23
LC record available at https://lccn.loc.gov/2017023622

Our books may be purchased in bulk for promotional, educational, or business use. Please contact your local bookseller or the Macmillan Corporate
and Premium Sales Department at 1-800-221-7945, extension 5442, or by
email at MacmillanSpecialMarkets@macmillan.com.

First Edition: October 2018

10 9 8 7 6 5 4 3 2 1

To my daughters, Rachel and Kate . . .
for the unconditional love that we share and your ability to
always make me laugh, no matter what

Contents

Acknowledgments

I have to thank my co-writer, Holly Robinson, first and foremost. Without her talent and expertise, I wouldn't have been able to organize, add on, delete, and shape my story into something worth reading. She understood who I was very quickly into the process. She also was there to encourage me during the many phases when fear kicked in and I honestly didn't know if I had enough courage to talk about my life's path in the only way I knew how . . . with complete honesty.

I have so many supportive friends who have also encouraged me over the years to write a book. But it was Clifford Ross who actually insisted on it. He told me whom to see and wouldn't rest until I saw them! Clifford connected me with Peter and Amy Bernstein, now my literary agents. I met them at their apartment one evening, sat on their living room couch, and they said, "So let's hear your story . . ." I brought my Flywheel co-founder Jay Galluzzo with me so that he could fill in with things that I would undoubtedly forget. An hour and a half later we left, and before I got home there was a contract in my inbox.

Thank you, Peter and Amy, for believing in me.

Back to Jay . . . my former partner, my friend, and my Flywheel co-founder. We shared an office for four straight years and were probably communicating through some form or another during the rare parts of the day when we weren't in that office. I attribute so much of Flywheel's success to our constant collaboration and absolute love for what we, and our third co-founder, David Seldin, were creating. He took the good with the bad, tolerating my moments of complete frustration and tears, probably because there were so many more moments of joy and laughter. His concept of adding metrics to the bike was genius and clearly a huge part of our success. He protected me, supported me, encouraged me, and respected me always.

Thank you, David, for pushing me at times when I didn't have the confidence to push myself. I've learned a lot from you, especially when it comes to relentless negotiating skills! Your wisdom and confidence is something I will always admire. The three of us were really the perfect team.

I'll never forget our first meeting with the Frankforts. We had the whole family come take a ride followed by a meeting in our dingy Flywheel offices while the grandchildren played in the Flybarre room. Feeling Lew's energy and hearing his excitement over the brand that we created was exhilarating. Thank you, Lew, for believing in us. It was that moment when I felt that we really created something important, and with you on our team, we could continue to introduce and spread Flywheel's empowering energy to more and more people nationally, as well as globally.

This book would not be possible if it weren't for all of my incredible riders with whom I have sweated through every pedal stroke. To those who have stuck with me since my Reebok/Zone/SoulCycle days, to all of the incredible people that I met at Flywheel—your energy and shared stories have inspired ME and kept me going every single day that I get on that bike . . . even when I'm not in the mood. The transformation miraculously happens every time, and you are a big reason for that.

To my Dad, who left me way too soon. Thank you for teaching me how to be everyone's "best audience." Your sense of humor conditioned me to be able to laugh through so much of my life and find humor in everything. Your expert status in your field as a physician taught me to strive to be the best. To my Mom, who was never easy(!), I know that your love for me was always there. You were a career woman at a time when most moms weren't, and I know that influenced me greatly. I also thank you for both influencing my style and instilling the importance of grace and class. That was all you.

If I hadn't tried my first spin class at Reebok, I never would have met Philippe Reines. I will always have a place in my heart for you. Four years after I started to really dig deep into my therapeutic process, I met you because I decided to try that Reebok spin class. As my relationship with you and spinning grew simultaneously I was able to muster up the strength to make a drastic move in my life. You set me up for success when I felt like a fish out of water. I can never thank you enough for teaching me everything from how to work a computer to how to enjoy life.

And lastly, I have to mention my daughters, Kate and Rachel. It is now twenty-one years since we have been a threesome. We never had to close a bathroom door in our home and it was pretty hard to have any secrets, for good or for bad. As you have grown into adults and are venturing out on your own, our bond just gets deeper. I have been able to seek out your advice, ask for your opinions, be your best friends, and still be your mother. I thank you for your love and support and your fierce loyalty. Kate—your ability to advocate for and express yourself with complete abandon is always impressive. Rachel—your sensitivity and incredible insights always blow me away. Despite all of the differences between you two, your senses of humor alone will always keep me going . . . and laughing to the point of crying.

Prologue

In February 2010, after nearly four months of intense collaboration and many sleepless nights, my dream had finally come true: my two partners and I opened our flagship Flywheel studio in the Flatiron district, in Manhattan. By October, Flywheel was off the ground and running. I couldn't have been happier. All three of us were thrilled with our concept and our rapidly growing business. We couldn't wait to get to work every single day and never minded putting in long hours.

One rare evening off, I decided to go out with my friend Josh to see *The Social Network*, which had just been released. The buzz around the film was off the charts. Josh and I are avid cinephiles, and we were eager to share the excitement of opening weekend together. We arrived early and, popcorn in hand, settled happily into our prime, center-row seats.

Prior to seeing the movie, I hadn't known many details about the founding of Facebook and how it had taken off as a business.

Now I was riveted by the story of co-founders Eduardo Saverin and Mark Zuckerberg. As the tangled, emotional story unfolded on-screen, my heart began pounding and I couldn't help but reflect on how every successful business is a personal story, too, about hopes and disappointments.

Watching the tale of Facebook's creation play out in that darkened movie theater prompted me to begin reliving my own experiences as co-founder of SoulCycle and Flywheel. I think that's the moment I first started thinking about the book I might write one day.

My path to success definitely wasn't an easy one. It was a journey with many low points, all of which I share here, including low self-esteem, nightmare scandals, and financial troubles. Along the way, I learned that it takes time and experience to truly know ourselves, our potential, what makes us happy, and how to achieve balance and contentment in life.

When I gave up my lifelong passion to be a professional dancer, I never imagined I'd be able to replace it with something that was just as important to me. Nor did I ever dream of the hurdles ahead and the strength it would take to conquer them. By sharing my story and the lessons I've learned, I hope to inspire you to find your true path, whatever that may be, and embrace it as a way of helping you succeed in life, love, and a career that inspires passion and feeds your soul.

Life wasn't meant for coasting. I hope this book inspires you to ride hard and have fun along the way.

PART I

REINVENTION

1

Follow Your Impossible Dream

I took a deep breath, squared my shoulders, and tried not to tremble as I looked the judge in the eye. *You can do this, Ruth,* I reminded myself. *It's time you stood up for yourself.*

For months, my lawyers had been negotiating with my husband Jeff's attorneys to hammer out a divorce agreement. Yet, despite the many hours and dollars spent, he and I still couldn't agree on crucial points, such as summer custodial arrangements for our children, alimony, and child support.

Now we were all gathered in a conference room with a judge. It was my turn to speak up and tell the judge what I needed. Since I had given up working when the children were born and Jeff was a successful attorney from a wealthy family, I was hoping to convince the judge to grant me enough financial support so I could stay home with our girls for a few more years.

My twin daughters, only six years old at that point, were everything to me. I had been completely committed to being the best stay-at-home mom possible. I wouldn't realize this until much later, but focusing on the children was my way of shutting out everything else that was going wrong with my life.

As I described my situation, I tried to speak confidently despite the tremor in my voice. The judge was an older woman, so I felt optimistic that she would understand my plight and give me some leeway.

I was wrong. The judge simply shook her head when I finished speaking, as Jeff and his lawyers glared at me. I wouldn't be getting any increase in child support, she told me, and I would have to go out and get a job.

I summoned the courage to reason with her. Perhaps she didn't fully understand. I wasn't asking for a great deal of extra child support or alimony, simply enough to allow me to continue maintaining a home for the girls so their lives would remain as stable and happy as possible. "Your Honor, I really don't have a lot of options," I said. "My only work experience at this point is teaching fitness classes, and the pay in that field is really not substantial at all. I don't see how I'm going to be able to support myself and the girls."

"Why don't you become a real estate broker?" Jeff suggested from across the table.

"Because I don't *want* to be a real estate broker!" I shot back. He knew that would be about the last thing I'd ever want to do. I realized that Jeff was trying to needle me because he was furious, but understanding his anger did nothing to lessen my own.

Between the ages of eight and twenty-two, I had followed my dream and trained as a dancer. When that didn't work out, raising our children became my next reason for being. My whole life had been about two things: wanting to find work that brought me joy, and devoting myself to motherhood. This next chapter now loomed before me like a black, uncharted sea. No matter how hard I tried, I couldn't picture the future.

However, I knew I was beaten. I could see from my own lawyers' faces that this judge wasn't going to budge an inch. I had no choice but to move forward. So what next?

The road to my divorce didn't truly begin until 1992, when I went to see a psychotherapist for the first time. By then I had been married for eight years. I wasn't especially happy in my relationship with Jeff. Ironically, however, I didn't seek out a therapist because my marriage was in trouble, but because my beloved father was dying and I was having trouble coping with the thought of losing him forever.

I realize now how odd it must seem that I never sought out any sort of counseling before that point, since my own mother was a therapist. But I suppose that's actually why I never looked for anyone else to help me understand my problems: my mother was always quick to offer her opinions on how I should live. I had spent much of my childhood feeling completely reliant on her. Why would I need a therapist?

It wasn't until my father was in the last stages of cancer and my mother was consumed by her own complicated cocktail of grief and anger that I realized I needed to seek emotional support elsewhere to help me handle the loss. I was thirty-four years old at the time and feeling overwhelmed by the nonstop demands of my twin toddlers and my husband.

"My father has always been the light of my life," I told the therapist during that first session, choking up as I tried to describe our relationship.

Dad had curly dark blonde hair, hazel eyes, and a slight paunch because he loved to eat. He was hilarious, and always described me as his "best audience." He had no trouble laughing at his own jokes; no matter how dumb they were, I'd collapse in giggles, too.

I loved it that my father wasn't afraid to make a fool of himself or break the rules. Once, when I was about twelve years old, he drove me to dance class. It was pouring rain and there was a broad, raised walkway to the studio's front door. As I was trying to figure out how to run from the car to the studio without getting drenched, my father suddenly drove the car right up the curb and onto the walkway, straight to the front door.

"Daaaaad!" I shrieked, but all he did was laugh. What choice did I have but to giggle and throw my arms around his neck when he delivered me right to the door of the dance studio, like my knight in shining armor?

It often felt like he and I had our own secret club, because we had experiences we shared with each other and nobody else. One of my favorites was our annual trip to Chinatown, where Dad and I always went to the Nam Wah Tea Parlor. He drove a boat of a car, a Lincoln Continental. Yet, without hesitation, Dad would make the turn onto Doyers Street and maneuver that huge rig along the winding, narrow road.

Every time, I'd yell, "Dad, we're going to drive on the curb!" Sometimes we did. But we always made it to the restaurant, where we had our regular booth with its cracked red vinyl upholstery and yellow stuffing protruding through the cracks. The waiters would wheel carts past us, and we'd point at what looked good and eat an impressive amount of food. When we couldn't possibly swallow another bite, we were left staring at the stacks of small, oval, mismatched plates that the waiter would count in order to calculate the check. We always marveled at how much the two of us could consume in one sitting.

People often ask who my role models are in business. I used to say I didn't have any. My father was a physician and all of his friends were, too. Despite growing up on Long Island, I never knew any hedge fund managers, bankers, or CEOs. What did I ever learn about business as a young girl?

Yet, when I reflect back on my father's passionate enthusiasm for his work, I realize that he was probably the first and most important role model I had. Dad grew up in a modest home in Brooklyn, yet he put himself through Brooklyn College and was so determined to become a doctor that he made it through medical school with flying colors. Eventually, he became a clinical professor of medicine at the State University of New York at Stony Brook, and he spent his career at both Long Island Jewish Hospital—my brothers were the first twins born there—and at the North Shore University Hospital in Manhasset, where my father was chief of gastroenterology.

He was a gifted physician, devoted to his patients, and a medical school professor who loved to teach. He was a clinician as well, and through extensive research he wrote a landmark paper on Crohn's disease. Despite being diagnosed with bladder cancer at the age of fifty-seven—I was still in college—my father had an unyielding optimism and a love of life. I'm convinced it was that optimism that kept him alive through two remissions and another thirteen years.

Consequently, I grew up with a profound sense of how essential—and wonderful—it is to love your work. I longed to find a career that offered me the same deep sense of satisfaction and joy that my father obviously found in his.

As I explained to the therapist during that first session, my mother provided a lifelong role model for me as well, but ours was a more complex relationship. Today, a portrait of her hangs on the designated "family wall" of my New York City apartment. The picture was taken in a studio founded by Louis Fabian Bachrach, Jr., one of the most prominent portrait photographers of the time. Bachrach is perhaps most famous for his portrait of President John F. Kennedy, taken when Kennedy was a senator and used as his official presidential photograph.

Mom grew up in a Jewish family in Washington Heights in Manhattan. She excelled in school and was admitted to Smith College when she was only sixteen. There, my young and impressionable mother was surrounded by many privileged young women whose cultural backgrounds were vastly different from hers, and she worked hard to acquire that same veneer of sophistication. Even then, my mother understood something about branding, as she sought to build an identity that would immediately communicate class and elegance to anyone who met her. Having her portrait taken at Bachrach studios was just one example of how she created and sustained this polished image.

In this portrait of my mother, she is wearing a suit with a small check and padded shoulders. Seated with her wrists crossed, holding a pair of wrist-length, white kid leather gloves, she looks perfect: all-knowing, strong, and definitely in control.

My close friend Jeff, an actor with an incredible sense of humor, comes over to my apartment once in a while, and whenever I'm sharing a particular challenge with him, he will sit and listen. Then he will stand up and, in complete silence, simply point to the picture of my mother and stare at me with an unwavering, deadpan, yet somehow terrifying expression. It makes me laugh every time.

I'm not sure why the laughter bubbles up. It's true that my mother adored me, but she wasn't an easy woman. In hindsight, I can see that she was narcissistic and often domineering. My father avoided conflict with her and did whatever it took to carve out time for himself at home. He used to hide out in the bathroom—always a gastroenterologist's favorite room—with a stack of crossword puzzle books. Sometimes he even pretended to be asleep while my mother was talking. Now I understand how this must have annoyed her, and in fact showed a lack of respect, but as a child, I could only see the humor. The reality was that pretending to sleep was a perfect escape for my father, who avoided confrontations of any kind with my mother. This was his way of coping. Little did I know that I was absorbing this coping mechanism as my own.

. . .

Because my twin brothers were active boys who were "always running in opposite directions," as my mother put it, she was at her wit's end trying to manage them. My parents were both thrilled to have a daughter when I was born.

Instinctively, I adopted the role of the "good girl." I learned early on that as long as I pleased my mother I could bask in a certain warmth and genuine love that she seemed to reserve especially for me. That meant I was a well-behaved child who did whatever I could to earn her approval. When Mom was happy, I was happy.

Because I adored my mother, I did everything possible to please her. When I got older, for instance, on weekends I would sneak into my mother's room to make her bed so that she wouldn't have to do it, knowing how happy this would make her. I did whatever I could to avoid her criticism, which she doled out as readily as she offered praise. I loved her with everything I had and spent as much time as possible with her, even if it was only to run errands, get groceries, see the "shoe man" who repaired her prized Ferragamo footwear, or sit beside her in the hair salon.

My mother kept the same hairstyle for her entire adult life, and it was always perfectly in place. As she aged, it turned a beautiful silvery gray, and she never considered coloring it, a fact she was proud to share with anyone who asked. Often, people would tell her that her hairstyle made her look like the actress Olympia Dukakis. That didn't thrill her. I don't think she wanted to be compared to anyone.

Mom also never saw the need for pedicures or manicures

except for special occasions, like my brothers' bar mitzvah and my wedding. She far preferred to tend to her nails herself, and frequently told me that she was horrified by the thought of anyone touching her feet. Whenever I happen to glance at my own natural hairstyle and unpolished fingernails, I think of her.

In the early seventies, my mother would occasionally throw elegant dinner parties at our house. She hired my best friend, Sandy, and me to be servers, specifically during the cocktail hour. Maxi-skirts were all the rage then, so Sandy and I decided these would be the perfect uniform for us at the party.

The only tough part of this gig was that I had to socialize with my parents' friends and I was pretty shy back then. Sandy helped share the burden, though, and we had our own laughs in the kitchen behind the scenes.

Dinner parties meant shrimp cocktail and a large crystal punch bowl filled with some kind of colorful, fruity champagne concoction with orange slices floating along the top. We got to indulge once the meal was served and we were "off duty."

Mom would bring in a chef to do the cooking. Beef Wellington was always a favorite entrée for these occasions. My mother loved being the Queen and the hostess; my brother used to say that she intentionally chose women friends who were unattractive, so that she could get the lion's share of attention from the men.

For the most part this was true, except for her friend Joan. Joan's husband was the chief of surgery at Long Island Jewish Hospital, so she was pretty much all that. She and her husband were wealthy, and Joan had the clothes to prove it. She wore only the top designers and I was always excited to see her, not only because I was anticipating what she might wear to the party, but because I was also eager to see Mom's reaction.

Sure enough, my mother would always have some negative things to say about Joan during the party recap that took place the next morning. "That Joan is such a phony!" my mom would often exclaim. "She always needs to be the center of attention!"

Dad and I would glance at each other, and I knew we were thinking exactly the same thing: Mom hated to share the spotlight!

Still, I am grateful to have acquired my mother's love of fashion. She had exquisite taste. As a child, I always got excited whenever she dressed up for an evening out with Dad, especially for hospital dances. My father was highly revered at the hospital where he worked, and Mom loved being his wife for that reason. She was good at looking and playing the part of a doctor's wife.

I loved watching my mother transform herself for those dances. Mom began this ritual at her vanity table in front of a makeup mirror. Still in her bathrobe, she would sit at this table, where I often played with her makeup when she wasn't using it, and begin applying foundation, eye shadow, mascara, and lipstick. She hardly ever wore makeup, but for big parties she made an exception.

Then she'd put on her jewelry—always elegant and understated—before adding the final touch, a spritz of perfume from the geometrically shaped glass atomizer that sat on her vanity tray. Now she was ready to get dressed.

Her clothes were classically tailored and free of unnecessary embellishments. One of my favorite dresses was her hot pink, double silk dress by the designer Donald Brooks. It was knee-length and perfectly simple, with a jewel neckline and long sleeves gathered into narrow wrist bands. I thought she looked beautiful in it.

She also had a spectacular coat hanging in her closet, made of seal fur. The coat smelled like her perfume (Joy) and was the softest thing I had ever touched. I would sometimes run it slowly across my cheek as I sat in her closet. The dark mahogany fur over that hot pink silk dress was perfection, at least to my girlish fashionista self.

The morning after the party, I'd wake up hardly able to conceal my excitement and impatience. I couldn't wait to hear all about it, especially what everyone had worn, right down to the tiniest details. My mother would patiently go through the dresses of every one of her friends and describe them to me. There were always one or two that fell under the "risqué" category, and I especially loved hearing about which of her friends had worn the "see-through dress" or any other garment that met with Mom's disapproval.

My mother loved shoes as much as she adored dresses. Her favorite pairs were organized by color and season and stored in their boxes. Sometimes we would take the train together to "the city," which is what we called Manhattan, and go to Saks Fifth Avenue to see her regular shoe salesman, Mr. Terry. He was short, a bit squat, and mustached. He always greeted my mother as if she were royalty, which made me feel special, too.

On one of these shopping excursions to New York City, my mother was wearing a smart suit designed by Anne Klein.

We went to a fancy restaurant for lunch and she happened to spot Calvin Klein, who was just starting his own fashion line. Mom saw him check out her outfit and whisper to his dining companion, "That's Anne's." My mother and I never forgot that heady moment of fashion glory.

By the time I was thirteen, another of the things we wholly enjoyed together was watching soap operas after school. *Another World* was one of our favorites; I was fascinated by the colorful, dramatic lives of the characters, and their lives became an important part of mine. The intrigue and suspense, the evil doings and romances fascinated me. While my mother would sometimes poke fun at the level of drama in these shows, I took the plots seriously—and was always stunned when she could predict what was going to happen next based on foreshadowing.

For instance, in a scene where a character fell off a ladder and suddenly started experiencing headaches, my mother immediately nailed the diagnosis: "Brain tumor!" I hadn't caught on yet that brain tumors were handy plot devices leading to hospital scenes with patients in bed, bandages wrapped around their heads and breathing tubes in place. As far as I was concerned, Mom knew everything.

We also bonded over my English homework. My mother was smart; she attended Smith College as an undergrad, but ultimately earned her undergraduate degree and MSW from Hunter College. Her brother once told me that she was forced to leave Smith when there were financial problems at home; this was something she never would have discussed with me or my brothers, and I only learned of it after her death.

Mom never would have wanted to tarnish that elite image she had worked so hard to cultivate. In fact, the one story she ever told me that didn't fit into the elegant persona she had created for herself was about the time she was coming home from Smith for a holiday break and her father met her at Penn Station, so drunk he could hardly stand up. Mom told me that she was absolutely mortified when he showed up at the train station, especially because she was with friends.

Her father was a paper salesman, and when I was a child he would bring me books of paper samples of the most beautiful textures and colors. I created all kinds of arts and crafts projects with them for hours. Sadly, whenever my mother talked about him, she compared him to the Willy Loman character in *Death of a Salesman*. That's all I ever really knew about my grandfather. I can only imagine all of the other stories she never shared.

Mom eventually had her own part-time psychotherapy practice and always made time to help me analyze the books I was reading and write papers about them. She was a wonderful reader and editor; as a result, writing became one of my strong points.

Even as a teenager, I continued to do all I could to earn my mother's approval. This wasn't easy. She was extremely judgmental of women who fell short of her impossibly high standards. Once, for instance, I was standing with her in a cashier's line at the grocery store. We were waiting behind another woman, the mother of one of my classmates, who was dressed in formfitting pants. As we left the store, Mom said, "That woman wasn't wearing any underwear. That's disgusting!"

"Disgusting" seemed to be one of her favorite words, even when describing her own body as it started to show her age. Because of my mother's sharp eye for fashion, I loved shopping with her, but at times I felt uncomfortable. As my body matured, she often made comments when I was trying on clothes, saying, "I wish I looked like that" or "My body is so old and disgusting now, I can't stand the sight of it."

I understand now that my mother probably felt competitive with me and resented my close relationship with my father. Because I adored him so, this was the one area of my life where I dared to defy my mother. Even as a child, I cultivated opportunities to share things with my father that left my mother out, like our love of music. In the fourth grade, I took up the flute and played it through high school. I thought it was so cool that my flute teacher, Mr. Harris, was in the orchestra of the New York City Ballet. Every time I attended a New York City Ballet performance, I would head straight down to the wall overlooking the orchestra pit and wave to him.

My father and I would often duet, me on flute and him on the piano. Even when we weren't playing, Dad always had music in the house. Classical, show tunes, and the Big Band sounds of Tommy Dorsey, Louis Armstrong, and Frank Sinatra were some of his favorites.

Dad and I also shared books and ideas in ways that never interested my mother. Although she had been the one to help me research, organize, and write my high school papers, my father was an avid reader and the real intellectual in the family. He had always loved reading literature—anything from Shakespeare to plays by George Bernard Shaw—and philosophy in particular. Once I started college, he would ask what books I was reading in my philosophy and religion courses, so that he could read the same texts. We then spent hours discussing them on the phone.

My mother was also jealous of anyone else I was close to, like my ballet teachers. I remember shopping with her once when I was about fifteen and running into a teacher we called "Miss Lynn," a professional dancer who had taught my ballet classes when I first started dancing in elementary school. When I was younger, Miss Lynn was like a rock star to me: an attractive woman whose career had brought her as far as Broadway, where she became a "gypsy"—a term used for Broadway dancers who traveled from show to show.

That particular day, Miss Lynn was standing on a pedestal in the middle of the store as we walked by, having a dress altered. I said, "Oh my God, Miss Lynn, hi! It's so good to see you!" and gave her a big hug.

"Hello, Lynn," my mother greeted her. Then she patted my former teacher on the stomach and said, "Oh, I see you've put on a little."

I cringed and walked away, knowing how that kind of comment could wound any woman, but especially a woman whose career was in dance. We dancers, for better or worse, are always acutely aware of our bodies. How we feel about ourselves is usually wrapped up in how we believe our bodies look to others.

While my father was modeling the importance of doing work that you feel passionate about and being able to communicate that passion to others through teaching, my mother was modeling other, contradictory lessons: that I should excel academically, yes, but that my primary responsibility was to cultivate my appearance and convey a certain level of class. That would be my most important asset when it came to attracting the "right" sorts of friends and, eventually, a husband who would provide for me financially while I raised our family. Ultimately, both of these role models led me to follow my dreams, though not quite in the way I would have expected.

In her ongoing campaign to ensure that I was physically attractive, my mother signed me up for ballet lessons when I was eight years old, "because you're getting a little bit of a belly, Ruth." She also was concerned that my posture needed improvement.

Ouch, right? However, Mom's decision to enroll me in dance classes was one that I will always be grateful for, not only because it ultimately led me to the career of my dreams, but because, right from the start, I loved everything about dance: the discipline, the music, the leotards, the rigorous athleticism. Most of all, I loved how dancing made me forget everything else, whether I was in the studio or on stage.

Of course, there was a parallel here that I didn't see at the time. My need to strive for perfection in dance—an impossible goal, since there is always room for improvement—mirrored my attempts to meet the expectations of my mother, who never thought I was good enough and always found something to criticize. At least when I was actually dancing, the rest of the world faded away, and the movement brought me some relief from striving so consciously to be the best at everything.

My passion for dance—and, later, choreography—stemmed from my love of music. I had been learning about classical composers like Chopin, Mozart, Bach, and Beethoven both in dance class and as a flute player. At the same time, one of my brothers began introducing me to contemporary bands. My collection of albums grew rapidly as I explored Herman's Hermits, the Beatles, and the Who. Every Friday night, my father would take my brothers and me to the record department of Korvette's, where we were each allowed to choose one 45 rpm record to buy. I still remember that they cost sixty-nine cents.

I would sit in my room for hours, learning the lyrics to every song as I watched record after record drop down onto the automatic turntable. Music opened up other worlds for me. I got through the sixties and seventies listening to the Beatles, the Rolling Stones, James Taylor, Carole King, Joni Mitchell, and Led Zeppelin. Music took me through my heartbreaks and helped me channel my inner rock star. These artists and their songs helped me identify and unlock my feelings of sadness, isolation, and depression, although I wouldn't really understand and learn to cope with these emotions until later in life.

My bedroom, about twelve by twelve feet, had always seemed like a safe haven. It had an alcove for my bed that made me feel like I was in a private sanctuary, especially because the linens were in bright green and yellow—my favorite colors back then—with a cheerful daisy pattern. Surrounded by my favorite things—dolls, stuffed animals, posters, pretty dresses—I'd listen to music and shut everything and everyone out of my secret world.

Now, dance was a way for me to inhabit music more fully. I let it flow through my body as I learned how to move with it and express my emotions—even the ones I didn't fully understand, and certainly wouldn't have felt comfortable sharing with my family even if I had. My parents encouraged and supported my new passion for dance by not only bringing me to classes but also taking me to Broadway shows. The innovative choreography of Bob Fosse was a huge influence on me—I especially loved *Dancin'*, *Pippin*, and *Chicago*. With lyrics and choreography that so openly exuded sex, they were a revelation to me.

Another of my favorite shows was Michael Bennett's *A Chorus Line*, with its story of dancers vying to make it on Broadway. One of the songs from that production, "At the Ballet," really resonated with me. The lyrics express how the dancer started taking ballet classes because everything seemed so beautiful at the ballet, no matter what else was going on in her life. I felt exactly the same. Whenever I watched dancers move across a stage, I felt transported. I literally couldn't sit still, because my body would physically respond to their movements. And whenever I was actually dancing, I was fully engaged in the moment.

By age thirteen, even though I knew I wasn't the most accomplished dancer in my ballet class, I still had dreams of being in *The Nutcracker*. Then another new door opened for me: my dance school added a jazz instructor that year, so I signed up for his class.

That's when I discovered where I truly belonged. I loved jazz dancing because there was so much more freedom of movement than in ballet. As I began mastering the new ways to move, jazz music unleashed a sensuality in me that I had previously kept tightly under wraps—especially whenever I was with my repressed, rigid mother, around whom I never felt comfortable talking about sex.

From that point on, jazz and modern dance allowed me to open up even more to music, and to express myself fully onstage in ways I wouldn't dare to do at home.

My high school years were frantically busy. I was an honors student, but I also spent countless hours taking dance classes and performing. I took the train from Manhasset into New York City nearly every day to study with the pros. I was pretty and fairly popular in school, where my biggest coup was making the varsity cheerleading squad when I was only a freshman. This was rare, and I had dance to thank for making it happen; because of my rigorous training, I could easily do all of the stunts.

By junior year, my days were split. I was attending a special dance school on Long Island and spending only half of every day at my regular high school. I was fortunate during this time to have some truly memorable teachers, like Helen McGehee, from Martha Graham's early company, and Bert Michaels, an original "Jet" from *West Side Story*, who would later go on to become a renowned choreographer and actor. When Bert came into one of my classes, he taught us "Cool," one of the most innovative pieces ever choreographed by

Jerome Robbins. That class still remains one of my life's high-lights because of the joy Bert demonstrated both in his dancing and in how he taught young students. After that, I was clearly able to see Jerome Robbins's influence on many subsequent dances by Michael Jackson and other famous dancers.

My dance teachers were powerful role models for me. At the time, I thought of them as people I could look up to in the world of dance. I realized only later that these teachers were also communicating other important lessons to me as well—lessons about persistence and resilience that I still rely on to this day whenever I'm facing a challenge. And, as I continued to perform in dance recitals and be exposed to these phenomenal people, my passion for physical movement to music was really taking hold.

Despite my many achievements at school and on the dance floor, my mother still wasn't satisfied with my accomplishments. She was alternately fearful for me and critical of me. For instance, when I took my driver's test and passed at age seventeen, I was ecstatic, but my mother could only react with concern.

"I don't want you driving on the highway," she pronounced. "It's too terrifying. Just promise me that you won't get on that highway, or you'll have an accident. I can't worry about that."

Naturally, I absorbed many of her fears, but I would pick and choose where I wanted to take risks. I actually did drive on the highway, much to her dismay, and only wish that was

Summer camp visiting day, 1968.   My parents

my biggest challenge. I also felt compelled to rebel behind my mother's back, even though I lived in fear of her wrath. I tried smoking pot at thirteen and routinely smoked cigarettes in the bathroom before taking a shower to eliminate the smell. But outwardly rebelling was never a possibility for me. I was too scared of her criticism and disapproval.

I maintained a 3.5 GPA in high school despite my frenzied schedule. However, I never tested well and bombed the PSAT—the preliminary college entrance exam. The test didn't actually count for much beyond determining which students would qualify for the National Merit Scholarship Program. Yet, when I shared the scores with my mother, she started screaming at me. Her terrifying tirade sent me running upstairs so fast that I tripped.

"I'm so embarrassed!" she shouted. "You'll never get into a good college now! What am I going to tell my friends?"

I tried talking to my father later about how hurt and humiliated I felt, but he refused to confront her. "Oh, you know your mother," he said, and faded into the background as he usually did to avoid conflict.

My mother signed me up for a special prep course to help me raise my test scores, and I added one more responsibility to my schedule.

Why do I bother sharing these things with you? Because one of the most important business lessons I've learned along the way is that many of us feel compelled to repeat our family relationships in the personal and professional partnerships we choose. It's wise to understand your own family dynamics when you're forming those partnerships. I should have paid closer attention to my relationships with my parents before choosing partners of my own—I might have protected myself better if I had.

As grueling as my schedule was in high school, dancing brought me so much joy that I was determined to continue in college. However, I also wanted a place where the academics would be challenging. Eventually I chose Mount Holyoke College in South Hadley, Massachusetts—an all-woman college rated among the top fifty liberal arts colleges in the country, and the sister school to my mother's alma mater, Smith.

At Mount Holyoke, I maintained a high grade point average despite my rigorous dance schedule. A local professional company even asked me to perform with them. One of my favorite solo pieces during college was set to a piece of intensely sexy classical music by the Argentine composer Alberto Ginastera.

I still treasure my dance teacher's comment about the way

I performed that intensely beautiful piece, because it described exactly how I felt: "Ruth, when you dance this on stage, you will burn a hole through the audience."

Despite my inherent shyness and lack of self-esteem, there was something about dancing to a piece of music that allowed me to enter an entirely different world. I could overcome my anxiety and move to the music without my usual feelings of doubt or self-consciousness. I loved the intensity and power of owning the stage in front of an audience and reveled in these opportunities to become whoever I wanted to be.

Naturally, having the mother I did, coupled with my choice to become a dancer, meant that I was extremely conscious of how my body looked. That's also a natural part of dancing professionally, where you can never be thin enough. This is especially true among ballerinas. Even with what felt like the thousands of calories I was burning each day with hours of dance practice, I tried to curb my appetite, at times practically living on diet soda and cigarettes, since my natural body type was not pencil-thin. At the time, my goal was an unhealthy one: I wanted to see the outline of my bones through my chest.

With dance, I felt confident that I'd found my life's passion. As graduation day approached, I told my parents that I wanted to move to New York City and become a professional dancer.

This was an ambitious goal—the dance scene in New York is possibly the most competitive in the world—but I was convinced that I had the talent and work ethic to pull it off. Besides, I had always wanted to live in the city. Here was my chance.

When my parents saw how determined I was to pursue what they perceived as an impossible dream, they weren't thrilled, but they agreed to help support my ambition by subsidizing my rent. In 1980, the summer after graduating with honors from Mount Holyoke, I found a sixth-floor walk-up apartment on the Upper West Side with a roommate who was working as a fashion writer for the *New York Post* and launched myself into big city life.

Throughout my first therapy session, the therapist quizzed me steadily about my parents and my childhood. After I had finished describing my childhood and my failed career as a dancer, she suddenly switched gears and asked about the state of my marriage.

"I don't know," I said. "I guess it's difficult sometimes, being married."

"Tell me a little more," she suggested. "What's it like, day to day, being married to Jeff?"

As I began describing our relationship, I found myself revealing deep-seated feelings of unhappiness with my marriage for the first time. Such a powerful combination of rage and sorrow coursed through my body that I had difficulty breathing.

Until this point in my life, I had believed my marriage was typical. I had been repressing my true feelings. Now, facing the imminent death of my father and my therapist's gentle probing, overwhelming emotions started bubbling to the surface.

That was the beginning of the end of my marriage. It was also the start of my reinvention, because the breakdown of my marriage forced me to resume my search for a career I could truly feel passionate about pursuing.

Lesson #1: Be Open. Role Models Are Everywhere

Recently, I received an email from one of our Flywheel instructors that made me realize I've reached a point in my life that I was striving toward all along—without knowing it. The instructor wrote to me before she left for China, where she will be a leader in expanding a new chain of boutique spinning studios.

"Thank you, Ruth, for being so understanding and supportive," she said. "I'll never forget my time at Flywheel. When times got hard it was always you and who you are and what you represent that kept me coming back. You have demonstrated outstanding leadership abilities and shown that you don't have to be hard on your employees to be effective. Kind, loving, supportive, but firm. I will certainly do my best to emulate these positive attributes in my own leadership roles to come."

This letter was incredibly gratifying to read. It reinforced the fact that I have reached a position of leadership in the

Dancing in a college performance, 1978

business world by doing things my own way, not by adopting a traditionally "male" style of leadership. Women are sometimes faulted for being "too empathetic," and even emotional, rather than confident and objective, but I have found that doing things thoughtfully and kindly has its own strengths. You can be effective with your employees, employers, and customers without sacrificing your warmth, generosity, or sense of humor.

People asked me for years who my business role models were. It took me a long time to realize that those at the top of my list had little or no business training themselves. In addition to my father, my dance teachers served as my earliest role models. They demonstrated a love of their careers and a profound joy in doing the day-to-day work of perfecting their craft. They were also endlessly, and creatively, reinventing themselves.

Once they left the stage, for example, my dance teachers didn't give up what they loved. Instead, they transferred that passion into nurturing new talent, and taught young dancers to be the next generation of performers. I remember one particular dance teacher in college, Hannah Wiley, who amazed me because she was gifted intellectually as well as on the dance floor. She showed me that to be a good choreographer you must be creative, mathematical, and architectural. She always pushed me to do my best, and yet she did it with a positive attitude and a keen sense of humor. I have emulated her teaching style as a spin instructor, while training other instructors, and as a business leader.

What's more, Hannah was a ballerina, and I was a modern dancer. She taught me how important it is for people in different genres to demonstrate a mutual respect when working together. That kind of appreciation for partners whose strengths are different from yours is an important quality in a business leader, too.

You may think you know nothing about doing business, and that's what's stopping you from progressing in your career. But inspiration is all around you. Think about the people you admire—your teachers, parents, friends, and colleagues—and list some of the qualities you admire about them. Ask yourself how you might develop those qualities, and how they might contribute toward your success as you pursue your goals, whatever they may be.

2

Let Failure
Be Your Best Teacher

To be an artist in New York City is to experience great highs and deep lows on very little sleep. At the age of twenty-two, I was confident about my ability as a dancer and felt comfortable onstage. I felt sure I could earn a place with a professional company.

Until then, I had to make enough money to keep myself going—a considerable amount, despite my father's help with the rent—so I took a part-time job at Teuscher, a high-end Swiss chocolate store in Rockefeller Center.

Although I had never worked in retail, the job was enjoyable. I liked chatting with people who came in to buy chocolates, often for special occasions. It was also my first opportunity to see the importance of providing—or perhaps more accurately, the perils of *not* providing—good customer service. The chocolates sold in the store were flown in weekly from Switzerland, and therefore ridiculously expensive—the store specialized in champagne truffles. But, because we were in Rockefeller Center, we often had tourists wandering in to ask for something more like chocolate-covered marshmallows. The owner was a real snob, though he wouldn't admit it; this sort of thing made him crazy. He would literally shoo the tourists out of his store, telling them to "go to Fanny Farmer."

Fortunately, I most often worked with the manager, Henry. I adored him. He was hilariously funny, often mocking the owner behind his back, but he was meticulous about his work. From Henry, I learned the importance of taking pride even in the simplest tasks, like the way the chocolates were displayed. Henry was my first and only friend whom I lost to the AIDS virus, a tragic loss, but certainly not unusual for that time.

During my free time, I trained hard, taking dance classes at the Clark Center on Eighth Avenue, Broadway Dance, the Ailey School, and Steps. I also searched for notices advertising auditions being held by modern dance companies around the city. I knew I'd be competing with the top dancers from around the world. But I'd had the benefit of attending a small, privileged women's college, one where my talent was nurtured by caring professors and instructors. As a result, I was naively optimistic.

"By this time next year, I'll be dancing professionally," I'd remind myself during tedious hours in the chocolate shop, or when I was schlepping on the subway from my apartment to work, then to dance class and back home during those long, exhausting days.

It wasn't until I showed up for my very first audition for a modern dance company that I realized this really was the big leagues. I was stunned to find myself surrounded by over a hundred dancers, all competing for a single opening. It literally felt like a cattle call.

It was immediately apparent that many of these dancers

were every bit as talented and experienced as I was, if not more so. There was absolutely no way for me to rehearse for the auditions, either. We were given choreography to learn on the spot, then expected to dance in groups of ten or so while the company director judged our skills and weeded us out—quickly, I might add. Sometimes I would make it down to the last ten, but that hardly mattered when they were only looking for one.

Suddenly, I was more nervous than I'd ever felt before. I didn't enjoy the auditions at all, and I wasn't surprised when I was cut.

Despite my anxiety, I continued attending every audition for modern dance and jazz companies I saw in the trade papers or found by scanning bulletin boards at the studios. I doubled down on my determination, vowing to work even harder in my classes so that I'd improve. I told myself that I would be less nervous with each audition I attended, too. It was just a matter of experience.

"I don't care if I have to do this for years," I thought, gritting my teeth after being rejected a second, third, and fourth time. "I'm going to make it."

As I continued pursuing auditions and taking classes, my social life started heating up. One afternoon, the most handsome man I had ever seen strolled into the chocolate shop. He was slightly older than I was, over six feet tall, and trim but muscular. With his classic looks, I decided he must be a model.

The stranger bought a few pieces of chocolate—expensive truffles—and I was so struck by his appearance that I could barely breathe as I rang up his purchase and passed the chocolates over to him. Henry and I looked at each other after the man left and let out deep, lusty sighs. Then we both laughed.

This man showed up in the chocolate store several more times, always buying just a few truffles. Eventually, I learned that his name was Alan, and that I'd guessed right: he was trying to carve out a modeling career in New York.

Then, one day, Alan called the store. Henry answered and held the phone out to me with a wicked grin. "Ruth, it's Alan. He wants to speak to you!"

I could barely hold the phone, I was trembling so hard, but when Alan asked me out to lunch, I managed to squeak out a yes.

Alan took me to Le Quercy, a little French restaurant in Midtown. I was shaking so much that I could barely meet his gaze or hold my spoon to eat the lobster bisque I'd ordered. I blamed my sudden, acute anxiety not only on the fact that Alan was so good-looking, but also on my lack of experience with men, other than one serious boyfriend in high school.

It wouldn't be until later on in my life, after many years of therapy, that I would become aware of the prevalence and consistent replaying of relationship triangles throughout my life. This pattern began in childhood. After all, with an on-going mutual adoration between my father and me, my mother often just served to get in the way, yet I was set up to always be the loser. She was his wife, and that wasn't changing any-time soon.

I played this pattern out time and time again. Ironically, this role was so familiar that it felt comfortable. No wonder I continued finding myself becoming one point of a triangular relationship over and over throughout my life.

One of the earliest examples of this dates back to senior year of high school. I had a crush on Jimmy, a tall, handsome classmate with beautiful blue eyes who had an even bigger crush on me. We dated quite a bit during our senior year, but something always prevented our relationship from progressing past a certain point.

Jimmy wasn't the best communicator, but I did know that there was another girl in the picture. The truth was that this triangle kind of worked for me. I was fully comfortable with my own sexual desires, and with my ability to attract others to me. But I was also saddled with a prudish mother who raised me to believe that sexually active girls suffered from a certain stigma. I never wanted to be "that" girl.

My biggest concern was senior prom. Would Jimmy and I go together? Or would he take Robin, the other girl? I won in the short term: Jimmy asked me to prom. I felt very happy and, more importantly, victorious. Robin, however, ended up with the bigger prize: she married him, after Jimmy and I lost touch in college. I always felt they were actually better suited for each other, though, so there were no sour grapes.

There were many more triangles to come in my life, but it would take me years to recognize the pattern.

My college years were devoted to studying and dance. The only college guys I ever encountered were at occasional fraternity parties at Amherst College, and I couldn't seem to relate to them at all.

Like me, Alan was trying to make it in a highly competitive field that attracted people from around the world. He had grown up in a modest New Jersey home and had never finished college; he drove a taxi to make extra money. Yet he had a sort of elevated air about him, exuding culture, confidence, and know-how.

Because I never could have imagined a man with Alan's stunning good looks being remotely interested in me, dating him shored up my confidence in auditions. It helped, too, that Alan was extremely supportive of my career, even coming to watch my dance classes occasionally.

While we dated, Alan and I went to countless parties together. He had lots of friends in the modeling world, so these gatherings were full of people so gorgeous they looked almost like another species. We also spent weekends at my parents' house in Old Westbury. My mother was nearly as enamored of Alan as I was. Meanwhile, Alan learned a great deal from my father about all sorts of subjects, especially wine and music. He absorbed it all, and I could see him blossoming and becoming even more sophisticated around my parents.

Alan and I went out for a year. During that time, it was lucky I had his support, because my confidence took one hit after another as I continued to be passed over at auditions in favor of more experienced and talented dancers, or dancers with a certain look.

Something else was starting to happen, too: I was beginning to have doubts about wanting to dance professionally. This wasn't only because breaking in was so difficult, but because I was beginning to realize that I didn't fit the mold. While it was true that I had been dancing for years, and even majored in it at college, the dancers I had known at Mount Holyoke also had other interests. Like me, they were mostly bookish and academic.

In New York City, however, the people competing against me for these rare places in dance companies were like Olympic athletes. They were specialists, hyperfocused to the point where everything they ate, thought, or did was related to dance. The more I was exposed to this world, the more clearly I saw how one-dimensional it was. I began to wonder whether this was the right career for me after all.

Alan's career as a model wasn't progressing much faster than mine was as a dancer. He had taken a job as a waiter at Jim McMullen's, an Upper East Side restaurant, a popular haunt at the time, where he began spending more and more time with a "friend," a girl who waited tables there.

As innocent as I was back then, it took several weeks before it occurred to me that Alan and this waitress might be more than just friends. When I finally asked him about her, Alan admitted that they had become involved.

I broke things off with him immediately, devastated not only by Alan's betrayal, but by the fact that I hadn't seen it coming. With doubts surfacing about my career in dance, and finding myself suddenly alone again, I was depressed and anxious. It felt like my life was over before it had really begun.

Nearly two years after moving to New York City, I decided to give up on my dance career. This had been a gradual process of disillusionment rather than a sudden decision. The rejections— one after another, piling up over the months—had eaten away at my confidence. At the same time, I was seeing more dancers and hearing stories about their lives. The lifestyle of a professional dancer, with its intense demands on your body, time, and self-image, turned me off.

I gradually stopped going to auditions. Because my goal was less certain and money was tight, I also started to cut back on dance classes. At this point I was twenty-four years old. Still young, but not so young for a dancer—that was another factor, too, in my realization that it was time for me to find another dream.

That dream had to start with landing another job, preferably one with the potential for advancement into a new career. But what?

At about that time, Jeff walked into my life.

Two months after breaking up with Alan, with my heart still in tatters, I went on a blind date set up by my best friend from high school. Sandy and Jeff had met while they were both students at the Washington College of Law at American University; one night, Sandy called to invite me to dinner with Jeff and another friend of hers at Nanny Rose, a restaurant across the street from my apartment.

From that first dinner, I knew Jeff was attracted to me. The feeling was mutual. He had grown up in the Midwest, but his family had relocated to Los Angeles. This made him seem exotic to me, since I'd lived in New York all my life. Jeff was also smart, attractive, confident, and ambitious. He had recently passed the bar exam and had already landed his first job at a prestigious New York law firm.

Jeff pursued me aggressively. I was flattered by his attention, especially because I was in such a vulnerable position. Having a man as powerful and driven as Jeff so obviously want to spend time with me was a sweet salve to my battered ego.

A few months after we started dating, Jeff invited me to fly to Los Angeles to meet his parents. As we pulled into the driveway of his family's mansion in Bel Air, I was stunned by the sheer size of the house, the beautiful views, the Rolls-Royce in the driveway, and the California landscaping.

His parents took us to the fanciest restaurants in the neighborhood and had a regular table everywhere we went. His father even had a regular chair at each table, always facing the crowd. I was impressed by how comfortable Jeff seemed in the sort of paradise I had always assumed was reserved for movie stars.

Jeff's mother was a senior partner in a Los Angeles law firm. She was a kind, lovely woman and clearly happy to meet me. I couldn't help but admire her generous nature, expensive clothing, and jewelry.

I was less fond of Jeff's father. He was successful in business, rough around the edges, chauvinistic, and needed a lot of attention. From time to time it also seemed like he had a mean streak that came off as hurtful. The more time I spent with him, the more I felt for Jeff and what it must have been like to grow up with him. During that first visit, all of Jeff's siblings were at the house and I got to meet them for the first time. One day, some friends of Jeff's parents came by the house. As his father went down the line, introducing all of us to them, he announced each person's name and profession, saying, "This is my son Jeff, the lawyer; my son Steve, the doctor;

his wife Cathy, the architect," and so forth. Then he got to me and said, "And this is Ruth, Jeff's girlfriend. She has great legs."

Even worse than his father's actual statement was the fact that I allowed it. I endured the chuckling and said nothing as feelings of anger and humiliation washed over me, probably because part of me believed that having great legs was the best thing I could offer at that time.

Yet, despite Jeff's father, I loved being among these accomplished people in this comfortable home, and wondered if love might provide the answer to my career dilemma. If I married Jeff, I could take care of him emotionally while he took charge of our lives and supported me financially. Having been so accustomed to deferring to anyone who exhibited authority, allowing Jeff to be in charge gave me a comfort level I needed. If I asked questions, he always had the answers. It didn't even matter if those answers were right or wrong. I didn't have the confidence to trust in my own instincts or potential. I could see a promising future with Jeff. We would have children—I had always wanted to be a mother—and then, perhaps when the children were older, I could find work that I truly enjoyed. What a relief it would be, I thought, if I didn't have to figure out my whole life right now.

Remember that book *The Cinderella Complex*, by Colette Dowling? Dowling's spot-on description of a woman's unconscious desire to be taken care of by others, because she's fearful of independence, described me perfectly at that point. My self-esteem had been battered by a critical mother and my failure to make it as a dancer. My heart had been shattered by Alan's betrayal. I was making ends meet by working for a catering company, a job I hated because it required me to sit all day in a dismal basement office. It's no wonder that I had no faith in my ability to make a life for myself and thought a man was the answer to my problems.

To add to that, I would be reenacting my own "perfect" childhood, as I'd described it to my first therapist, if I married Jeff and supported his ambition while raising our children. My father had worked long hours as a physician to support us, while my mother's part-time work schedule revolved around taking care of home and family. It was the only sort of family model I knew, and it was comforting in its familiarity.

Jeff was starting to look more and more like the Prince Charming I'd been waiting for all my life.

After I stopped dancing, I needed to find a way to exercise as I phased out my dance classes. I had tried a few gyms and hated them. There is absolutely nothing more boring to me than exercise that feels like *exercise*. In searching for a work-out alternative, I began trying different fitness studios around the city.

These days, there are thousands of health and fitness clubs, and their numbers are still on the rise. According to the website Statista, in 2015 there were 36,000 health clubs in the United States, with about 55 million members. The industry generates more than $80 billion in revenue annually nationwide.

But boutique studios were a new trend back in the late eighties and early nineties. These studios grew quickly in popularity because they were easier to open than large gyms, and they cost less to equip and run. For clients, boutique fitness studios were an advantage, too, since they offered small classes you could pay for individually, without getting locked into monthly gym fees.

I finally found a small studio on the Upper West Side that I loved, mainly because the woman who ran it, Lee Martin, was so charismatic and energetic. (Coincidentally, the studio was located on the second floor of a building on West 72nd, between Columbus and Amsterdam; years later, we would open our first SoulCycle studio on the same block, nearly right across the street.)

A former actress, Lee was in her mid-twenties and a great advertisement for her own classes. She was petite and in amazing shape, with slender but muscular thighs and crazy washboard abs. Her studio, Bjorkman & Martin Studio of Dance and Exercise, was one of the hottest new studios in New York City in the mid-eighties.

Lee had instructors working for her, but I rapidly discovered that her classes were the ones I loved best. She offered a combination of calisthenics, isometrics, stretching, aerobics, yoga, and—most importantly for me—dance. These workout sessions exercised every part of my body and let me move to music in new ways. Lee, like my own mother, and like Jeff, too, had an extremely authoritative, "know-it-all" personality, which only added to my comfort level around her.

"The goal is not to be thin, but to be healthy," Lee used to say.

She was prone to yelling at students in class to work harder. At the same time, she was careful to teach us how to move in ways that would protect us from injury. The agony and effort I put into those classes was well worth it. Almost immediately, I could feel how these new movements were reshaping my body and making me feel invigorated, even euphoric.

Lee's classes also set my mind free. I emerged from them feeling less stressed out about my day-to-day responsibilities and more optimistic about life in general. This wasn't just exercise, I realized: it was a way of being.

Given her acting background, I wasn't surprised to discover that Lee's classes attracted many celebrities despite the cramped studio space. It wasn't unusual for me to walk into a class and spy an actor whose face I recognized standing right next to me.

A few months after I started taking Lee's classes, she surprised me by saying, "You know, Ruth, you really should be teaching here. You're very gifted."

To me, this was the ultimate seal of approval. Because Lee reminded me so much of my mother—charming, confident to the point of being domineering, attractive—earning her praise made me feel like I had really arrived on the dance aerobics scene, just as my mother's praise had always made me feel like a "good" girl.

Maybe this was my path forward.

I had never taught fitness or dance classes, but I had certainly taken enough dance classes to know how to do it. I had also choreographed solo and group dance performances when I was in college, so that part of teaching came naturally to me.

Still, I was extremely nervous the first time I stood front and center, ready to lead the class in that tiny room with a

Me and my fellow aerobics instructors at
Bjorkman & Martin, 1985

mirrored front wall. The people who came to Lee's studios
were a discerning crowd. Many were already making it as actors and singers, and nearly all of them were energetic, Type
A people. They never had trouble expressing their opinions,
including critical ones.

It's also true that if people are accustomed to taking classes
with a certain instructor they love—whether those classes are
aerobics, Pilates, yoga, spinning, or anything else—their first
instinct is to be suspicious, critical, or even dismissive of a
new teacher. They assume the new instructor won't be any
good. A teacher has to prove herself, and that's what I set out
to do.

One of my favorite aspects of teaching at Bjorkman &
Martin was making the playlists of music I'd use in my

classes. I had grown up surrounded by music in every aspect of my life, from my early childhood spent playing the flute to dancing to every genre of music. At Lee's studio, we used a turntable to play albums. I received endless enjoyment out of choosing musical selections that would inspire me to put a lot of thought and care into choreographing my classes. Lee's playlists taught me that you didn't have to limit your choices to the almost canned-sounding, pulsating "gym" music that was so prevalent in the group fitness classes at the big-box gyms.

During that time, I spent many hours every week at a store called Vinyl Mania on Amsterdam Avenue and 73rd Street, searching for the right music to inspire my students. I also had a slight crush on the Michael-McDonald-lookalike in-store DJ, who would spend hours spinning countless remixes for me until I decided what I wanted to buy. My objective was simple: I knew that if I could help other people lose themselves in the music, so they didn't think of what they were doing as "exercise," they would stick with the classes and I would be a successful teacher.

I felt the trepidation among the students in my early days as an instructor, and there were a few rough patches. Over the next couple of months, however, I started winning people over. Before long, people were eagerly signing up for my classes, and I gradually began to feel accepted.

Unfortunately, that's when Lee's true nature emerged. She had a fragile ego—also like my mother, I realized later—and, if an instructor appeared to be popular or successful, she would feel threatened enough to interrupt their classes and take over. She would literally walk right out onto the floor and say, "You know what, class? She doesn't know what she's doing, so I'm going to take over and teach you the right way."

I had witnessed Lee undercutting other instructors in this way when I was taking their classes. Once my classes started selling out and I began developing a following of my own, she started doing it to me, too.

Fortunately, most of the studio's clients knew Lee well enough to roll their eyes and say, "Okay, Lee's taking over, here she goes again," without thinking much about it. I would get upset, of course, as did the other instructors, but we never once stood up to her. She was the boss and we loved what we were doing. We didn't want to take the chance that she would dismiss us.

Teaching at Lee's studio provided a number of valuable lessons for me. The first was that I could earn an income while moving to music and expressing myself creatively, even if I wasn't a professional dancer. The second was that I could put together an inspiring playlist of music and lead other people to move to it, so they could feel motivated and be physically and mentally transformed by the experience.

The third was that an instructor could inspire almost a cult following, something I would see over and over again as I dove deeper into the world of boutique fitness studios. All of the students and instructors—including me—looked up to Lee, literally wanted to *be* Lee, and seemed equally intimidated and impressed by her.

Oh, and a fourth useful lesson? Celebrities are just ordinary human beings. So many actors came to Lee's studio for classes that I eventually stopped being nervous around them, even when it was me teaching at the front of the room and demonstrating new choreography. In the studio, the celebrities worked hard and sweated like the rest of us. Some picked up steps quickly, while others had to struggle. I taught James Taylor, Carly Simon, and the actress Diane Lane. Ben Stiller and his sister Amy came often, as did Kevin Bacon, Lesley Ann Warren, and Andie MacDowell.

The actress Jennifer Grey was a regular student as well. She had appeared in a few commercials and films by then, but she was interested in becoming an instructor at the studio to stay in shape and supplement her income. I was training Jennifer when she landed the lead in the movie *Dirty Dancing*. We never saw her again.

But probably the most essential lesson I gleaned from this job was that people who treat their employees the way Lee did are often doomed to drive their businesses into the ground. Eventually that kind of negativity will catch up with you. I started teaching at Lee's studio around 1984, and the business closed by 1989 because Lee had managed to alienate everyone who worked for her.

One by one, we fell victim to her enormous ego. She ultimately drove everyone away and ended up sabotaging her own business. I believe I was the last one standing, so to speak; I stuck with her until the bitter end. That's probably not very surprising, since I was well versed in that dynamic. But I did learn a valuable lesson through this experience, which is that it's essential to remember that your employees are your most valuable asset.

Lesson #2: Failure Is Underrated

Even *before* I started my own companies, I had hit bottom many times in my life: when I gave up my dream of being a dancer in New York, when my first serious boyfriend betrayed me, when the catering job I'd been so excited about turned out to be a nightmare, when my marriage ended and I couldn't see how I'd ever support myself, to name a few.

It can be difficult to feel optimistic about your future if you're young and struggling to find the right career, if your job offers no chance for advancement, or if you're trying to launch a business and are having trouble finding investors or taking hit after hit because your companies go under. However, if you can learn to see every end as a new beginning, you will survive your losses. What's more, each time you fail, you will discover, as I did, that failure can teach us much more than success.

It's easy to succeed, right? When we succeed at something, we feel good about ourselves. Proud of our accomplishments, we sometimes become too complacent. When we fail, however, we have to learn how to pick ourselves up off the floor. We must acquire essential new skills and values; we have to learn how to be patient and resilient and reinvent ourselves. Each time this happens, we become stronger.

When you fail, let yourself feel the pain. Acknowledge it. Wallow in it for a while and allow some empathy for yourself. Cry. Share your pain with friends. Then tell yourself that the only direction you can go after hitting bottom is up. Whether you're in despair about failing at a relationship, a job, or a financial decision, learn from your mistakes, then say, "I'm going to prove I can get to a better place."

Being able to reinvent yourself is a matter of overcoming your own self-doubt enough to take new risks. The only sure way to fail in life is to stop trying. You need to keep putting yourself out there no matter what happens, because otherwise you'll miss out on valuable networking opportunities.

How do you keep going after you've been kicked to the curb?

This may sound counterintuitive, but the most important thing you need to do is embrace failure. Respect yourself for being the sort of person who goes out into the world, takes risks, and sometimes fails—but makes the most of those failures to learn something new.

For instance, I remember a particular jazz class I was taking when I was about fourteen years old. The class was full and the teacher, Eddie Zawacki, was good-looking, charismatic, and flirtatious. We were all in awe of him.

We were doing high kicks in that class, moving across the floor one at a time. Well, I kicked my leg so high and so hard that I fell down, smack on my butt. Everyone in the class started laughing at me.

Eddie raised his voice and commanded the class to stop laughing. He then made an example of me, saying that everyone should always have that much enthusiasm and abandon, because that would give us the ability to take risks in everything we did in life. His inspiring speech always stayed with me.

The second thing to remember if you're going to keep going after a setback is the importance of focusing on your own health and well-being. Exercise, get a lot of sleep, and treat yourself to a facial or a massage occasionally.

"Wait, I can't spend money on a massage or an exercise class," you may think, if your particular low point includes being between jobs and feeling broke. But, trust me, it is during times like these that you need to do things that are just for *you*. It will be money well spent. Or, if you truly are strapped financially, find things to do for yourself that cost no money but offer the same benefits: hike a new trail, go for a run in a nearby park, or just dance in your apartment with a group of friends. The point is to do whatever you can to get yourself to a positive place, because that's how you'll fuel your own resilient spirit.

If you respect yourself enough to take care of your health and appearance, you will feel empowered. That self-empowerment will, in turn, lead others to see you as a person who is worth talking to, investing in, or hiring. Good things are ahead of you. Keep your eyes open and take care of yourself so that you can be ready to make the most of new opportunities that come your way.

3

Trust Your Intuition

Becoming more involved in teaching at Lee's studio coincided with my blossoming romance with Jeff. By the time I was ready to quit working at the catering company and start teaching at Lee's studio full-time, I had decided to marry him. I was twenty-six years old and couldn't imagine a better future for myself than the one Jeff was offering: a stable home, children, and a husband who adored me and was clearly driven to work hard.

Those seemed like good reasons at the time. However, if I had to advise my own daughters about marriage, I would tell them to really try to know themselves and some of their own personal and professional life goals before getting married. Honestly, my primary motivation for getting married when I did wasn't just because I loved Jeff, but because I felt so insecure about my own abilities that I couldn't imagine fending for myself in the world.

I would also tell my daughters—and you—to trust your intuition. Many times, people have gut feelings about business decisions and relationships but ignore their own emotional reactions. I have discovered the hard way that if I have a good feeling about something, whether it's a person or a strategic career move, it's probably a good decision. And if I don't, I'm probably about to make a terrible mistake.

I was old-fashioned in some ways and never had any intention of living with Jeff—or any other man—before marriage. However, after we'd been going out together nearly a year, Jeff brought me back to my apartment one night after dinner. He and I walked up the six floors to my place, and, as I opened the door, the hallway light shone into my bedroom, illuminating no fewer than fifteen mice running all over my floor, disturbed by renovations on the first-floor business.

I didn't scream, but I didn't set foot in that apartment, either. I looked up at Jeff and said, "I'm coming over to your apartment tonight, and I'm never coming back here."

I remember calling my parents after moving in with Jeff to apprise them of my new living arrangement. Knowing how traditional they were, I was nervous about telling them. But it wasn't just that. I was a very young twenty-six, and I didn't want them to think I wasn't their little girl anymore. I didn't want to believe that, either.

Although my mother had never supported the idea of living together prior to marriage, she seemed to take my announcement in stride, perhaps because she was impressed by Jeff and felt confident that he would take care of me. As for my father, while he tried to project a certain comfort level about my new arrangement, I could tell that he was feeling like he was losing "Daddy's little girl."

Jeff was delighted with our new arrangement. He lived in a much nicer place than mine, in a high-rise building with park views in a desirable part of the city, and it was easy to accommodate my few possessions in his apartment.

We got engaged soon after that. Jeff wasn't a man who ever asked a question he didn't know the answer to—that's one of the qualities that make him such a great attorney—so I knew he was waiting for a strong hint before he'd pop the question.

One day, we were walking across 57th Street and passed a jeweler's window. We stopped to look at the diamond rings and I pointed to one of them. "I really like that ring," I said.

"Well, that's an engagement ring," Jeff said.

"Yeah, so?" I said, grinning up at him.

"So, do you want to get married?" He was so nervous that he could barely utter the words.

"Yes," I said.

He smiled back at me, a bit shocked. "I guess we're getting married," he said, and that was that.

We called my parents right away to share our news, and they were absolutely thrilled. My father and Jeff couldn't have been more opposite in temperament, but they definitely had similarities, which I suppose is one reason I wanted to marry Jeff. Both were confident and driven. Like my father, Jeff could also be very silly and always had the ability to make me laugh. He could repeat a dumb joke five times and I'd laugh every time. I loved being his audience.

Jeff looked up to my dad, too, and valued in him qualities that he so needed and that his father never had. Dad loved Jeff because Jeff made him feel important and appreciated.

We'd had an easy time adjusting to life together before our engagement. I suppose that was largely because I was submissive and eager to please. If Jeff and I ever had an issue about anything, I deferred to him to avoid conflict—much as my father used to do with my mother, I realize now.

Once we began making plans for our wedding, however, things became more difficult. Jeff had strong opinions about decisions that I naturally assumed would be mine, like choosing a china pattern. When we argued, he was like a dog with a bone—certainly a useful trait in his profession as a lawyer.

Perhaps if I had been a more confident person, I might not have felt so belittled and bruised by our arguments. It didn't help that I shared what was going on with my mother. When I told her about our fights, she would side with me and tell me to stick to my guns, because that's what she would do. It became an unhealthy triangle, with my mother siding with me and fueling my ire, causing even more tension between Jeff and me.

The only decision Jeff did not take part in was selecting a wedding dress. My parents took me to Kleinfeld Bridal, where the sales staff brought me one dress after another to try on. The one I eventually chose was a simple, off-the-shoulder, floor-length satin dress with an appliqué across the bodice.

It was then, while I was trying on dresses, that my intuition kicked into high gear. I remember looking at myself in the mirror and thinking, "Oh my God. This is real. I'm getting married and I don't know if I'm making the right decision."

This feeling of despair was so powerful that I confessed my doubts to my mother. She said, "If you want to call it off, we will call it off."

I shook my head. "How can I do that, Mom? How could I do that to Jeff?"

And—although I never quite admitted this—I didn't know what *I'd* do if Jeff didn't take care of me. I was truly afraid that I lacked the skills to make a good living on my own. I had already tried and failed at being independent. Not only did I feel a strong pull toward the lifestyle I knew Jeff could provide for us, but I also hoped that we could take care of each other's emotional needs and he could supply me with the confidence I lacked. In return, I would be a devoted wife and the best mother I could possibly be.

I tried to rationalize my doubts away, as all of us are prone to do sometimes. Surely, I thought, the stress between Jeff and me was temporary, caused by having to make so many seemingly momentous decisions leading to our wedding day. In addition, Jeff was on the brink of leaving his steady job and starting his own law firm, and I knew he was anxious about that.

I managed to convince myself that things would be fine again once we were married and on our European honeymoon.

Eight months after our engagement, Jeff and I were married at the Garden City Hotel near where my parents lived, in front of about two hundred guests. I don't have any memory of enjoying the day. It all felt very awkward.

I had planned a low-key but elegant wedding with the help of my parents. Being their only daughter, I knew that they wanted to make it as beautiful as possible. I didn't even learn until weeks after the wedding that my mother had just been diagnosed with breast cancer because she didn't want anything to mar this special day. (A month later, she had a lumpectomy with a good result.)

Despite our efforts, it wasn't an altogether happy day. In the morning, when the families congregated for pictures, Jeff's father made it known that the event didn't meet his standards. It wasn't nearly as lavish as he would have liked. I was crestfallen by his opinion, and by his decision to share it with whoever would listen. I also was worried that my parents might catch wind of this. It just felt so hurtful, and I wanted to shield them from his input. A couple of my friends served as bridesmaids; the other bridesmaids were my soon-to-be sisters-in-law. Adding to the awkwardness was the fact that I hadn't maintained many close friendships from my college days, leaving me with a pretty small group of guests; because most of the people in attendance were Jeff's friends and family members, I felt isolated and alone.

As the rabbi began speaking the final words at the altar to seal our union, Jeff began sobbing tears of joy. I looked at him, somewhat surprised by this emotional outburst and feeling uncomfortable because I wasn't sure what emotions I was experiencing. I realized I was neither happy nor sad. Mostly what I felt was numb.

Should that have been a clue that I was making a mistake? Should I have heeded my intuition and run away before the rabbi pronounced us husband and wife?

Those questions didn't occur to me. I kept telling myself that Jeff was a good man, a smart attorney who would go far in life, and he adored me—all of which was true. This was love, I decided, and of course love wasn't always smooth sailing.

I clung to the belief that our love would grow and flourish again once we were away from our families and the stress of the wedding was behind us.

I was wrong.

After we were married, I saw and experienced Jeff's temper and outbursts, often at times when they were least expected. Whenever he got angry or frustrated, I noticed a pattern in my reactions: I would immediately start to feel diminished, afraid, upset, and ultimately responsible. Then I would withdraw, thinking that if I just stopped trying to defend myself, Jeff would have no one with whom to engage. But the reality was that my attempts to withdraw only made things worse. We became trapped in a vicious cycle. While I was certainly used to my mother's ire, she expressed it through silence and by cutting me off. I had never experienced this kind of loud yelling and it frightened me. My automatic reaction to both styles of displaying anger was to hide—if not physically, then emotionally. I became an expert at retreating and repressing, a survival method I had learned at a very young age, and this contributed to the relationship dynamics with both Mom and my husband.

While I was solely focused on my own unhappiness in our marriage, what came across was that both of us were unhappy. Just as Jeff's way of handling frustration resulted in pushing me away, my desire to run away did nothing to help him feel secure in our relationship. We both lost out in the end.

Nobody really knows what goes on inside another couple's marriage. In fact, even the two spouses within a marriage often have vastly different perspectives of the relationship. There are two people, living different lives, and then there is their union, a unique third entity they create together. Partners must nurture that union for it to survive. Neither Jeff nor I had the necessary emotional tools to do that.

I knew Jeff loved me. He probably thought he was trying to communicate with me when he got angry. He couldn't fathom why his loud voice, physical gestures, and unpredictable moods terrified me. After all, he never struck me. How could I feel afraid or abused?

And yet, I did. He was a skilled attorney and I viewed myself as a failed dancer. I didn't have the self-esteem to stand up to him, and I certainly didn't know how to argue my point of view successfully or communicate my feelings. Looking back, I'm actually amazed I stuck it out as long as I did. But the truth was, I had a mother who harbored a lot of anger, no history of divorce in my family, and nothing to compare my marriage to. I thought, "This is the way marriage is, so I'd better get used to it."

Jeff had started his new job after the honeymoon, so he was gone every day, but most nights he came home tired and irritable. It seemed like nothing made him happy. I knew he was under a lot of pressure, but unfortunately, my go-to response was always, "What am I doing wrong?" The unhappier he was, the unhappier I became, because I couldn't "fix" things for my husband—or in our relationship.

I tried talking to a few close friends, but they didn't seem to want to hear about it. I remember telling one particularly close girlfriend about what I was experiencing, but she didn't even react. She just changed the subject. It wasn't until years later that I understood the truth: the experiences I tried to share with my good friend were unfortunately familiar because of what was happening in her own marriage, so she couldn't bear to consider them too closely. She still hasn't. Our friendship has faded over the years, although I sometimes still see her at social events, where I'm distressed to see the toll that years of stress and unhappiness have taken on her face and demeanor.

Other married women friends of mine had similarly dismissive responses when I shared my turmoil with them. As time passed, I gained more insight into their situations. I realized their reactions were less about avoiding my problems, and more about being unwilling, or unable, to confront the issues in their own troubled relationships.

As a last resort, I felt compelled to share my worries with my mother. "That sounds terrible!" she said, but she never suggested that I leave Jeff. She never gave me the confidence to believe that I could live on my own, perhaps because she couldn't imagine being independent herself. Despite her domineering, confrontational personality, my mother was weak and fearful. She loved having Dad take care of her.

I reminded myself constantly that things could be worse. Jeff adored me, and I was accustomed to that powerful adoration from my father. I think being put on a pedestal was probably necessary at that time in my life, because I couldn't get up there on my own; I hadn't yet found my own true identity. It would be many more years before I understood this.

Besides, if I left Jeff, what would I do?

Exercise and soap operas were my escape and my salvation. I was now teaching full-time at Lee's studio. I was addicted to

All My Children at the time and lived for each episode that I taped on the VCR. I remember coming home one evening and situating myself in front of the TV, waiting for my escape. Lo and behold, the VCR must not have been set properly that day and the show wasn't recorded. I literally had a temper tantrum that ended in tears. Afterward, I knew I had to examine why my reaction had been so extreme. I knew that something must be very wrong.

As with my mother and Jeff during the time we were making wedding plans, I again found myself caught up in a bizarre triangle. Now, instead of Mom and Jeff trying to control me, it was Lee's powerful, dramatic personality pitted against Jeff's clever legal mind. This was largely my fault. I deferred completely to both of them: to Lee, because I looked up to her so much as a teacher, and to Jeff, because I admired his work ethic and I was financially dependent upon him.

Two strong personalities never work very well together. Jeff couldn't stand Lee. One particularly telling memory stands out. The instructors at Lee's studio had put on a performance for our students one night. Jeff arrived at the studio afterward to pick me up while we were still moving benches and tables back into place.

Lee snapped her fingers at him and said, "Jeff, move that bench."

Jeff looked at her with nothing short of rage. "I will never move that bench, Lee," he said, "and don't you ever snap your fingers at me again." And there I stood, in the proverbial triangle, not knowing whom to please.

Soon after that, Lee pulled me aside. "You really should leave him, Ruth," she said. "This marriage is not good for you."

Maybe not. But my relationship with her wasn't that great either. Lee's fragile ego and her inability to celebrate the successes of her instructor staff had cost her nearly every employee. I was one of the few who stayed with her until the very end—no surprise.

When Lee's studio closed in 1989, I had to look elsewhere for work. A customer of Lee's opened an exercise studio downtown in Tribeca, where she offered a variety of group fitness classes, so I started teaching step classes there. Little did I know at the time that her new venture was completely funded by her marijuana business. One day she showed me suitcases of pot in her closet. I was astounded.

Step aerobics—a form of exercise done to music using an elevated platform—had been developed by a fitness instructor named Gin Miller. Gin had suffered a knee injury; when her doctor recommended that Gin step on and off a milk crate to help strengthen her muscles, she saw the value of the exercise for everyone. By the early nineties, step classes had become all the rage in New York.

Because step classes had an element of choreography, I enjoyed teaching them. However, the business never really took on a community feel and struggled to find a compelling identity. As a result, I never felt fully invested and lost interest after a year or so.

Next, I took on private clients, an endeavor that often took me into lavish apartments and townhouses around Manhattan. I thought I would enjoy personal training, given the flexibility of my hours and the decent pay, but it ultimately proved to be more exhausting than fulfilling, given how much time was devoted to hearing clients talk about their personal problems.

Of course, if a personal trainer really jells with a client and enjoys that client's company, a close bond forms. I had one client for over fifteen years who, to this day, remains a wonderful friend. Our relationship definitely became a two-way street and we shared a lot; at times, I was seeing her three times a week.

All of these teaching and training experiences provided illustrative examples that proved to be useful later on at Soul-Cycle and Flywheel. For instance, working at Lee's studio made me realize early on how building a community is integral to the success of any fitness business. Your community creates a support system for both your customers and your employees, because if you create the right environment, people will want to keep coming back. This means forming an extended family of sorts, one where everyone is treated with equal importance, respect, and loyalty.

Creating a supportive, safe, fun community is probably paramount to the success of many different sorts of entrepreneurial endeavors, but I think it's particularly true in the fitness industry. This sort of business typically runs seven days a week, from early morning into late evening. Ultimately, the people you work out (and play) with in your fitness studio will become your social life, if not your family.

In our new technologically dependent society, building community through your business is more essential than ever. We tend to be disconnected from each other in any personal way because we're busy texting or sitting behind a computer screen. In a successful boutique fitness studio, people will put away their phones for an hour to exercise together—and they will want to talk and socialize before and after the classes.

Socializing becomes even more natural and fun after sweating together, and as a community, we spur each other on through the energy we contribute to our workouts. Witnessing this community in other people's fitness studios provided me with an essential hands-on lesson in what success looks like in this industry. Much later, I would begin to deliberately think about how to build community in my own businesses.

Meanwhile, personal training also taught me that what people want, first and foremost, is to be listened to, because they often don't feel like they're getting recognized for whatever they're doing in their lives, whether it's working at a stressful job, staying home to raise children, caring for elderly parents, or dealing with difficult relationships.

The experience of being a personal trainer definitely impacted the way I taught spin classes later, because it demonstrated how important it is to incorporate mindfulness into exercise, and to support clients by giving them personal attention and shout-outs. Sometimes I even share my own personal challenges during class, knowing they will resonate with others, as a way of encouraging students to build a sense of community and acceptance.

Recently, for instance, I had a pretty serious argument with a friend that didn't end well. I was expressing feelings of disappointment, but instead of offering any words of understanding, she just shot everything right back at me, putting me on the defensive. Ultimately, I felt like she didn't hear a word I said.

I had to teach a class soon afterward, and during the class I spoke about the importance and power of saying "I'm sorry."

I didn't describe my personal situation; instead, I addressed the issue more generally, because I knew that others must have shared this kind of experience.

Not long after that class, I received the following note from one of my riders:

> *Just want to say that I found you particularly inspirational this morning—your Ruthisms were simply wonderful! When you were talking about "I'm sorry," you did it in such an impactful way that I thought I would have to repeat your sentiments to my girls (assuming I can remember how you said it). When your kids were younger, did you speak to them in that insightful, soulful way? If you did, how totally awesome for them! I'm too busy policing and nagging to cover inspirational stuff. Mental note to self to change that after today, so* THANK YOU!

I still had things to work out with my friend, but I was pleased to be able to turn what had been a negative experience for me into something productive and positive for others.

About the same time I started building a small client base as a personal trainer, I also decided to start trying to get pregnant. I was twenty-nine years old and running out of time. One day, I said to Jeff, "I think we should start our family."

Jeff had been ready to have children for a while, so he was pleased and excited. It still amazes me that I was naive enough to believe that having children would bring us closer together, but I fully bought into this idea, harboring a secret hope that parenthood would magically transform us into a happy family. At that time, I never in a million years considered myself a candidate for divorce. There had never been a divorce in my family; I couldn't even imagine the possibility.

It took me three years to get pregnant despite the fact that we saw specialists and passed all of the fertility tests with flying colors. One reproductive specialist put me on Clomid, but all that did was make me gain ten pounds. The next step was Pergonal injections. Fortunately, by the second shot I was pregnant.

Finally, it felt like I was beginning my "real" life. I would be a mother and I was convinced that focusing on family life and the well-being of my children would grant me a deeper, more fulfilling purpose than anything I'd done so far.

Then came a shock: about seven or eight weeks into the pregnancy, the doctor informed me that I was having twins. Immediately, I burst into tears, hysterical because my mother had said that twins were an impossible responsibility, especially if they were boys.

Eventually I calmed down, reasoning that having two children at once was better, actually, since I was already considered on the "advanced maternal age" end of the spectrum for that time. From then on, I embraced my pregnancy. I ate well and continued doing Pilates and taking long walks for exercise. Jeff, too, seemed more settled and content. When we were together, he was nurturing and protective of me.

For the first year after Kate and Rachel were born, Jeff was a doting father, changing their diapers and holding them. However, because he was working during the day to support us—and long hours at that—he wouldn't get up at night to feed them. I was so fatigued from the lack of sleep and my new nonstop responsibilities that it felt like I was swimming through fog.

Any time things felt like too much, though, I quickly reminded myself that this was my role now. I owed it to my children to play it to perfection.

My father's cancer had come roaring back by 1993, and I started therapy that year to help myself face the enormous void his death would leave. With the therapist, I also started the unsettling process of exploring the depths of my unhappiness in my marriage.

The therapist helped me see the startling truth: from my honeymoon throughout the years we had been married, I was subjected to behavior from Jeff that was unequivocally unacceptable. Yet I had allowed it. I had spent my entire marriage as the victim of a man with an intense temper.

While I was eventually able to take responsibility for my contributions to the dysfunctional dynamics with both my mother and Jeff, it would take many more years of maturation, experience with relationships, and therapy. Meanwhile, the girls were small, and I was struggling to hold on to any threads of happiness in my life. Exercise continued to be the best survival tool for me.

My next exposure to a boutique fitness business was when I started taking classes in the Lotte Berk Method in the early nineties. Lotte Berk was a German dancer who had fled the

Nazis in the 1930s with her British husband. The couple moved to England, and, when Lotte was injured and could no longer make a living as a dancer, she combined her ballet barre routines with rehabilitative therapy and created an innovative exercise method that sculpted the bodies of her students. Her disciples went off to teach her method in various places nationwide.

In 1991, Burr Leonard and Mimi Fleischman, a pair of sisters who had been taking classes at a Lotte Berk studio, started their own barre classes, modifying them somewhat to protect the joints of students who needed lower-impact workouts. Today, there are about seventy Lotte Berk studios in the United States and Canada, with many more barre-based spin-offs.

The classes I took were held in a fancy townhouse on East 67th Street in Manhattan. Students had to walk up a couple of flights of stairs to a small room with a ballet barre and a mirrored wall. The only difference between this room and a classic dance studio was the carpeted floor. The business was run by Fred DeVito and Elisabeth Halfpapp, who also taught many of the classes and were the clear favorites among the instructors and customers.

The Lotte Berk Method classes were ultra-challenging and never got any easier. Just like in dance classes, there were always ways to use the method to become stronger and more competent, and students would strive to earn a "shout-out" or some personal praise during the class. Once again, I saw how important it was that students were recognized and felt cared for, something that could be accomplished just from having the teacher call their names out in class, perhaps only once.

I also appreciated the comfort of having an exercise community of my own. I started to notice the same people taking classes in their regular time slots and looked forward to greeting them and sweating together. Having celebrities in class always validated the business as well. Occasionally, for instance, I would notice Ann Reinking, probably Bob Fosse's most revered dancer, in a class with me. It didn't get more thrilling than that. She had been one of my Broadway idols when I was growing up; if this class was good enough for her, then I wanted to be there, too.

In addition to their studio in Manhattan, Fred and Elisabeth also opened a studio in a former barn in Bridgehampton, Long Island. Jeff and I had bought our own house in Bridgehampton by 1994, and I had been spending summers there with the girls since they were toddlers. During my Lotte Berk days, I went to classes in the barn religiously. (Of course, I had no idea at the time that we would open our first SoulCycle Hamptons location in that same barn thirteen years later.)

I credit both Elisabeth and Fred for being at the forefront of boutique fitness long before I co-founded SoulCycle. Elisabeth, having been a professional dancer for many years, was certainly a great role model, showing me how someone could turn her passion for dance into a very successful business after giving up her stage career. She and Fred also went on to create Core Fusion at the Exhale Spas, developing their own signature barre method class—and providing more role models for me, though I didn't know it yet.

My father died at home in 1993. My mother had become difficult for me to be around because she was so terrified of losing him and being left alone. Her narcissistic point of view of my father dying seemed to be, "How dare you leave me? How could you do this to *me*?"

For his part, Dad continued to repress whatever anger he felt toward my mother, eventually shutting down physically and emotionally. As the illness continued to advance, he even stopped speaking.

My father's rapid decline was terrible to witness; for instance, he couldn't enjoy eating anymore, and that had always been one of his greatest pleasures. I used to make special trips to Barney Greengrass on Manhattan's Upper West Side to buy him his favorite pickled herring. Sometimes, it would be the only thing he'd eat. I felt overwhelmed by grief as I watched him diminish before my very eyes.

A couple of weeks before he died, my father and I had our last conversation. I was lying next to Dad on his bed when he said tenderly, "I want you to know how much I have loved our thirty-five years together."

"Well, I've loved our thirty-five years together, too," I said. By this time I was bawling.

"I want you to promise me you'll take care of Mom," he said.

"But I want another thirty-five years with you!" I said.

He was too weak to answer me. We simply held each other.

Jeff was extremely affected by my father's passing because Jeff had idolized him, too. He tried to help me through my grief. My father died on March 19 and my birthday is on March 27; Jeff arranged a dinner date for us at Union Square Cafe, but I couldn't fathom celebrating. Despite our shared sorrow, I had never felt more disconnected from my husband. I barely spoke at dinner.

Summers out on Eastern Long Island provided a peaceful oasis from our household in New York that was anything but, because I could spend three months in the country with our girls. Jeff worked in the city during the week and commuted out to us on weekends; I also had support from our nanny, Judy, who helped out with child care during the day in the city, but lived with us full-time in the summer. She felt like part of the family and loved Long Island as much as we did.

We shared lots of outdoor time and laughter and slept well. The sunsets were some of the most spectacular I'd ever seen. Every summer, the girls and I would pick an exceptionally beautiful day, wait until just before sunset, and hold a special photo shoot on the grounds of the elementary school in Wainscott. Photographing them had become a hobby of mine. They were my favorite subjects. And the small-town feel of that spot, with its little white schoolhouse, the bright green grass, and a worn barn in the background, provided an absolutely perfect backdrop as I recorded how fast my girls were growing up. Soon, they would start school; I wouldn't let myself think about how to fill the empty hours ahead.

I made friends with some of the other mothers and we planned activities together, both with and without children. Then, in 1994, after my father was gone and we'd been summering on Long Island for five years, Jeff and I decided to buy a house in Bridgehampton. It was a lovely second home and I was delighted with it.

I thought having this summer house would make me happier. But, like all material acquisitions, the thrill was fleeting. It wasn't long before our new house, with its too-thin walls, was filled with anger.

. . .

In 1996, when the girls were six years old, I joined the Reebok Sports Club, an upscale fitness club near Lincoln Center on the Upper West Side. The club offered fitness training, a variety of group classes, and a sumptuous spa. Many of the women in my classes were stay-at-home moms, too.

The gym became my sanctuary, and my workouts allowed me to handle my husband and children with greater patience. The twins were a joy to be around, of course, but still busy and exhausting. Jeff's law practice was well under way and required him to devote even more hours to his career. Often, he was so wiped out from his long day that he'd come home and immediately retreat behind the closed bedroom door, making it hard for me to take a break.

I sometimes longed to point out that I'd been with the kids all day. What made him think I could *keep* handling them? Yet I didn't dare disturb him, anxious to keep the peace.

For the first couple of years at the Reebok Sports Club, I limited myself to using gym equipment and taking group fitness classes because these workouts were familiar. I had to pass the room where people were spinning and sometimes paused to listen to the music—usually techno tunes with a great beat and no lyrics.

Despite the lure of working out to music, for a long time I was too intimidated to sign up for a spin class. The idea of pedaling a bike with a crowd of people in a darkened room to a thumping beat seemed completely foreign. Plus, the spin room was like a smaller club within the bigger sports club.

The classes all had regular riders, and everyone seemed to know everyone else in this tight community.

One day, I mustered the courage to sign up. The instructor, Glenn, was a disciple of Johnny Goldberg's—a South African professional cyclist known in the spinning and cycling worlds as "Johnny G." Johnny G helped pioneer spinning as the result of an accident: he had been training for "The Race Across America," a cross-country bicycle race from Los Angeles to New York City, when he was nearly killed on the road during night training.

After that, Johnny G decided to do his night rides and build endurance indoors on a stationary bicycle. With the help of John Baudhuin, another avid cyclist who also happened to have an MBA, he went on to help design and manufacture the first run of spinning bikes. Spinning classes were first offered at Crunch gyms in New York in 1993.

I didn't just love spinning when I first tried it in 1996: I was immediately and completely hooked. Partly this was because we were spinning to music. Glenn's playlists of techno, club, and other lyric-less music, combined with the power of pedaling, moved me beyond the point of exercise to really feel a shift in my mood and perspective, sometimes within minutes of starting each class. Music has always been front and center in my life, so I suppose that wasn't surprising, especially since dance had always been my favorite type of workout. Now, as I moved to Glenn's music, I wasn't dancing across the floor, but I still felt exhilarated. Spinning allowed me to escape my own life and fully inhabit the moment in a way no other form of traditional exercise ever had.

I also thought Glenn was really cool, with his long hair and lean body. He didn't teach the way my other fitness instructors did. He had a captivating aura; he was more Zen than high-powered or hard-core. Glenn didn't even seem to own a pair of bike shoes, while everyone else did.

Glenn would sit on the podium wearing army boots and nod his head to this amazing techno music he played for us, occasionally issuing instructions about the choreography we were doing on our bikes. Despite his minimal instruction, everyone seemed to know what to do.

"Choreography" might sound like a stretch to describe what happened when we were spinning, but it really isn't. Whether we were on a standing run or a seated sprint, I understood that Glenn had put a lot of thought into his playlist and into exactly how we should ride to the music he'd chosen for us. As a former dancer, I found that aspect of spinning especially intriguing and appealing.

Spinning immediately reminded me of a dance class, because we learned the routine and performed it as a group facing a mirror across the front wall of the room. I felt the tremendous power in the mirror image of a group moving together in perfect sync with the music, and the motions of spinning completely brought me back to the days of doing what I loved most.

My dance instructors used to teach the class a routine, and then you were pretty much on your own to perform it. Glenn did the same thing. Because he so often sat on the podium rather than on a bike, he could watch us in the same way a dance teacher would. The riders wanted to be good for him, just as dancers are always seeking approval from their dance teacher. Both scenarios tapped into the competitive nature of the participants. You wanted to be the top rider/dancer with the best possible form while conveying a look of ease, as if you were expending no effort at all. I knew that I could do this and be good at it.

Plus, there was something magically transformative about being among other cyclists in a darkened room, surrounded by music and the energy of everyone pedaling to the beat. The classes inspired a kind of restful mindfulness I had never felt in an exercise class before. I could disappear inside my head while pedaling hard and feeling myself grow physically stronger. Every class was a complete mood changer, so empowering that I felt like a different person when I emerged from the spinning room, drenched in sweat but smiling and exhilarated.

The best part? Spinning didn't feel the least bit like exercise. It was much more than that: it was an experience where I moved to music and emerged each time feeling more in touch with my own feelings and physically and emotionally stronger.

Before long, I abandoned my other classes and workouts to devote my gym hours to spinning.

Spinning quickly became a big part of my daily existence, giving me forty-five precious minutes to escape my stress and mingle with a completely different group of people who were not part of my ordinary world. My grief over my father slowly began to recede; spinning was helping me feel more like myself again.

Soon after I began spinning, I noticed that one of the men

in my classes kept blatantly staring at me. His scrutiny made me feel flattered, if a little uncomfortable, but I didn't give it much thought. He was only a kid; he didn't look much older than his mid-twenties, and I was already thirty-seven.

Then, one day after class, we were walking down the steps to the main floor and he said, "Good class."

When I responded, he introduced himself as Philippe. He was obviously nervous; I tried to put him at ease as we walked down the steps side by side. Philippe was handsome, with light brown hair, classic features, and a lean body—kind of a Tobey Maguire look-alike.

Beyond his obvious physical appeal, what really drew me to Philippe was his razor-sharp intelligence and acerbic sense of humor. We began chatting after every spin class. I learned that he was Jewish, twenty-six years old, and had grown up with a single mother in low-income housing in New York City. His father had abandoned him at birth, and his mother had no choice but to work full-time to make ends meet. He was predominantly raised by his grandmother until he was twelve; after she passed, he was mostly left on his own, in a sense abandoned by every adult in his life.

Philippe wrote his own script. He dropped out of college after two years and was headed in no particular direction when we met. We were two people at completely different points in our lives, yet we were equally lost and in need of companionship.

It took me a while to realize that Philippe was interested in being more than friends, I guess because that possibility seemed so unlikely to me. I was an exhausted mother. We were over a decade apart in age and from completely different worlds. Besides, Philippe only ever saw me sweating in gym clothes. How alluring could that possibly be?

Our friendship continued to blossom over the next few months. The girls were in first grade by then. Philippe began walking me home from spin class. It was the dead of winter, and so freezing cold that we could see our breath with every word. Even so, sometimes we ended up sitting on a bench in Central Park, talking for hours before I had to pick up the children. Our conversations flowed effortlessly and he made me laugh—something I sorely needed.

Eventually I told Philippe how sad I was about my father and how unhappy I was in my marriage. He was very kind and gentle with me, and I couldn't help confiding in him. I suppose I was starting to fall for Philippe by then, even if I wasn't perceptive enough to know it. I certainly never entertained the idea of being with him in a romantic way—I was married and, more important, a mother—but I was grateful to have such a caring confidant. I even remember telling Jeff about my "spin friend," as Philippe was often a part of my day. What I wasn't facing was the momentum building between us and how I couldn't fathom stopping the train.

I'm not proud of what came next: Philippe and I began having an affair. However, I would never cheapen our intimacy by using that label, because nothing felt haphazard, thoughtless, or temporary about our relationship. I knew I was embarking on a huge change in my life.

Beginning a relationship with Philippe was no way to stay in my marriage. It was a way to blow it up—and it did.

Lesson #3: Forget Fear and Trust Your Intuition

Trusting your gut goes hand in hand with feeling confident. But how do you learn to listen to your intuition if you're afraid you might be wrong about what it's telling you?

Two strategies will help. The first is to give yourself space. Step back from the situation and try not to think about the decision for a while—even a weekend off will help give you a clearer perspective. Make important decisions only when you're feeling calm and grounded.

Next, make a list of pros and cons. Ask yourself *why* you want to do something—whether it's breaking up with a partner or launching a new product. List all of the reasons you think it's a good idea, even the smallest, most petty ones imaginable. ("I like his dog!" "I want to take that new job because they give out free cookies in the lunchroom!") No reason is too small.

Now list all of the reasons why making this decision could be the worst idea *ever*. Again, don't be afraid to write down the reasons that might seem stupid to someone else. This is your list and nobody else ever has to see it.

Finally, try to counter every reason *not* to do something with a reason to do it. For instance, if you're thinking about divorcing your spouse and you list "financial security" as a reason to stay, counter that argument by saying, "I will crash and burn financially if I leave," and then say this: "But that's my fear talking. If I have financial difficulties, I can find a roommate or move to a cheaper city. I will figure things out."

Too often, your fear gets in the way of your intuition. The trick is to separate your rational and irrational thoughts so you can go after what you really want.

Lesson #4: To Build Successful Relationships, Build Your Own Self-Esteem

Forging successful relationships while building your own self-esteem is tricky. So often, our confidence can be shattered by a bad relationship—whether that relationship is with an intimate partner, a friend, or a business colleague. On the flip side, positive relationships of any sort can lead to you feeling empowered. So which should you work on first? Your relationships or yourself?

In my experience, while you might get lucky and form solid, positive relationships that support your own development, you're far more likely to seek out and sustain good relationships at work and in your personal life if you get to know yourself first. Doing so will require you to spend a significant time on your own at some point in your life. Because I married early, I didn't learn this lesson until I was older, but once I had to live alone and support myself, I realized the value of being self-reliant. As challenging as my journey was at times, learning how to live independently led me to have much more positive relationships in my personal life and in my business circles.

I don't think that I was ever truly equipped to be in a healthy, balanced relationship until I realized that I didn't have to be in one for financial or emotional support. When you take *need* out of the equation and make a relationship about *wanting* to be with someone else, the chances of that relationship succeeding are going to be much greater, because you'll make wiser choices about the people in your life. Whether you're choosing a friend, a lover, or a business partner, it's paramount that you choose someone who is supportive and respectful and can listen to your opinions without the need to dominate your interactions. That's the only way that you will continue to grow and evolve in your professional and personal life.

4

Want to Move Forward? Let Go of the Past

The year of my affair with Philippe was both exhilarating and terrifying. I knew it was only a matter of time before Jeff found out. Yet I wasn't strong enough to ask for a divorce, knowing how much pain I would cause him and how angry he would be, especially since I was still grappling with the fact that all of this was actually happening. I was also fearful of the impact a divorce might have on our daughters, who were about to start elementary school.

Eventually, though, Jeff started to suspect something was going on and confronted me. I was guilty and grief-stricken as I told him about Philippe, and Jeff was understandably hurt and furious.

Things got messy and painful after that. They stayed that way for a long time. To this day, I wish I'd handled things better, but at that time in my life, I needed a catalyst to leave my marriage. Perhaps I subconsciously wished for Jeff to find out about the affair, because just picking up and leaving on my own with two small children seemed too formidable. I really didn't believe I could survive on my own.

I felt like a complete outcast for a long time after separating from Jeff. The women I'd known at Reebok put two and two together when they saw me with Philippe; not surprisingly, we became the source of jokes and gossip. Worst of all, my girls were in school, and suddenly I had to explain to the teachers why I was attending teacher conferences alone. In that entire class, only one other child had divorced parents.

People say to me now, "Wow, you were so strong, leaving your marriage." I certainly didn't feel that way at the time. But, in retrospect, it did take courage to ultimately choose the vast unknown over the relative security of being someone's—anyone's—wife.

What gave me the strength to tell Jeff the truth and leave him, instead of trying to salvage my marriage? As the girls got older and their personalities continued to develop, I was realizing more and more that I didn't want them to live in a household with so much unhappiness and marital strife. That was probably the biggest motivating factor.

It's interesting that I couldn't make the decision based on my own needs, yet I felt entirely comfortable making it for the sake of my daughters. I just didn't value myself enough at that time to consider that what was best for me might also be best for them.

When Philippe and I fell in love, I had hoped for a future with him, but it was not to be. We broke up after an intense two-year relationship. Although he disagreed with me at the time, I knew Philippe had a lot of self-exploration to do, and he needed to do it without me. As conflicted and scared as I was to venture forth alone, something was telling me that I had a lot of my own self-exploration to do, too.

Philippe's first step was to go back to school. After graduating from Columbia, he followed his dream to work in politics. I'd always known he was exceptionally bright, so it came as no surprise to me that he moved up the ranks quickly to become press secretary as well as a political consultant to Hillary Clinton. When she became secretary of state, Philippe was named deputy assistant secretary of state for strategic communications.

Philippe had been incredibly supportive when it came to helping me make the transition from marriage to living on my own, handling everything from finding me an apartment to teaching me how to use a computer and manage my finances. We were in constant touch during this time and he was my rock. We have always stayed in touch through the years; I thought Philippe was the perfect choice to advise and protect the U.S. senator, first lady, secretary of state, and Democratic nominee for president. I knew she was in good hands.

Each of us played an important role for the other, and Philippe and I both learned a great deal through our relationship. Once things ended with him, I found myself, at the age of thirty-nine, completely on my own for the first time. I was sad, but also strangely invigorated, finally free to do all of the things I probably should have done in my twenties but never did because I was too busy dancing.

Other than my newly precarious financial state, the biggest downside to being on my own was that I couldn't seem to stop myself from longing for an "ideal" partner. I dated many other men after things ended with Philippe. Some relationships lasted years, while others were short-lived. I still believed on some level that I needed a man to take care of me, so every time I broke up with someone, a few months later I'd find myself with another guy. I entered each relationship believing it was "the one," only to repeat the same tired pattern, losing myself as I tried to be that man's angel in some way, doing whatever it took to make him happy.

Of course, that never worked any better with these new relationships than it did with Jeff. I just couldn't see the pattern yet. I had a lot of growing up left to do.

The summer after I started spinning at Reebok, I had searched for a way to keep it up on Long Island, near our second home. I found a boutique spinning studio in East Hampton called The Zone, owned by Richard Gossett and Dacey Eric. This husband-and-wife team was the first to take a stab at creating a boutique spin business on the East Coast. They quickly created a strong community of devoted riders.

The Zone felt like summer camp, and when the season was over, you could feel everyone's sadness at having to say goodbye. Riders always pleaded with Richard and Dacey to open a studio in New York City, because there was nothing like it there, but they had their hands full managing the business in East Hampton.

Through the years, I had gotten better at spinning, and in the summer of 1999, Richard and Dacey asked me to teach at The Zone. I was excited by the opportunity, but anxious, too. This would be a real test of my abilities.

The students in the spin classes at Reebok—like the students in Lee Martin's classes, or in any other boutique fitness studio—tended to be critical, discerning, intimidating, high-powered individuals with successful careers—or, at least, successful spouses. The riders at The Zone presented my toughest crowd yet. This place attracted the top .01 percent. The Zone riders were picky, and I knew they were probably going to have that weird mindset kids get when there's a substitute teacher, saying to themselves, "I know I'm going to hate her."

That first class was every bit as difficult to teach as I had anticipated. A small group showed up, mostly supportive friends and strangers. There would have been more riders, except that several people walked through the door, saw a new instructor, and walked right back out again without even giving me a shot.

Despite this rocky start, I fully believed that with my love of music, my dance background, and my passionate commitment to this form of exercise I would find a way to win people over. And I had a bigger goal: to create spin classes that would take riders to a place of reflection and meditation, even as they grew stronger and more confident.

As I continued teaching at The Zone, I did my best to channel Glenn. He had a confident, cool vibe that I wanted to emulate. Thankfully, the teaching got easier with every class, as I began to really understand how to put together playlists that were pleasing to my students.

In spinning, there are different things you can do on the bike depending on the music. For instance, you can ride out of the saddle for eight counts, then sit for eight counts, or you can pedal standing up for four and sit for two. A great spin instructor choreographs the movement of the riders to the music in sequences that make the ride challenging but fun.

When spinning classes first became popular, instructors always played electronic music without lyrics like Glenn did. This was a kind of techno music that could put you into a sort of trance state as you rode. I also played techno music at first, but gradually I started to recognize the power of music and pedaling combined, and all that it could do for the rider mentally and physically. That led me to wonder how a playlist *with* lyrics, and with references to our past and present, might take riders even deeper into their journeys.

I began experimenting with my playlists, adding songs from an array of genres ranging from rock to blues, from classic crooners to reggae. In a single class, I might play Neil Young, the Commodores, Led Zeppelin, and the Bee Gees. The more risks I took, the more people seemed to be flocking to my classes.

By "risks," I mean I might have a room full of people in their thirties and play Frank Sinatra for them. Conversely, my students might be over fifty, and I'd play the top contemporary hit. I found that if the beat of a song was good and the lyrics were relatable, that song became a successful motivator.

As I had when dancing, I let the rhythms and moods of the songs dictate the movement. Bruce Springsteen's "I'm On Fire" might not be the song that gets you out of your seat at one of his shows, for instance, but it can certainly keep you riding a steady "flat road" while you are navigating through all kinds of emotions. George Michael's "Faith," on the other hand, might inspire you to rise out of that bike seat and move to the beat with intervals timed to the count of the measure.

Before long, I was choreographing my spin classes in ways that were similar to how I had once choreographed dances. The result was moving "as a pack," as we sometimes say in class. The visual of this movement in the mirrors surrounding the riders created additional power and energy in the room, because we were all generating it and feeling it together. When we were sprinting, we were sprinting together, and there was a rush of energy that surrounded every rider, just as we were all challenged together when we were tackling a slower, heavier climb.

I felt strongly—and still do—that this combination of music and choreographed movement lifted indoor cycling out of the "exercise" category and into a whole other experience. So often, riders line up after class to ask me, "What was the first song you played today? What was the last one? Where can I find that remix?"

I love it when they ask me that, because it shows that the time and thought I put into a great playlist paid off for my riders. Creating a great playlist is no easy feat. There are the tempo and mood choices, female vs. male vocalists, soloists vs. bands, and then the sequencing of it all. Often I will make my playlist the night before my classes, and then edit and even sometimes completely redo it the next morning. If I don't feel the music, my riders won't feel it, and the experience just won't be up to par.

Creating playlists for my spin classes has allowed me to draw upon a lifetime of music experience. Hearing a rider say,

"I can't believe you played that Police song! I didn't think anyone knew that one!" gives me so much satisfaction. I also like the idea of exposing people to music they've never heard before, because I know how powerful music can be. Creating these playlists is still one of the greatest pleasures of my profession. Playing inspirational, recognizable music with lyrics became part of my signature ride. Spinning wasn't a new form of exercise, but I was transforming the workout into something more.

It wasn't long before I had my own following at The Zone.

That fall, I returned to the city and resumed taking classes at Reebok, only to discover that Glenn was moving to Florida. I was devastated. Glenn was my guru and had been an important figure in my life, playing an enormous role in helping me work through my divorce emotionally and mentally, while also introducing me to a whole new way to work out.

We all felt his absence keenly. It became clear that none of the other spin instructors were as dynamic on the podium as he was, or had the charisma to build a community of riders who rode together not only in the same room, but also on the same beat, feeling the power and strength of riding as a pack. Glenn had made us stronger physically; more importantly, he had encouraged us to become empowered mentally.

There was only one thing to do: try out for his job.

I mentioned my desire to another instructor. When he encouraged me to follow through and audition, I put together a few songs, rode for the managers at Reebok, and was floored when they hired me in two minutes.

I had a job! Now, between teaching spin classes and child support from Jeff, I could make it on my own. It wasn't a grand living, but it was a start. What mattered most was that I was finally doing work I loved.

And, without knowing it, I had made a significant career move—one that would lead me to co-found not one but two incredibly successful national businesses.

In 2004, I had been teaching spin classes at both The Zone and Reebok for a few years when I first met Julie Rice. A year later I met Elizabeth Cutler; she and Julie would become my first business partners. By this point, Marion Roaman had acquired The Zone after Richard and Dacey decided to get out of the business. She changed the name to ZoneHampton; the studio eventually moved to a new location in East Hampton.

There were moments during those difficult years when I would come home in tears because I was so exhausted from teaching multiple spin classes for very little money while at the same time trying to manage life as the single mother of twins. Money was so tight that, during the summers when I was teaching at ZoneHampton, I had to stay in the house designated for instructors. It was a damp, rundown place and, like most of the other instructors, I hated it. I hated being away from the girls, too, who were spending weekends and vacation time with Jeff.

I met Julie at the Reebok Club. When she showed up in one of my classes, I noticed her immediately; all experienced spin instructors spot the strongest riders in the room pretty quickly, and it was evident that she was a seasoned rider. It was a pleasure to have her in my class.

By that point in my teaching career, I felt confident as an

instructor. I had been honing my method over the years. Still, I was surprised and flattered when Julie introduced herself one day after a ride and said, "Your class is amazing." She told me that I was the first instructor she had found who was better than any of the spin instructors she'd had in Los Angeles, where she had been living before moving to New York City. There, Julie was a regular rider at Body and Soul, a small boutique spin studio in West Hollywood with a cult following. Tevià Celli, one of its founders and a legendary spin instructor, ended up teaching for us at Flywheel in LA.

Julie quickly became not only a regular in my class but a friend. We shared a deep love of spin—maybe even an obsession—and that helped us form our first strong bond. I was completely in awe of her. She appeared to be everything that I felt I wasn't: hip, opinionated, sharp-witted, happily married, and outwardly confident about everything she did. She had a unique style, especially in clothes, and her prior experience working for a Los Angeles talent agency run by Benny Medina meant that she was connected with a lot of celebrities and was never short of great gossip.

It wasn't long before I was friends not only with Julie but with her husband, Spencer. The three of us often ate dinner together, hung out at their apartment, or went to movies. Julie and Spencer both had a great sense of humor and always made me laugh. This went a long way whenever I showed up at their door in tears because of a broken heart, which happened more than once. Julie always managed to turn things around, so that by the end of our conversation, I no longer even wanted to be with the person I'd been pining away for!

The fact that Julie always seemed so sure of herself was another powerful draw, since I was the sort of person who always second-guessed herself. I began relying on Julie for advice about everything from boyfriends to shoes and considered her the sort of close friend you can trust in any situation.

She and I had endless conversations about our dream to open our own boutique spin studio in New York City. I'd had my experiences at The Zone in Easthampton, and she'd had hers at Body and Soul. We were both disenchanted with the spin classes offered by big-box gyms, including Reebok, and knew that we had what it took to open a successful spin studio in New York. With Julie's connections to the celebrity crowd and my experience as an instructor with a popular teaching method and a big following, we had a lot to offer. The only thing we lacked was capital.

We talked about applying for a business loan and looking for locations, but neither one of us had enough business experience for any landlord to want to take a risk on us, and we certainly didn't have the capital to fund a start-up venture. Julie wasn't working, Spencer was starting a new career, and I had no money to spare. We were stuck, though we continued to dream about our own studio anyway.

Through my years of teaching at the Reebok Club, I started noticing that "spinners" were unique exercisers in that they only really wanted to work out by spinning. There they all were, paying an enormously expensive gym membership, yet using only the spin room. That clearly indicated to me that a boutique fitness business offering only spin classes could definitely have legs! I began constantly thinking of ways in which the class experience could be improved and could warrant a higher price.

As a group fitness instructor at a gym, you're pretty much left on your own once your class begins. At times this can prove to be quite challenging for the instructor. The sound system fails at times, or the mic might go out. People sometimes walk in late and need help setting themselves up. For all of these reasons and more, I believed that having other staff around to support the instructor would be one key way to improve the overall experience for riders.

Another common phenomenon at gym classes was riders not only entering late, but also exiting the room whenever they felt like it. This proved disruptive to the rest of the class as well as the instructor. In my imagined boutique spin studio, I had additional staff, a better sound system, and more attentive customer service, all of which would allow me to really take the experience and discipline of spinning to a whole other level for my riders.

In addition, coming from my dance background, I naturally drew parallels between spinning and dancing, and wanted to borrow certain inherent qualities one would find in a dance class and carry them over into a spin class.

First and foremost, there was a certain respect for the dance teacher exhibited by everyone in the class. Nobody ever entered a dance class late or left early unless the teacher was informed of this before the class started, because otherwise you would convey disrespect to both the teacher and the discipline.

It was also a given that class members would applaud the teacher at the end of class, again out of respect. The camaraderie from the shared experience of the dance class was equally present in the spin class. After moving, exerting, and sweating together, we would applaud not only the instructor, but also ourselves for getting through it!

Little did I know that the opportunity to create the unique boutique spin studio of my imagination was just around the corner.

In the summer of 2005, I was teaching at The Zone when I met another woman, Elizabeth Cutler. She took my classes regularly there. Then, to my delight, she showed up at Reebok in the fall and started taking my classes there, too.

One day, Elizabeth approached me after class at Reebok and told me that she loved my classes. Furthermore, she wanted to open a spin studio in New York City, one where the classes would be like mine. Not only that, she wanted me to be her partner as the face of the business, and offered to put in the seed money to get us started. "What do you think?" she asked.

I didn't have to think about it at all. This was my dream, and it was happening! "Done," I said. "I'm in."

Elizabeth and I started scheduling some brainstorming sessions where I shared the thoughts I had about what would make a boutique spin studio succeed based on the observations I'd made throughout the past five years of teaching. I could hardly contain my excitement as we scribbled our notes on paper napkins at various New York diners.

Then, one day, I thought of Julie and the conversations we'd been having. "Listen," I told Elizabeth, "I know another woman who might be interested in joining us. I think she could be a real asset to our partnership. Would you be interested in talking to her?"

I gave Elizabeth the hard sell on Julie not only because I really believed in what Julie could bring to the partnership, but also out of my strong sense of loyalty to her as a friend.

"Sure," Elizabeth said. "Let's meet."

Not long after that, the three of us set up a preliminary meeting, and I introduced Julie to Elizabeth.

Our first meeting took place in the fall of 2005 over lunch at the SoHo House. Elizabeth's husband ate lunch with Julie, Elizabeth, and me. We all talked about our visions and ideas, and Elizabeth instantly knew Julie would complete our dynamic trio.

Elizabeth had made a good profit on an investment she'd made on an all-natural soda company, and she agreed to back our start-up venture financially during its initial phase. We all hugged after lunch and parted ways, three great partners. I couldn't wait to get started.

The next time we met was at Elizabeth's apartment. It was clear that Elizabeth and Julie had hit it off, and I was thrilled to be in the company of two such energetic women who exuded confidence. At this meeting, we discussed the terms of our partnership, and over the next few months, we continued meeting periodically to discuss details about how the business would be run and, after some deliberation, chose the name SoulCycle for our new business. The name seemed perfect, because spinning for me really is a profound mind-body exercise. I loved the idea of creating a boutique fitness studio with a name that would clearly reflect the intent behind my teaching, which was equally about fitness and mindfulness.

We eventually landed on using a wheel as the logical symbol for our brand, because the image represented cycling on a bike as well as the different cycles of life.

Elizabeth had a friend who was a graphic designer and lived in Australia. She felt strongly about using her to help us with our visual ID. We went through many different design iterations of the wheel that would become our logo before finally landing on the one that felt right. After deliberating between green and yellow, we eventually chose yellow and white for our colors.

Next, we had to find a location. Coincidentally, the space where we opened our first SoulCycle studio was on 72nd Street between Amsterdam and Columbus, right across the street from where I had taught at Lee's studio, Bjorkman & Martin. Elizabeth found the space through a realtor and the three of us went to look at it together. It was a former dance studio on the street level at the back of the building—just a little hole in the wall, really. But it had one great selling point: a bank of windows facing the courtyard. Lastly, the price was right.

Finally came the exciting frenzy of ordering equipment and rehabbing the studio to accommodate thirty-three spinning bikes—all that would fit—plus a front desk and a tiny back office. Fueled by adrenaline and enthusiasm, we worked night and day, brainstorming about things like how to market our business, where to find other instructors, and how I'd train them.

We were very budget conscious. The studio was mirrored on the front wall, and we papered the back wall with a black-and-white photograph of a road. We spent hours upon hours going through stock photographs in search of that perfect road, finally landing on one that helped create the feeling of an infinite, open horizon in what was a very cramped space. Another perk was that the back wall of the space had windows. Although we needed to put bars in front of them, we were able to camouflage the bars with some tall bamboo plants, and it was great to have daylight pouring into the space through the greenery.

Meanwhile, our office was literally a cubicle, with a wall of cubbies separating us from our front desk, a cheap IKEA find. Julie decorated the shelves with tall glass vases filled with lemons, and we chose candles scented with grapefruit, which quickly became our signature scent.

All three of us were excited about our collaboration. Each of us brought something unique to the partnership. Elizabeth provided the start-up money and some real estate experience, while Julie brought her talents in design and marketing, as well as her celebrity contacts. I was the only one of us with any background in teaching a spin class; I brought six years of experience, a steady following of enthusiastic students, and my breadth of knowledge and skills in dance, music, teaching, and choreography.

By the spring of 2006, we had a name, a brand, and a finished studio. The three of us officially opened our Soul-Cycle doors, and I held my breath.

I was the first and only SoulCycle instructor. What if nobody showed up to take my classes?

Lesson #5: Forgive Yourself

Getting involved with another man during the last months of my marriage was something that caused me to suffer a lot of guilt and distress. However, it also taught me the importance of learning how to forgive yourself after "life happens." I also realized how absolutely essential it is to explore the reasons that drove you to make certain decisions in the first place. I understand now that I was overwhelmed by trying to meet our family's needs. Taking spin classes was the first step toward finding something that was just for me. Spinning became a time I could let go of it all, even if it was only for forty-five minutes. As this cathartic form of exercise became an essential part of my daily life, I started to consider what a viable product this could be for other people. Without even realizing it, I had found my new passion and was starting to hone a teaching method that would become the basis of two nationwide businesses.

Regarding my affair, I look back on that now and understand that my grief over my father, coupled with the problems in my marriage, made that period a traumatic time in my life. In retrospect, I'm not sure I could have left my marriage without both spinning, which gave me the strength and confidence I needed to get myself unstuck, and Philippe, who showed me that it was possible to have a different kind of intimate relationship.

It's easy to play the blame game, but a relationship always takes two. I can now take responsibility for what I contributed to the breakdown of my marriage. What's important is that Jeff, my girls, and I have all arrived at a far better place, and we did it by working together. Jeff continues to be supportive of our daughters in every way, and Kate and Rachel love and cherish their relationship with their father. I have also embraced Jeff, his wife Kathy, and their two wonderful children. Kate and Rachel have become loving stepsisters to Jeff and

Kathy's children. On occasion, we all even share holidays together.

Jeff and I certainly communicate on a different level than we did during our marriage, and we have continued to co-parent effectively and respectfully. I am so proud of that and consider it one of my greatest accomplishments.

Never underestimate the importance of forgiveness, compassion, and understanding, whether it's with family, business partners, or employees. Some people never get there. Though it took a long time and a lot of work, I am proud to say that Jeff and I did.

I have forgiven my ex-husband for the hurts he bestowed during our marriage. It was more challenging to forgive myself for my own mistakes, but ultimately more important. You can't move forward without forgiving yourself and letting go of the past.

Lesson #6: Sometimes It's Best to Ignore "Good" Advice

After my divorce, people would hear I was teaching fitness classes and make dismissive comments about how "nice" it was that I was finding a way to exercise. Or they'd offer advice about something else I could try that would certainly be more lucrative, as Jeff did when he told me that I should become a realtor if I wanted to earn some "real" money.

It's true that there are many ways to make a decent living. You could go into sales or high tech, or work your way up in banking if earning money is your main goal.

If, however, you want to feed your soul as well as your

bank account, you may have to take risks and ignore the well-intentioned advice of others. I knew I couldn't work in an office. I needed music in my life, and I needed movement. Once I discovered spinning, I needed that—and, more importantly, I wanted to teach spinning to others so that they might find the same mental and physical outlet that I did.

Was I thinking, way back then, "Oh, good, I can start a business and make millions of dollars by spinning"?

Absolutely not. Even when Julie and I started playing around with the idea of opening our own spin studio, I wasn't considering the money. I was simply thinking about how wonderful it would be to make a real career doing something I loved with a great friend.

When I reflect on what might have happened if I'd listened to Jeff and sold real estate, or done something else that others might have considered a "real" job, I realize how lucky I am that I was stubborn enough to follow my own path. Otherwise, I never would have started two successful businesses.

The one key ingredient all successful enterprises share is passionate leadership. If you are going to become one of those passionate leaders—whether you're working for yourself or for someone else—you must do something that satisfies your soul, not just your wallet. This means defining "success" as living a life where you're excited to get up every morning and feeling content with the work you've done by the end of the day.

Interestingly, as Flywheel continues to grow, I still witness this lesson played out on a regular basis. We see so many people become part-time instructors who also have full-time careers in law, finance, academics, and any other field you can imagine. They nearly always end up leaving what are often very lucrative and impressive professions to become full-time indoor cycling instructors. Yes, the pay is less, but the opportunity in this field grows every day. They are taking a risk initially, but they are making a smart move in the long run by following their true passion. I feel gratified every time I hear another spin instructor's story, because I get to see how fulfilled they feel at Flywheel. One of the by-products of self-esteem is that you learn how to rely on your own gut instincts instead of feeling the need to always go to others for advice and decisions. Nobody can know you better than you know yourself. Trusting your instincts will invariably lead you down the right path and will likely bring you great success. Think about it: whether it's your partner, parent, or friend offering you personal or professional advice, that person probably has ulterior motives, even if they're subconscious.

For example, when Jeff suggested I sell real estate, I am sure that his main concern was for me to be able to shoulder greater expenses for our family after the divorce. In his mind, he was thinking practically. He had little faith in where the fitness field could ultimately take me financially.

Likewise, years later, I had a serious boyfriend who advised me that SoulCycle was a bad idea when we were getting the business off the ground. He was extremely bright and accomplished in the world of finance, and his opinion always mattered to me when it came to business. Something in my gut told me he was wrong, fortunately, and I kept following my path—as you should follow yours.

PART II

REJUVENATION

5

Respect Yourself Enough to Protect Yourself

By the time we opened our first SoulCycle studio on the Upper West Side in the spring of 2006, I had been divorced for ten years and I was forty-eight years old. It had been a quarter century since I'd given up on my dream of becoming a professional dancer.

In the course of those years, especially when I was financially on the edge and struggling emotionally, I experienced some dark hours. I was convinced my life was going to be bleak and joyless. Instead, here I was, thrilled to be the cofounder of a brand-new business—one I passionately believed in—with my friend Julie, whom I wholeheartedly admired, and with Elizabeth, who seemed kind and whom I hoped one day I could count as a good friend.

I won't lie. Those first months were precarious. We had perhaps a half-dozen people—or fewer—in each class. Determined to get every new person who walked through that door hooked on SoulCycle, I taught each class as if it were sold out, with full-on energy and excitement.

I felt acutely responsible for growing the business. As "the talent," and as someone who had already inspired a large and loyal following at Reebok and in my Hamptons spin classes, I would be the face of our new studio. I had been honing my method of teaching spin for years, and it was wholly my own. The pressure was on: Would my way of spinning be enough of a draw to support an entire business?

My teaching style at SoulCycle was really a continuation of the method I'd been developing in my classes at Reebok. One of my main concerns, then and now, was to keep my riders safe by teaching them to exercise in ways that would prevent injury. Fortunately, my years of dance training provided a solid foundation of knowledge to draw upon.

Whether a person was on or off the bike, safety started with the proper alignment and engagement of the rider's abdominal muscles. After that came correctly positioning the rider on a bike to maintain alignment, and then teaching riders to be conscious of how fast or slow they were going, how much or how little resistance was being used on the bike, the amount and intensity of intervals, etc. My end goal was to help each rider develop not only a leaner, stronger body, but a clearer and calmer state of mind.

Elizabeth, Julie, and I were adamant about wanting to offer our riders full-body workouts. We talked often about how to do this. One day, Elizabeth said, "Why not add a set of hand weights to the bike, and incorporate them into the workout?"

When Elizabeth first suggested the idea, I was hesitant. This had never been done in a spin class before, and my first instinct was that it would be too precarious for riders to pedal without holding the handlebars. But Elizabeth felt so strongly about adding an upper-body workout to spinning that I decided to try to make it work.

Eventually I concluded that if we could guide our riders to significantly slow down and maintain a moderate amount of resistance on the bike while they used the hand weights, and made sure they were engaging their abdominal muscles while sitting up, they would be working from a place of strength and protecting themselves against injury.

The three of us hopped on the bikes one day to try this new method. I put on some music and began to choreograph an arm sequence on the spot, making sure to exercise the muscle groups in the back and arms in a way that would prevent riders from knocking into each other. I had spent years teaching upper-body sequences with free weights when I was an instructor at Bjorkman & Martin. Now I simply incorporated weight sequences that could work on the bike, while staying mindful not to knock into the rider next to me. We were thrilled with this addition to the workout, and it stuck.

Our new method of spinning with arm weights was so unique that it caused a bit of controversy among critics in the fitness world. Many instructors originally refused to buy into this concept as being safe and/or effective. Eventually, however, using arm weights while spinning became a popular method and was adopted by numerous indoor cycling businesses.

As it turned out, about 80 percent of my riders at Reebok left their memberships at that beautiful, full-service gym to take classes with me at our comparatively cramped little studio in the back of a random building on West 72nd Street. Although I was amazed and delighted by this, I wasn't altogether surprised. It had been clear to me at Reebok that many of the spinners only spun, despite having so many other workout options at that facility. I'd had a feeling that they wouldn't mind giving up their gym memberships.

Spinning has always attracted a certain type of person. At the risk of generalizing, I can say that the majority are Type A personalities—people who strive for perfection rather than ever settle for anything. The result is that, through spinning, I have met many actors, musicians, dancers, and other celebrities, as well as icons of the sports and business worlds—people whose drive and diversity have really enriched my life.

Several of our first SoulCycle followers were celebrities. Personality-wise, they ran the gamut from quirky and reticent to loud and outspoken. I always found it important to get a quick read on what they wanted or needed so that they could feel as comfortable as any other rider in our spin classes.

At SoulCycle, one of the first celebrities to join us was actress Kyra Sedgwick, who had been one of my students at Reebok. She was a joy to have in class, always focused and ready to work hard. Kyra really felt the journey.

Another celebrity rider was my dear friend Katie Couric, whom I first met in the summer of 2005 while teaching at ZoneHampton in East Hampton. Katie had accompanied another woman, a regular rider I'd known for years. As so often happened after class, people congregated outside the studio to socialize for a bit before getting into our cars.

I had remained in the lobby that morning and was talking to someone about the fact that I was going through a particularly hard breakup of a four-year relationship. Katie overheard our conversation and shouted across the room, "I'm going through a breakup of a four-year relationship, too!"

The next thing I knew, I was in Katie's bedroom in East Hampton, where she began showing me books about narcissists. We realized very quickly that our ex-boyfriends shared a lot of personality traits and both fell into that category.

There's nothing like a shared hardship to bring people together, and that's exactly what happened with us. To this day, not only has Katie remained an incredibly good and loyal friend, but she continues to support my businesses with unrelenting enthusiasm. I'm really honored to know her, and I have the utmost respect for the path that her career has followed and the risks she has taken. She is always a source of inspiration for me.

Our SoulCycle celebrity clients also included TV star Kelly Ripa, model and actress Brooke Shields, Chelsea Clinton, and film producer Jane Rosenthal. Caroline Kennedy would often come and ride with her own group of friends, too, including Janet Elder and Maureen Dowd, longtime writers for the *New York Times*. They were all a pleasure to know.

Football legend Tiki Barber became a big fan of my classes at SoulCycle as well. I marveled at his incredibly lean and strong physique, but the main thing that struck me was the intensity of his focus in class. I suppose this is the kind of focus all professional athletes must bring to the game, because it's such an integral part of their success when they perform, but it always amazed me to watch how Tiki's eyes never wandered around the room when he was spinning. He would stare at one point in front of him and work as hard as he possibly could. After working with him, I often asked my classes to focus on the ride as if they were professional athletes, because I found his absolute dedication to fitness so inspiring.

Since our space was quite small, there was always staff around, ready to help take on the responsibilities that we used to have when we taught group fitness classes at the gym. It was a total luxury for us to have people ready and able to take care of everything we needed, whether it was a faulty mic or the need for another towel. All we really had to do as instructors was enter the room, get up on our podiums, and lead—or, for some, perform—for groups of people who wanted someone else to be in charge of their lives for forty-five minutes.

Gradually, I realized that the unexpected side effect of having instructors worry only about executing the best classes possible was that boutique spin instructors were becoming celebrities in their own right. When I think of the "rock stars" today who built this status on a spin bike, I can see how the roots of it all began.

We knew the potential was there for our newly minted spinning business to snowball as word spread about SoulCycle. We were hoping that our model was different enough from what was already out there for our momentum to pick up fast, and we did everything in our power to build on it quickly. For example, in addition to exclusively offering spin classes, we decided to offer a pay-per-class format instead of the more traditional monthly gym membership.

First, though, we had to devise ways to let people know SoulCycle even existed. One major sticking point when we were negotiating our lease was the fact that we were located in the back of the building, but the landlords refused to allow us to post signage outside. We came very close to giving up on the space as a result, but because we were impatient to get our enterprise started and couldn't find a better location at the time, we went ahead and rented the studio. Little did we know that eventually this lack of signage would prove to be an advantage: it created an exclusive aura, typically reserved for nightclubs, where you have to be in the right crowd to even know it exists. I certainly never anticipated a lineup of big black SUVs outside the studio on a daily basis after the word was out, but that's exactly what happened. We were unintentionally becoming the club you couldn't get into . . . a club for discerning members who wanted only the best.

Elizabeth had put up the money and negotiated the space. Julie's responsibilities included running the front desk, much of the marketing, and making connections with as many influential people as possible.

Of course, the irony was that our studio was far from posh. Our riders entered SoulCycle through a long, narrow hallway, walked past our one bathroom with no shower, and ended up standing in a cramped space in front while they signed in. We were charging more money than anyone was used to paying for a fitness class back then. On top of that, our riders were shelling out additional cash for water and shoe rentals.

Being in such a cramped space also meant riders had to wait for the previous class to exit the studio before they could enter. This led to sweaty bodies rubbing up against those about to sweat; it was, for lack of a better word, gross. But no one seemed to care.

In the early days of SoulCycle, there were a number of other problems as well. We felt better hiring people we knew at this early stage of the business. Some were aspiring actors and surely needed work. They were young and enthusiastic, but often partied just a little too hard at night, which sometimes led to them forgetting to come in the next morning or oversleeping. Julie would cover and do whatever needed to be done at the front desk while I taught.

Then there were the recurrent issues with our sound system. It would suddenly break, or the mic would cut out. And, when it did work, poor Tony, who rented a space upstairs for his private training gym, was constantly complaining to us about our music being too loud. (It probably was.)

Despite these glitches, SoulCycle began growing, slowly at first, then exponentially.

Before starting SoulCycle, I didn't even know what "branding" meant, but now I never underestimate the importance of a company's identity, visual and otherwise. Julie had a great eye. She did a wonderful job creating our "look," from the jars of lemons on our shelves and the mantras on the wall, to the style of our retail wear when we began a clothing line.

One day, Julie walked in with a small plant that she placed on the top shelf of the cubby unit. Being my mother's daughter and an arbiter of good taste, I remember thinking, "Wow, that's a little tacky. Not at all Julie's usual style."

But then she explained it was a "money tree," adding, "It's going to bring us good luck!"

I laughed and decided to put my faith in this meager-looking plant, too. Why not?

We added "keeping the faith" to our many other tasks during those long, long early days. Julie and Elizabeth papered the neighborhood with fliers and created press kits in our signature yellow folders with a logo sticker slapped on the front. They were sent to as many magazine and newspaper editors as we could think of. Julie also continued reaching out to whatever celebrity contacts she still had from her career as a talent agent, often offering them free classes.

I loved the heady excitement of being part of something bigger than myself and threw myself into doing whatever I could to help the business edge into the spotlight. All three of us were over the moon any time SoulCycle appeared in the press. Even the smallest mentions made us feel so proud.

For instance, I remember how thrilled we were when a writer from the website DailyCandy signed up for class. At the time, every new and trendy business appeared on this blog, and we were dying to get into it, too. We couldn't decide how cool to play it with the writer, or whether it was better to let her know that we were aware that she was riding at Soul-Cycle or not. She seemed unfriendly and unenthusiastic when she left the studio. However, that clearly didn't represent her experience. In the end, we were featured on the site and given a very favorable review, a huge boon since the website targeted the audience we were trying to reach.

One of our biggest and most important press events took

place in the spring of 2007, when we held a fundraiser on behalf of the Democratic presidential campaign of Senator Hillary Rodham Clinton—with Bill Clinton as the speaker. The event was suggested by one of our riders, Ellen, who happened to be the daughter-in-law of Representative Nita M. Lowey, a Westchester Democrat. Representative Lowey praised the SoulCycle event for being healthier than the usual pigs-in-a-blanket cocktail party.

I could barely wrap my mind around this idea. Here we were, this brand-new, hole-in-the-wall business, yet Clinton had chosen to host a fundraiser here. The attention from the press would be huge.

I was teaching the class of riders who were paying to hear former president Clinton speak. Hoping he'd ride with us after his speech, I researched his favorite music and made a playlist with it to use during class. The list included Fleetwood Mac's "Don't Stop," Joni Mitchell's "Chelsea Morning," and Nina Simone's "I Wish I Knew How It Would Feel to Be Free." Clinton's people were leery about having a photo taken with him surrounded by a bunch of sweaty, scantily clad women. We handed out long-sleeved white T-shirts for everyone to wear during the event, printed with the phrase "Exercise Your Vote."

After President Clinton finished his speech, I mentioned that I had curated a playlist with some of his favorite songs. He asked me to play it again, and as he was toe-tapping, he sang along to Nina Simone's song. Afterward, I asked him to sign my CD, and he was happy to do it; that CD sits on my shelf to this day.

About thirty-five people paid $2,300 each to ride that night.

Mr. Clinton wore a suit and didn't end up spinning with us, but he talked about the importance of exercise and his wife's presidential platform. As Julie, Elizabeth, and I took pictures with him, we all knew this was a game changer for SoulCycle. *The New York Times* even picked up the story. We were definitely on the fitness map now.

Our clientele was continuing to expand rapidly, not just because of the brand or the celebrities people might rub elbows with while riding, but because our small posse of instructors was the best in town. In the beginning months, I had tried out different spin classes all over the city as I went on a mission to find the best possible SoulCycle instructors. I was looking for people who truly felt and understood music well enough to count and move to it. Beyond that, I was also searching for a certain allure or charisma on the bike—a personality, a voice, a physical presence.

As time went on and we began making a name for ourselves in the spin world, we no longer had to travel in search of instructors. Everyone wanted to teach at SoulCycle. People started approaching us and asking if they could apply to teach at our studio.

We began holding frequent instructor auditions, during which Julie and I would watch applicants ride to a few songs while we assessed them. Elizabeth occasionally joined us as well. It very quickly started to feel like we were the judges on *American Idol*. No doubt we really were "casting" to a certain extent, as every ride is more than an exercise class—it should be a complete mind-body experience, with the instructor driving.

Our *New York* magazine SoulCycle picture during our first year

In addition to recruiting and training instructors, I weighed in on decisions about the studio design and equipment and was responsible for creating SoulCycle's schedule of classes and matching classes to the right instructors. Julie liked to give her input in the scheduling as well and often had good insights. I also taught the bulk of the classes, and Julie and Elizabeth left it up to me to manage anything that happened inside the studio.

Although I'd never had any formal business education, my instincts were good when it came to managing our instructional staff and determining what time slots would be best for them, given the demographics of each class. As we slowly built up a cadre of instructors, I prepared a training manual and worked with each teacher for six to eight weeks. Instructors were also expected to take as many classes as possible as part of the training process.

My emphasis was to solidify and communicate the techniques I'd been using for years. I always embraced each instructor's unique personality, as well as his or her interpretation of the ride, yet I constantly emphasized the importance of structuring the rides to ward off any chances of injury to our riders.

More often than not, I would have to strip away whatever teaching methods these new instructors were using and start training them all over again. There were plenty of spin instructors out there with no education in anatomy and physiology. My goal was to show them how to help riders warm up safely before moving into interval training of any sort. This was especially important as we were introducing the use of arm weights.

I also taught SoulCycle instructors how essential it is to relate to riders on a personal level and make them feel noticed. New riders had to be set up and taught how to spin; I emphasized the importance of letting each rider know he or she should work at an individual pace, and reminded our instructors that learning to spin was a process, just like learning to do anything else.

"One inspirational word from you, and they'll work harder," I told our instructors. "Make eye contact with your riders when you're up there and give them shout-outs. A single word of praise can make a rider's day." I stressed the importance of always making the ride for and about the riders—not the instructor.

Another big part of the training process was teaching instructors how to make a playlist. I stressed how important it was to have an eclectic playlist covering a range of genres, so there would be something for everyone in the classes. Julie and Elizabeth asked why I didn't just give the new instructors my existing playlists, since I had some great ones, but I shook my head.

"My music inspires me, but it won't necessarily inspire another instructor," I said. "If the music choices don't motivate the instructors, they won't be able to motivate their classes."

Finally, one of the most challenging things for me in training these new instructors was teaching them how to incorporate a mindfulness aspect to the ride. This wasn't an easy concept to communicate, much less teach. For some instructors, it seemed to come naturally. To others, it never really became a part of their style. It took time and experience on that instructor pedestal before someone felt comfortable enough to share thoughts and words of inspiration.

I understood this, because for me it had taken time as well. It's scary up there, facing a roomful of people you don't necessarily know, who are probably judging everything from your hair to your voice to your legs. What I started to realize in my own development as a spin instructor was that the easiest way to inspire and transform people was through sharing my own experiences and challenges. Odds were good that most people out there were experiencing similar challenges of their own. I learned that being able to show vulnerability to a class of riders often inspired and encouraged them to feel safe and allow it for themselves. All of this contributed to that end result of transformation and empowerment at the finish of every class.

Just as I tried to take care of our riders by training the instructors properly, I did everything I could to help our instructors feel respected and cared for, too. Perhaps this was so important to me because of my background as a dancer. Dance requires extreme discipline and dedication, and the instructors are respected, even revered. It never occurred to us to question anything the dance teacher asked of us; we just did it. Now, I wanted to instill the same sort of discipline and respect at SoulCycle between the instructors and riders.

At Reebok, it was typical for members to walk into a class late or leave early. In deference to my hardworking instructors, and as a way of instilling discipline in our riders, I made a rule at SoulCycle that if riders showed up two minutes late without calling us ahead of time to tell us so, they would lose their bikes. Riders were expected to be there at the start of class and, barring extreme circumstances, to finish the entire session. I also expected there to be applause at the end of every class, again as in a dance class, as a way of demonstrating our appreciation for the efforts made by everyone involved. We were on this journey together.

When I reflect on the most successful spin instructors I've known, they are inevitably the ones who share something of themselves with riders—or even bare it all. We were fortunate to find two dynamite instructors early on who could do just that.

At the end of September 2006, Elizabeth told Julie and me about an instructor she had met out in East Hampton named Stacey Griffith. Originally from Los Angeles, Stacey had been in the fitness business for many years, teaching in various group fitness genres as well as doing some private training. She had a tumultuous past, and as a result, hadn't quite found her path. SoulCycle gave her the perfect platform.

While she had a rocky start with us, Stacey eventually came into her own as her popularity at SoulCycle began building. As so often happens, people who struggle against adversity and get through to the other side make the best fitness leaders and mentors, because they have so much to say. Stacey was a fine example of that. She brought her mantras and life lessons to the bike, and her classes almost became more motivational talk than physical exercise. But certain riders loved this, and she became a shining example of how inspiring and powerful a role model one can be on a bike.

Stacey was an important draw for SoulCycle early on. After my departure, she became a huge success.

Three months after Stacey joined us, I brought another instructor into the fold. Laurie Cole was recommended to me by someone I had worked with at both ZoneHampton and Reebok. I trusted his opinion and asked Laurie to come into SoulCycle for an audition.

Hiring Laurie was a no-brainer. Although it took her some months to build a following, she was determined to be successful with us, and she was. Laurie was a charismatic instructor with a great sense of music, and her playlists were always diverse and motivating. It didn't hurt that she was an actress; Julie referred to Laurie as a "Courtney Cox look-alike" who knew how to work her personality on the bike. Laurie soon became another powerful force at SoulCycle.

It was now up to Laurie, Stacey, and me to create magic daily in subpar conditions. The three of us had very different teaching styles, and each of us appealed to a different cadre of riders: Stacey was the coach, Laurie was the self-appointed guru, and I was considered the soulful legend.

Together, we made a dynamic team.

Julie and Elizabeth spent a lot of time outside of the office once we started hiring staff for the front desk, so they weren't as visible to the riders. During those early months, especially, I taught a crazy number of hours—up to twenty classes a week. I taught so many classes that it wasn't unusual for me to over-hear clients refer to SoulCycle as "Ruth's Studio," especially the people who had followed me from Reebok.

By opening in the spring, so close to summer, it was defi-nitely a challenging time to fill classes. New Yorkers tend to vacate the city and escape to the Hamptons, Cape Cod, Nan-tucket, Europe, and other popular vacation destinations. As a result, those first six months consisted of classes that often had six or eight people in them. Teaching small classes re-quires much more energy than teaching large ones. As the instructor, you have to be engaged and compelling enough to make up for all of those empty bikes in the room. Despite my exhaustion from "bringing it" every time I got on that po-dium, I was determined to build the numbers. As the average group size began slowly increasing, I felt so gratified. My hard work, along with Julie's and Elizabeth's, was paying off.

Spencer, Julie's husband, called me "The Fountain of Ruth." The amount I was spinning, as well as the fact that I was blessed with genetics that allowed me to appear a good ten years younger than my age, meant my body had never been more toned.

Ironically, I had also never felt more wrung out. I was working long hours, and by the time SoulCycle opened its doors, my daughters Kate and Rachel were sixteen years old and facing the tough challenges presented to children growing up in New York City.

Thanks to Jeff, our daughters attended private schools and were receiving a fine education, but many of their fellow classmates had absent or overworked parents. These children had plenty of money and often very few boundaries. As late-night parties, drinking, and boys began presenting complex issues for my daughters to navigate in their own lives, I faced an uphill battle. It didn't matter how many hours I was working. I was still on the clock as a mother full-time, struggling to keep tabs on the whereabouts of my children, instill the right values, and create constant reality checks. I wanted Kate and Rachel to understand what the "real" world was like for people who didn't benefit from the same level of privileged upbringing they and their classmates were enjoying.

At the same time, Kate and Rachel were adjusting to the fact that their father had remarried in 2002 and now had a three-year-old son. Soon Jeff would have another child, a daughter. Despite his growing family, Jeff's commitment to Kate and Rachel never wavered, but his time and attention were naturally split. As a result, I often overcompensated, doing anything I could to assure my children that they were loved. This took a great deal of time and energy. I had continued to date men after the divorce, but nothing developed into a permanent relationship. Previously, I had often given too much to my boyfriends in attempts to please them. Now I found myself holding men at arm's length. When it came to choosing between the man in my life and my daughters, I always erred on the side of the girls' needs, saving most of myself for them rather than sharing my whole heart and soul with anyone else. Even my longest relationships suffered due to my unwillingness to blend any of these men into the life I lived with my daughters.

My top priority was still motherhood. I made it a point to always be there for breakfast with Kate and Rachel, and to always be home at the end of the school day, with dinner waiting. Not having a husband or nanny meant that juggling the start of SoulCycle with family life was very challenging. Julie and Elizabeth had young children but benefited from having both husbands and additional help from nannies or extended family.

There's no question that I was sometimes tired and irritable during our start-up phase. My daughters were, too. Both girls were swamped with homework, with Rachel often working until two in the morning. She was also playing basketball after school, so she operated in a constant state of exhaustion.

Kate was entering an all-girls school as a sophomore the same fall we opened our first studio. She often came home in tears and told me stories about being excluded from conversations, parties, and the various cliques. This broke my heart, and I made a special point of always being home in the afternoons, with my arms open, in case she'd had a hard day.

Elizabeth and Julie both marveled at the fact that my children were already teenagers. Julie, especially, was always curious about what was going on with Kate and Rachel and told me she was taking mental notes to prepare for her own daughter's teen years. I did my best to offer whatever parenting insights I had, though I knew her journey would necessarily be different from my own as a single mother working long hours to support both our new business venture and my daughters.

According to the U.S. Bureau of Labor, the odds of a small business surviving aren't as slim as you might think: about 75 percent of new businesses survive their first year, and half of them are still viable after five years.

Sure, fifty-fifty odds might not sound that great, but it's the old "half-full" or "half-empty" perspective: this also means you have a 50 percent chance of creating a successful enterprise— provided you're smart about keeping costs down and putting money back into the business so it will grow. We kept our costs reasonable when starting SoulCycle. Thanks to Elizabeth's initial financial investment, we also avoided taking on huge start-up debt. We spent zero dollars on advertising, counting on word-of-mouth. We were also creative. For example, Elizabeth's solution to the lack of signage outside was to paint a big rickshaw bright yellow and park it by our outside entrance.

In the early spring of 2007, Julie and I began talking to Elizabeth about opening a studio somewhere in the Hamptons. We knew it was a good idea, but we needed her approval since Elizabeth had seeded the business. She and her husband also had a lot of experience in real estate investments.

Julie and I made a solid argument for choosing the Hamptons as our second SoulCycle location. Our current clientele and target demographic basically migrated out to Eastern Long

Island for the summer—just as Jeff and I always had—and stayed put until after Labor Day, when their kids returned to school. What better way to keep our old clients and gain new recognition from the elite crop of New Yorkers who could afford to summer there? Plus, they could bring their friends.

We also knew that the demographic in the Hamptons reached well past New York; it was international. Extending our reach into the Hamptons could drive a huge growth spurt for SoulCycle.

Elizabeth was easily sold on the idea. In a way, she was our target audience, since she already owned a house on Eastern Long Island. The three of us took a road trip to look at spaces, our enthusiasm building as we fantasized about our new plan. The realtor had told us about a barn available in Bridgehampton that sounded perfect.

It was love at first sight. The barn was big, bright, and airy, with the perfect rustic feel. We nearly lost the property to another bidder, but Elizabeth managed to wrangle a deal, and the barn was ours. Her perseverance and real estate experience really paid off.

I couldn't have been happier about the prospect of teaching there. Not only was the space ideal for a spin studio, but I was used to spending my summers in the Hamptons. I had created some of my favorite memories with my daughters there.

The next logical step in our plan was to find suitable summer living arrangements for Julie and me. Neither of us had much money at that point, and the business was paying for the rental, so it seemed reasonable for me to share a house with Julie and her family.

Elizabeth, Julie, and I took another road trip out east together and worked with a broker who showed us seven houses in a single, exhausting day. One home had four bedrooms; the rest all had three.

We discussed our options on the way back into the city, tired out from our long day. I didn't want any sort of luxurious summer rental, but I hoped we could rent a house with four bedrooms, so there would be room for my daughters as well as Julie's toddler, husband, and mother-in-law, who would be acting as the children's nanny. I longed to have my children spend at least part of the summer living with me.

There was just one problem: the only house available that would be big enough to accommodate my girls was a mess and ultimately depressing. Any other four-bedroom rentals were too expensive. We finally opted for one of the three-bedroom choices in Sag Harbor. I would not be able to accommodate my girls, unfortunately, but at least they could stay at Jeff's house, and we figured out ways to see each other during the summer.

The Sag Harbor house featured two bedrooms upstairs and a larger master bedroom on the main floor. It was the logical choice for Julie and Spencer to stay in one of the upstairs bedrooms, with Julie's mother-in-law and their daughter in the other bedroom across the hall. Their family could occupy the entire floor.

Taking the larger master bedroom downstairs at least served as a small consolation for having to stay in this three-bedroom house without my daughters. I even had a separate entrance, which offered more privacy for all of us.

I settled in as best I could. We had some good times in

that house. I remember coming back late after some random dates to find Julie and Spencer watching TV in the living room. They often wanted to hear a recap of my evening. It was like coming home to my parents, which was ironic, considering I was so much older and in such a different place in my life than they were.

By early fall 2007, I was back in New York City and business had really picked up. With SoulCycle attracting the elite New York heavy hitters, it wasn't surprising that classmates from the private school Kate and Rachel attended knew about the business through their parents. As a result, these parents sometime brought their kids to classes on weekends or holidays.

I was always happy to see them, since Kate and Rachel were so proud of me. Whenever they overheard their peers talking about SoulCycle, they always jumped in and told them that their mom had started the business. I loved being a career role model for my daughters the way my father had been for me.

Meanwhile, the studio was booming. We could barely fit everyone into our classes; they were nearly always sold out, with waiting lists besides. Julie was pushing us to start thinking about expanding, and we all started talking about where we might locate a second studio in the city.

Elizabeth dragged her heels on this idea. I was resistant, too, worrying about whether we had enough really good instructors. We were barely coping with the riders we had, and I argued in favor of keeping up the quality of our classes rather than growing too fast.

Eventually, Julie was able to convince Elizabeth to do it, and I was outvoted. They were right to do so. In hindsight, I can see that I was being too risk-averse—that was always my nature. The truth was that SoulCycle was on a roll, and it was a good time to capitalize on our progress. We chose an Upper East Side location for the next SoulCycle studio, since so many of the riders we had added from our summer in the Hamptons lived in that area.

I was thrilled by our rapidly growing business and more enthusiastic than ever about making SoulCycle a success. Unfortunately, things didn't go as I'd hoped. Our partnership ended so abruptly that I was left feeling wrung out and exhausted. What was I going to do now?

The ensuing months passed in a blur. Everything seemed to fall by the wayside, other than my classes at SoulCycle and endless meetings with lawyers as Julie, Elizabeth, and I worked out the necessary legalities involved in severing our partnership.

Eventually, we drew up a separation agreement and signed it in December 2007. During this time, the new studio space on the Upper East Side was in the process of being renovated and equipped, and I continued teaching classes at SoulCycle. Nobody except Laurie Cole—not the riders, not the other instructors—knew that I was no longer a partner in Soul-Cycle. And I told Laurie only because I considered her a friend at the time.

I was operating under the assumption that once the agreement was signed I would leave SoulCycle, but I had trouble envisioning what I would do next. My girls were seventeen by then; soon they'd be in college, and I'd really be at loose ends. The thought of going back to teach at the big-box gyms depressed me. I couldn't believe that the business I'd helped create and nurtured with such passion and excitement was no longer mine. What would I do without SoulCycle? I returned to the studio on 72nd Street to pack up the rest of my belongings. Julie happened to be at the front desk; after our conversation that day, I decided that my best option was to stay on as an instructor at SoulCycle, at least until I figured out my next career move.

For the next two years, I did stay on as an instructor at SoulCycle, but my emotions about my new, more limited role were all over the place and boiled over at unexpected times.

During the spring of 2007, for instance, my daughters were touring colleges. With the two of them looking at different schools, that meant a lot of visits. Jeff and I worked together to divide and conquer. Jeff handled most of the trips that involved flights, and I took the drives.

I didn't own a car, so I had to rent one for each of these college trips. At that time rental cars didn't come equipped with GPS systems, and I don't always have a great sense of direction. On one of these trips, I drove Kate to Schenectady, New York, to visit Union College. It was a disaster. We got lost on the way.

I began yelling and crying and ultimately had to pull over to the side of the road until I could calm down enough to keep driving. Poor Kate bore the brunt of my emotions at that moment. But I couldn't bottle them up: I didn't have a husband; I no longer had a business; and I didn't even own a car, let alone one with a GPS. My kids were going to college. I felt alone, completely overwhelmed, and terrified about the future.

To get through my intense feelings of loss over the ending of the SoulCycle partnership, I focused on doing what I loved most: teaching. As always, during the forty-five-minute classes with my riders, real life was suspended, and there was nothing but positive energy. Every class gave me as much as I gave the riders. I had developed close relationships with many of these people over the past seven years of teaching, and it was hard to give that up.

Teaching others in spin class always helped me remember that everybody out there faces challenges, every day. Whenever I'd start thinking my challenges were too big to handle, I'd talk to my riders and learn what was going on in their lives. Spinning helped me feel strong enough to face the rest of my life and keep moving, just as it had when my marriage was falling apart. I was part of an incredible community of people who came every day and did this form of exercise, exerting ourselves and bonding as we talked about various issues and grew stronger together. The courage of my riders always inspired me.

My friendships, especially with two new staff members at SoulCycle, also kept me going. Sue Molnar started with SoulCycle in January 2008 and was a great addition to our instructor pool. She was a rock-and-roller from South Carolina with a Southern drawl and an infectious laugh. She had an authentic, homespun quality, and I bonded with her immediately, especially since Sue and I were close in age. Like me, she related to her riders on a more social, peer-to-peer level, rather than as a guru or mentor. Sue and I both started to do more and more theme rides, which became very popular and turned into a mainstay on the schedule, though the themes were always changing.

Our Upper West Side studio also added a new manager that winter. Kate Hickl had recently moved to New York City from Texas and was a yoga instructor at the time. She was smart and extremely capable and did a great job for us.

In the summer of 2008, Kate came out east to manage our Bridgehampton studio and did a wonderful job there, too. I'm not sure anything could fully prepare a person to deal with the Hamptons' clientele. They were a discerning group and demanded the best instructors and classes. That was largely true of the SoulCycle riders in the city, too, but everything was heightened out on the east end of Long Island. However, Kate handled the stress with ease, and she and I became fast friends that summer.

Kate would typically pick me up from the jitney stop when I was coming out from the city, and I got a kick out of the way she drove. She was always barefoot, with her left foot up on the seat and her right foot on the gas pedal. I figured that that must be how they drove in Texas.

During our drives, we shared studio gossip and talked about our lives. I was grateful for our friendship, especially as Kate was the voice of reason whenever I was feeling down or frustrated.

I'll always remember our lunch toward the end of that summer at a health food restaurant in Sag Harbor. "I just don't know how much longer I can stay on at SoulCycle," I confessed.

"Whenever and wherever you go, Ruth, I'm going with you," Kate said.

I thanked her and readily agreed, grateful to have such a loyal friend. But the truth was that I remained clueless as to the "when" and "where."

Eventually, Kate decided that she really wanted to teach spin classes, so I trained her that summer. It didn't take long. By that fall, she was teaching and helping us recruit new instructors to prepare for the opening of our Upper East Side studio.

Life continued to be busy for me outside of SoulCycle, as my twins were both exploring college choices. We had been a wonderful, bonded triad, and when they left for college the following year, I felt stunned by my own solitude.

At the same time, I knew it was finally the right moment for me to focus fully on my next career move. There was just one problem: I didn't know what it should be.

Lesson #7: Want to Make Better Business Partnerships? Look at Your Family Dynamics

You never want to enter into a business partnership that repeats your failed personal or professional relationships. Unless we make an effort to understand our past, many of us replay our family dynamics and repeat our relationship issues in our romantic partners, friendships, and business associations.

An emotionally withholding father, for instance, might cause you to subconsciously choose the same sort of husband or partner, because that's a familiar personality type. In my case, I had a domineering mother, which meant I still hadn't figured out how to stand up for myself personally or professionally.

You don't need to be friends with your business partners. They don't even have to be people you'd necessarily want to socialize with, but there does have to be a certain level of mutual respect.

Ask yourself this: Will these partners treat me as an equal? Do they respect my talent and areas of expertise so that I will be empowered to make decisions? Will these partners understand the need for balance in my life and the importance of downtime when I need to take it? What is their approach to conflict if we have a disagreement?

Communicate clearly with your business partners about everything from your expectations of who will assume which responsibilities to how you'll resolve conflicts, especially around money issues and time constraints. Be sure your opinions are heard and valued from the outset, and the partnership will have a better chance of success.

6

Stay Open to Opportunity

I stayed on at SoulCycle until the summer of 2009. I was teaching in the Bridgehampton studio that summer when Jay Galluzzo, who was then working in private equity, began taking various classes there. Although I didn't know it at the time, Jay observed what was happening in the Bridgehampton barn and was blown away by SoulCycle's business model.

That fall, Jay returned to the city and spoke with his private equity partner, David Seldin. He told David all about the spin business, laying out the facts and figures until David saw the opportunity there.

What's more, Jay had a fresh idea: he wanted to add technology to spin bikes so that riders could choose to efficiently measure their progress. On the bikes we used at SoulCycle, riders could turn the resistance up or down, but there was no real way to measure what sort of output or goals riders were achieving. In Jay's view, riders were often cheating themselves out of the best workouts possible, pedaling without enough resistance to achieve their fitness goals.

Jay's concept was to add metrics to the ride by attaching computers to the bikes that would help riders calibrate their resistance and measure various aspects of their workouts. The computer would give the rider a points tally at the end of class, combining the metrics and ultimately representing the energy output. With this technology, riders could strive to achieve their personal bests, measure how hard they were working at any given point, and understand what they had accomplished by the time a class ended.

Throughout the fall, Jay worked on this concept—which he named Tricera Revolution—in earnest. He and David also began developing their platform for Tricera Partners, a boutique firm focused on partnering with entrepreneurs to bring new concepts to market and help operate them. Flywheel was the first Tricera project; they developed an exploratory plan and an informational presentation, hired a designer to work on a plan for the studio, found a developer to begin thinking through the tracking/competition technology, and set out to look for the perfect partner to lead the creative and cultural side of the business. Ideally, they were scouting around for a popular spin instructor who could understand this new idea and train instructors to introduce the technology successfully to riders.

They first approached a well-known spin instructor from Body and Soul in Los Angeles. When they inquired about her method for making class playlists, however, she just laughed and said she made them only minutes before each class, because they were completely dependent on her mood. This was a bit too improvised for them, so they wrote her off.

Next, David and Jay went to another SoulCycle instructor.

She approached me one afternoon and said, "Hey, I'm going to have this meeting with these two private equity guys about starting a new spin studio. You should come with me."

"Wow, that sounds interesting," I said. "Sure, I'll go."

The meeting was taking place at a townhouse on 63rd between Lexington and Park. On the way over, I asked the other instructor a million questions about who these people were and what they wanted to talk about, but all she knew was that one of them lived in this townhouse, "so the guy must have money."

The townhouse belonged to David, who opened the door and introduced himself before leading us to his office. The other instructor and I sat on one side of the table, with David and Jay on the other. They ordered a massive spread of top-quality sushi from Jewel Bako and then started sharing their ideas, giving us the hard sell and then asking our opinions.

"Do you think people would be interested in bikes with technology?" Jay asked. "And is there enough demand for a different kind of spin studio?"

We both assured them that it sounded interesting. I also told David and Jay that I thought there was plenty of room in the market for a new spin studio—especially one that brought something unique to the marketplace.

As we walked out of the townhouse that night, I said, "This feels like a dream that's too good to be true, doesn't it?"

The other instructor was more skeptical. "Yeah, I don't know if I want numbers on a bike."

Still, she was interested enough to meet with Jay and David again, so the four of us organized a series of conversations to talk details.

"We want you to be in charge of creating the whole method of spinning on these bikes," Jay said.

The more I talked with Jay and David, the more appeal their idea had. It seemed like the perfect fit for me. When they finally presented a formal offer, the other instructor said, "Sorry, I'm not interested." Down the road, I learned that both David and Jay were thrilled that I had decided to tag along with the instructor who invited me to the initial meeting. I was their top choice, so her declining made it that much easier for the three of us to move forward.

I grinned. "I'm in," I said. "But I need to have my lawyer look at the contract."

I was a late bloomer in business, but I had learned this much: I needed to protect myself, because nobody else was going to do it for me.

The negotiations did not go smoothly. David and Jay had been private equity partners for a long time, and through the next few weeks, I learned why their partnership was so valuable and successful: it was a good-cop, bad-cop kind of relationship, with David being the hardheaded one during negotiations. At some point, my attorney, Lance Harris, and I gave up trying to reach an agreement with him. Lance called me and said, "Ruth, what do you want to do here?"

I said, "You know, I don't think I want to keep going." I was feeling absolutely gun-shy due to David's hard-nosed communication style.

"Okay, I completely understand," Lance said. He then sent David and Jay an email saying, "My client has decided to go in a different direction, thank you very much." It was not a negotiating tactic at all. I really meant that I wanted out.

Literally thirty seconds later, my phones began ringing: both my cell and my land line. I also started getting emails and texts, all from Jay. I didn't know what to do, so I didn't respond to anything for a while. Another lesson I had learned at this point in my life was that you don't always *have* to respond to people just because they might want to speak. Especially in heated moments, it's always beneficial to wait, breathe, and respond only when you're feeling calm and ready.

Eventually, however, I listened to one of Jay's voicemails. "Ruth, if you could just call me as soon as you get this message, I'd appreciate it," he said, sounding panicked. "I really need to talk to you."

I called him back. "Just meet with me," he said. "Coffee, lunch, whatever you're comfortable with, okay?"

Two days later, on a cold Saturday, we met at a coffee shop on 57th Street on the Upper East Side and seated ourselves in a booth for two. "Okay, what do you want to talk about?" I said.

Jay started by apologizing for David's tough negotiating tactics and said he wanted to qualify something. "I can guarantee you that when David is on your side he will protect you like a lioness protects her cubs."

I wasn't certain I believed him. "I'm still not sure it's the right partnership for me."

"Look, let's just talk about what you want in the contract and what you don't want," he said. "Then I'll talk to David."

I couldn't see the harm in it, so I started going through my list of demands. I eventually agreed to join them if they would promise me a salary and a certain percentage of the business.

Jay accepted all of my terms, but I wasn't going to take his word for it. I wanted our agreement put in writing.

"I appreciate you agreeing to these things," I told him. "However, we still don't have a deal. I want to talk to my lawyer, and he will finalize everything. If and when there are continued negotiations, my lawyer will take over." Again, I was employing my hard-won lesson about not rushing into an answer. I wanted to grant myself plenty of time and get legal advice before I signed a formal agreement.

"Of course," Jay said.

I sat back in my chair and finally allowed myself to smile at him. I was pretty proud of myself at that moment. I'd done it: I had stood up for myself, and I'd found a promising new venture. Most importantly, my first true business partnership was born.

By the fall of 2009, David and Jay had found a space near the Flatiron Building they wanted to show me. David knew the owner of the building and felt the rent was a good deal.

I agreed to look at the space, but I was completely opposed to the location. "I think we should look for a place on the Upper West Side," I said. "I have a following there. I don't know anybody in this neighborhood. At least if we start on the Upper West Side, we'd have a guaranteed group from the beginning, because I know a lot of my riders would switch studios."

They were willing to look at alternatives, but at the same time, they kept producing statistics about the neighborhood's demographics. Our only workout competition in the Flatiron district was a private training gym across the street, and that

Jay Galluzzo and me, Flywheel co-founders

actually presented an opportunity for us to leverage synergy between the two companies, not a threat.

Around the same time we were discussing locations, we were deciding on a name for the business. My daughter Kate had chosen to transfer to Tulane University. While I was visiting her there, David and Jay arranged a conference call with me so the three of us could decide on a name. We had all been scanning over the parts of a bike in the hope of finding inspiration. Prior to the call, I had arrived at the "flywheel" and considered suggesting that for the business.

Before I could speak up, though, David had apparently arrived at the same word. Jay loved it, and the three of us decided it felt right.

After a few more conversations about where to open Flywheel's first studio, David and Jay persuaded me that the Flatiron area in Manhattan, close to Union Square and subway stops and an easy walk from the Empire State Building, had the right density of people to provide us with a steady stream of customers. I ultimately deferred to them because analyzing demographics fell within their domain of expertise, not mine. I had to trust them.

Thank goodness I did. David and Jay were right on target. Within the first few years of opening Flywheel, boutique fitness businesses started popping up all over the Flatiron district. Today the area is saturated with every kind of fitness offering you can imagine.

I was still teaching at SoulCycle and had kept my meetings with Jay and David under wraps for obvious reasons. However, at one point Kate Hickl pulled me aside because she'd heard rumors that I was leaving. "If you ever leave, I'm leaving with you," she declared, reminding me of her original promise.

I confided in her finally. "Good. I'm out of here when you are," Kate said after I'd told her about Flywheel.

"It's a deal," I said. "I'll tell David and Jay that I want you on board."

Soon after that conversation, I stopped teaching at SoulCycle completely. I was now able to start work on Flywheel in our temporary offices on 22nd Street, a block away from what would be our first flagship studio. Until that studio opened, I had a few months where I wouldn't be working as a spin instructor anywhere. I was concerned about not teaching for the sake of both my physical and emotional health. I was also nervous about holding on to some of my riders in the interim between the two businesses.

Then I had a sudden inspiration: I decided to approach the Jewish Community Center on the Upper West Side and ask if I could use their spin room to teach my followers for a few days each week. I'd had a great working relationship with the riders and staff there during my pre–SoulCycle days.

The facility wasn't exactly top-notch. It had a mediocre sound system at best, a bunch of bikes arranged kind of haphazardly, and a slippery wooden floor that was hardly ideal for bike shoes with cleats. However, Flywheel paid the JCC a nominal fee and we didn't charge the riders, so everyone benefited.

I'll never forget the group of riders who came during this interim period. Based on all that had happened, I treasured nothing more deeply than loyalty, and these people were all committed to me as a teacher.

Teaching during this transitional time was valuable for me, because it served as a preview of who might choose to ride with me at Flywheel and who might not. For instance, a very close friend told me that she wasn't coming to my classes because she didn't "like the facility" at the JCC. It was hard to wrap my head around that one. I would have thought that her desire to support me would have been more important than a less-than-perfect studio.

But this became a reality check, helping me brace myself for the inevitable disappointment when certain people didn't follow me to Flywheel. Over time, I learned not to take people's choices personally. Change is difficult. I had to accept that Flywheel couldn't be everything for everybody.

Lesson #8: Protect Yourself When Things Look Rosy, So You'll Be Protected If Things Fall Apart

I've seen it happen over and over again: friends or family members excitedly plot out a new business idea and passionately carry it through—only to have the business fall apart over personal or professional differences.

Don't make the same mistake. Even if you're working with a family member, as soon as you and another person form a business for profit, your company will be a general partnership and should be treated as such. Each individual partner will be liable for debts whether they agreed to them or not, and each partner will also be liable if something goes wrong and a lawsuit is involved. You need to sign a legal agreement with your business partner(s) so that none of you will encounter nasty surprises along the way.

Your agreement should be signed and sealed before any money starts being generated by the business. It should include:

- A clear description of each partner's current and future contributions to the business, whether those contributions will be financial or contributions of time. That way, it will be clear if one of your partners isn't meeting expectations.
- A plan for how you and your partner(s) will resolve disputes
- A plan for how you will handle profits and compensation—for instance, if one of you puts in more money, how and when will that money be repaid?

- A statement of each partner's power and whether business decisions will need to be made jointly
- An exit strategy—what if one of your partners dies, or decides she/he doesn't want to be involved anymore? The terms of dissolution, if your business stops being profitable or you want to end your involvement

Lesson #9: The Choice Really Is Yours

For many years, I felt like I had no choices. My parents guided me to work hard in school, and I never slacked off because I was afraid of disappointing them. My dance teachers kept me perfecting my technique and my husband dictated our social schedule.

But the truth is that this lack of choice was an illusion on my part. The option was always there for me to say "no." I just didn't realize it because I was so busy trying to please everyone. Or, to put it another way, I was always anxious about doing something wrong. I didn't want to disappoint my parents or displease my husband. My anxiety often clouded my ability to make the right choices for *me*. I was too busy reacting to other people's expectations and needs.

How do you make clear choices that are right for you, especially when you feel anxious about making a decision that might upset someone else?

Researchers have demonstrated in animal models that anxiety can literally shut down connections in the brain, making it tougher for us to screen out unnecessary information and make good choices. When you need to make a decision about something—whether it's work-related or not—make sure you've gotten enough sleep, cut down on the distractions around you, and do whatever it takes to put your body and mind in a more relaxed state. (For me, that means exercise.)

Remind yourself that there is usually no need to make a rushed decision. Timelines are often imposed by other people. If you can, slow things down and step away from "automatic" decision making. Paying close attention to your thoughts and emotional state will allow you to make more mindful choices that are right for *you*.

We must include ourselves in the equation of who is being pleased. Pleasing everyone else at the exclusion of ourselves always backfires. It's just another way of silencing your own voice, and you'll only be truly happy when you speak up so others can hear you.

7

Flywheel Takes Flight

When selecting the first bike we were going to use in our flagship Flywheel studio, I wanted to go with what was familiar to me, and to all of my riders, for that matter. It was the Schwinn bike we used at SoulCycle and at other big-box gyms.

David and Jay wanted to consider different options, but nothing else ever felt quite right to me.

There were quieter bikes, operated with a belt instead of a chain, but I felt strongly that the grittier, noisier effect of the chain was really part of the spinning experience. For lack of a better description, the sound it made was "badass." Since spinning always induced a certain empowering effect, this sound amplified the fact that riders were working hard to become stronger.

Prior to opening the studio, we had the bikes shipped to us. We hadn't realized upon purchasing them that some assembly would be required. There happened to be an empty warehouse space right next to our studio; since it wasn't rented out at the time, the landlord let us use it to build the bikes. David thought it would be a great bonding experience.

It was, but probably not in the way he intended. As it turned out, it was January, and there was no heat in the space. We were all freezing despite being bundled up in jackets, scarves, and gloves. It took an entire day to complete the project. And then, after we thought we were finished, one of us realized that the bikes were not assembled correctly. We ended up having to hire a crew to disassemble the bikes and rebuild them the right way. For a while we were all exhausted, pissed off, and ultimately sick with colds and coughs, but at least we had something to laugh about later.

David's wife, Stacey, and one of her business colleagues, Bob Rademacher, were instrumental in helping us design and build Flywheel's unique tech platform, from the booking software system right up through the TorqBoard. I was extremely grateful that they were both present the first time I tried riding a bike with the screen attached to it, because they were so familiar with this exciting new technology and could walk us through how it all worked. I admit to being nervous before I tried spinning on a bike with metrics. One of my favorite things about taking a spinning class had always been the ability to close my eyes and achieve a meditative mindset while listening to the music and the sound of the wheels spinning. That was the surest path to the mental transformation I'd always guided my riders to achieve, and I knew my Soul-Cycle followers loved it. Part of me was doubtful that people would want to look at a computer screen with numbers on it. Wouldn't that detract from the overall immersion experience of spinning to music?

But when Jay presented me with the first technology-equipped Flywheel bike, I gamely climbed onto it and started spinning to one of my favorite playlists, trying to imagine myself in front of a group of riders. For them to love this new way of spinning, I had to love the bike first and teach them how to use it properly.

To my delight, I recognized immediately that this studio bike was a game changer. Just as Jay had promised, it would make the rider accountable.

"Torq" became our word for "resistance." The Flywheel bikes were equipped with a small screen, which displayed resistance ("Torq"), cadence ("RPMs"), power output, and a final points tally ("Total"). There was also a large flatscreen in the front of the stadium called the TorqBoard where riders could opt to see how they stacked up against one another during the class, as well as compete in races if they chose.

The consistent consensus among all of the riders I have known at both SoulCycle and Flywheel is that we spin for both our minds and our bodies. Before Flywheel, spinners never used technology like ours. The emphasis in my teaching was more on the mindful and meditative aspect of the ride. Now that we were introducing the idea of computer screens on the bike to keep the rider accountable, I was thrilled to have the chance to make the physical component equally effective. Whether the Flywheel riders chose to look at the computer screen or not was entirely up to them. Having two "TorqBoards" mounted at the front of the stadium showed the metrics of each rider as we rode through the class, but again, whether riders wanted to look at those metrics or close their eyes during the ride was completely up to them. Riders could opt out of having their scores appear on the TorqBoard as well.

My intent was to train Flywheel instructors to speak to

both the Zen and Type A riders, using cues to help those interested in strength-building to push harder as well as encouraging other riders do some mental de-stressing. Either way, I wanted all of our riders to finish the class in an exhilarated state. Our decision to keep the lights dim also assured riders that no matter how they chose to ride they would not be scrutinized or judged. They could be in a personal space surrounded by infectious group energy.

With Flywheel, I was able to feel even safer and more secure about the upper-body workout portion of the class as well as all of the other movements. Being able to measure your work output and actually know where you should be in terms of speed and resistance gives the instructor more control. The ride felt ultimately safer. I also opted to use a weighted bar for arm workouts. This gave our riders more stability and control, and less opportunity to flail around and harm the riders nearby. I suspected that riders would either love this new technology or hate it. There would be nothing in between. I could only hope enough of them loved it to make this company a success. What I neglected to consider was that there would be a whole new group of people who had never been exposed to spinning in any form, and that they could make our business a success.

Besides offering an exciting new technology, Jay, David, and I wanted to create a completely different kind of spin studio at Flywheel. We spent many hours brainstorming the ways in which we could build on what SoulCycle had done right—then still more hours contemplating how we could improve on their model and do it better. Every decision we made was aimed at building customer satisfaction and loyalty.

The three of us worked together constantly, collaborating and sharing ideas. Once construction was completed, we moved from our larger office a block away into a former electrical closet at the studio. It was tight, but we didn't want to spend money on superfluous luxuries if we could put that money into the business instead.

One of the first decisions we made at Flywheel was to improve the space itself. We wanted to create an environment that would be welcoming to people of all shapes, sizes, ages, and personalities. We deliberately designed the Flywheel studio to have wider hallways, to give everyone plenty of breathing room so sweaty bodies wouldn't be crammed together. We also spaced the bikes out a bit more for greater ease of movement—and eliminated the awkwardness of having to ride with another person's butt in your face.

Another important improvement we made was to streamline the registration and payment process. At Flywheel, we decided to include the spin shoes and a bottle of water in the price of the class, so that people didn't have to keep taking out their wallets. At the same time, we still charged less per class than at most other spinning studios.

Our hands-on customer service included training employees to walk around the room before class started, so everyone could be set up properly and feel comfortable asking questions. Another big improvement was our decision to create an easy-to-use online registration system. We set up small laptops along a shelf so people could reserve classes ahead of time and then check themselves in when they arrived, eliminating long check-in lines before classes. Using laptops was also completely consistent with our state-of-the-art bikes.

Perhaps the most important difference between Flywheel and other spinning studios, however, was apparent in the very nature of the classes we taught. We wanted Flywheel to appeal to as broad a demographic as possible: to men and women of all ages, to professionals and retirees, to fitness fanatics and people getting off the couch for the first time. I was determined to open our doors to the widest possible audience—all colors, shapes, and sizes, as one of our T-shirts reads—by eradicating the myth that you had to be in shape before taking a spin class.

In all of the years I'd been in the fitness business, the most important lesson I'd learned was that a successful enterprise depends on customer satisfaction, so that became my primary goal at Flywheel. Kate Hickl came on board and started teaching for us right away; she also helped me train other instructors.

I carefully chose the rest of our teaching staff based on auditions. If they auditioned well, I put them in a training program. And if I sniffed out an oversize ego, I wouldn't hire them. Occasionally a big ego did slip by me, but those instructors ultimately didn't last.

One of the key qualities I looked for in Flywheel instructors was an ability to empathize with riders and look after both their safety and psychological well-being. I wanted instructors who wouldn't make the classes all about them. They needed to be comfortable with themselves, without having to be the center of attention.

Flywheel instructors had to be fit, too, of course. This point was made clearer than ever during one of our early auditions, when I pursued an instructor recommendation from one of our avid Flywheel riders. This candidate was a ballet dancer for the Dance Theatre of Harlem and had "legs up to here," according to the person who referred him, "so he'd be great on a bike."

I was excited about this candidate. Dancers always have the built-in advantages of knowing how to count music as well as how to move to the beat. I was really looking forward to meeting this potential instructor and assumed he'd be perfect, so I made arrangements for him to take my class.

"I can audition you right afterward," I told him. He hadn't taken a Flywheel class before, and I thought it was important for him to experience one before we proceeded to the next step of trying him out as an instructor.

When the dancer arrived, he was as tall, long, lean, and strong looking as he'd been described to me. It was difficult for me to assess his potential as an instructor during my class, however, since it was full, and I had a lot of people to watch and teach.

After class, the dancer and I chatted. He told me he'd loved the class and wanted to learn how to teach for us. I told him I just wanted to see him ride, and asked him to take me through a few songs on the bike so I could hear his voice and get a sense of his presence and technique. I asked for his iPod, plugged it in, cued the music, hit "start," then moved to the rear of the stadium to watch.

After about two minutes on the bike, the dancer dismounted and continued instructing his invisible class as he stood next to the bike. "Great job!" he called out. "Looking good! How are you all feeling?"

I felt baffled and almost thankful that no one else was in the room, so that I could hold it together and not break out laughing. This guy was offering nothing by way of instruction. Not a word about form or counting, nothing about intervals or standing runs. I finally stopped the music.

"Why are you teaching this class to me while you're standing next to the bike?" I asked.

"Well, after taking your class beforehand, I'm just too tired to ride," he confessed.

Needless to say, that was the end of that particular audition.

Despite how this might sound, I certainly wasn't insensitive to the demands of the job. I wanted Flywheel instructors to be able to identify when they were getting burned out and let me know, so I could schedule some time off for them. Once in a while, I'd hear about an instructor starting off a class by telling his riders that he'd already taught two classes that day—never a good idea.

"Your riders are looking to you for inspiration," I told our instructors. "If you're not feeling good, they will know it immediately. You never, ever want a rider having to ask if you're okay. The classes aren't about you. We're here to serve our clients."

During training, I also reminded our instructors how important it was to pay attention to each rider as a person with a unique situation and individual goals. "You need to know why each of your riders is here, what they're looking for, and how things are going for them," I said. "The more personal we can make the spinning experience, the better our customers will like it."

In addition, I stressed the importance of listening to everyone's complaints—instructors and riders. If someone had a complaint, our job was to hear it and do whatever we could to follow up and rectify the situation.

Finally, it was important to me that Flywheel instructors knew they were truly valued by the company as more than just "the talent." I'd been around New York City's performing arts scene long enough to know that creative people—actors, dancers, singers, and writers—are typically not well-compensated financially or given benefits like stocks and health care.

The Flywheel instructors needed to understand that they were the most important part of the business so they could give 100 percent. They had an enormous responsibility: it was up to them to create the magic that would draw our customers. While of course there were other benefits for people who chose to ride with Flywheel, I knew that nothing could rival what a great instructor could bring to each rider's experience. Jay, David, and I knew that our instructors would play an important role in our company's rise—or in its crushing defeat.

At Flywheel, therefore, we paid our employees a decent salary. More importantly, we tried to set up health care plans and stock option packages for most of the instructors, both of which were unusual benefits in the fitness industry. This helped build loyalty among our staff.

In February 2010, we officially opened the first Flywheel studio. We had been working for twenty-four hours straight to get the studio set up, but even then the place was barely ready. Everything was literally held together with duct tape and zip ties.

For the inaugural class, we invited all of our investors from our friends and family round. We also came up with a list of people whom we considered "influencers"—those who could help spread the word. The remaining riders were made up of people who had followed me to SoulCycle and were now just waiting for me to open my new business.

On opening day, we were all sick from working in that freezing-cold adjunct space for so many days straight, but it didn't matter. Teaching the inaugural class was nothing short of thrilling. It was the moment I'd been waiting for since November 2009, when we first started to work on the Flywheel concept. With everything that had led me to this night, it simply felt monumental.

I think everyone felt that way. The excitement in the room was palpable. People were so impressed with the look of our space and couldn't wait for the ride to begin. I gave a welcome speech, expressing gratitude and appreciation for everyone's support and patience in getting this new business under way. I was filled with nervous energy as I went down the list of those I wanted to thank. Most important among them were David and Jay, for presenting me with this opportunity, and my good friend and fellow SoulCycle instructor Kate Hickl, for sticking by my side and helping me lead the creative component of this business.

"Is everyone ready?" I asked the crowd then.

The hooting and hollering was through the roof. The lights dimmed, the music began, and I immediately found my "zone" as I led the class on their first Flywheel journey. The music was loud and the mic was clear, a spin instructor's dream. It didn't matter that a lot of the bikes were making a weird clicking noise and the tech was having problems. We didn't even care that Jay had apparently forgotten to turn on the

Kate Hickl and me, loyal friends and co-
workers from SoulCycle to Flywheel

AC, which meant that by song two we were all riding in what felt and looked like a steam room. It was a magical class and everyone experienced that magic.

Afterward, we had a champagne toast, and we all drank to Flywheel as we dripped with sweat. The minute everyone left, we went right back to work, scraping glue off the floor and preparing for our grand opening to the public.

Of course, it wasn't all smooth sailing during those first weeks. You can't anticipate everything in business, and some things are bound to go wrong.

One of the biggest mistakes we made was in the way we set up the studio initially. David had a sports background, and he had come up with the idea of changing the way the bikes were arranged in the studio. Instead of all of them being on one level, he suggested a stadium design. By placing the bikes on tiered platforms in a half circle around the instructor's bike, there would be no such thing as a "bad" bike, because everyone would be able to see the instructor. The instructor could also see every rider and make sure each person was safe and getting the most out of the experience.

Many spinning studios were dimly lit, but we decided to bring the lights down even more at Flywheel. We wanted all of our riders to feel comfortable, no matter what sort of athletic shape they were in, what their bodies looked like, or what they were wearing. Unfortunately, the poor lighting led to some near disasters, like the time a rider fell off one of the platforms after dismounting her bike and sprained her ankle. That night, Jay, David, and I went straight to martinis to commiserate once we closed the studio. We quickly installed lights along the rails after that to prevent someone else getting hurt.

There were marketing missteps, too. In the early days of Flywheel, we offered a lot of corporate rides: we would approach neighborhood businesses and offer free classes to their employees as a way of letting them know about the studio. During one of those events, a number of SoulCycle devotees happened to be among the company's employees. The Flywheel instructor teaching that class was talented but new and relatively untested.

I had been excited about this particular ride, but the

instructor gave such a bad class that many people left saying they'd never come back. People seldom grant you a second chance after that kind of experience. I vowed after that to only offer corporate classes taught by our strongest and most trusted instructors. It was an essential lesson on the importance of offering only the highest-quality classes.

A third mistake we made was probably our biggest. I had a popular pro athlete who often rode in my classes before Flywheel. Coincidentally, his representatives knew David. They ended up approaching us with an interest in investing with Flywheel. Given what I'd learned from Julie about the importance of press and celebrity contacts when building a brand, we thought it would be great to have a name like this football player's associated with Flywheel.

Instead, it turned into a nightmare. The athlete became part of a widely publicized scandal that ultimately affected his image in the public eye as well as our desire for him to be a representative of our company. We had no choice but to cut him loose from the Flywheel partnership. We would have to rely on the strong appeal of our unique product and the Flywheel experience instead of a celebrity name and hope for the best. We later proved that if you have a great product people will come—with or without celebrity names attached to your business.

At some point in the venture, we decided that it might make sense to have our own custom bike, and we thought we could do it for the same amount that we were paying Schwinn—or maybe even a little less. When it came to the design, we wanted it to be close to the Schwinn as far as the settings and feel went (chain-driven), but we wanted to alter the look to differentiate it. David took a trip to Taiwan and engaged a factory to design the bike to our specifications.

Instead of silver and red, the colors of the Schwinn bike, we went with all black, with our logo in a turquoise blue. This gave the bike a much sleeker look. We also made sure that the materials could combat heavy moisture because of the amount of sweat the bikes had to withstand, and that the design kept the technology protected. It was also crucial to make sure the bike was heavy enough so that even a large person wouldn't be able to move it while riding—something that happened occasionally with the Schwinn.

When the newly designed bikes arrived, they were definitely not perfect. As we started to use them, riders expressed various complaints. One was that the horizontal bar below the seat was too wide and set too far forward; if someone set the settings furthest to the back, the bar made contact with the rider's inner thighs.

Imagine the irony: Here we were, trying to create an environment at Flywheel where "all shapes and sizes" felt accepted and comfortable. Yet if your inner thighs were a certain width, they rubbed up against this bar. Not good.

There was also a problem with the placement of the computer screen. It wasn't as clearly visible as it was with the Schwinn.

We performed a series of tweaks and installed replacement parts to correct what didn't work during that first month of usage. Fortunately, our riders were patient and stayed with us until we got it right. Though not an easy process, the end result was a fully branded, custom indoor cycle design that was another evolution away from "gym spin" and what was being offered at other studios.

We even ran a contest for our riders to come up with the best name for our newly branded bike. Many participated and there were a lot of great ideas, but the winner was clear: Firefly.

Despite our early missteps, Flywheel quickly gained in popularity. Within a month, our classes were starting to fill. That was a turning point for the business: I knew that once classes started selling out word would spread fast.

It did—so fast that David, Jay, and I decided to open a second studio immediately. We wanted our next location to be on the Upper West Side, since many of our riders lived in that area. After evaluating various choices, we struck a deal with the Jewish Community Center where I used to teach. We took over their spin room and rehabbed it to create another unique Flywheel space in record time, opening the second Flywheel studio on my birthday, March 27, 2010. We announced it as one of the best birthday presents I had ever received. And it was.

Looking back, I attribute our early success in part to two factors. The first was my knowledge of the spinning business, acquired as I co-founded SoulCycle, and the way we built on that knowledge and improved upon it, especially in the areas of customer service, studio design, technology, and employee morale.

The second and most important reason we succeeded is because we started Flywheel from an authentic place, a place with passion and heart. From the beginning, Jay, David, and I wanted to create a business that felt like a family. We treated everyone equally, whether we were speaking with a customer, an instructor, or a maintenance person.

The three of us felt strongly that if our employees were happy Flywheel would succeed. If anyone who worked for us—and by now, that included a group of instructors, facilities coordinators, tech people, and operational employees at both studios—had an issue with something, we'd call them into the office to discuss it.

"Hey, how are you doing?" we'd ask. "Let's talk about where you are right now and what you're thinking."

The joke was that Jay and I were the mommy and daddy of Flywheel. I found that interesting, and probably pretty true, given that a lot of the human resource management skills I used were skills I'd learned as a mother. We nurtured our employees and encouraged them to voice their thoughts and behave confidently around us, the same way I had done with my daughters.

I've read Sheryl Sandberg's book *Lean In*, and while she makes many good points, I was coming from a different place. I wasn't interested in trying to compete with men by acting like them. I went in the opposite direction, using qualities that are typically attributed to women. I was warm, respectful, and maternal toward our employees rather than aloof, authoritative, and controlling.

For the first time in my life, I felt like I was being completely true to myself. I no longer needed a man to support me emotionally or financially. I had raised my daughters to be independent young women and they were both in college. I was happy to once again be working long hours and then getting up the next morning and doing it all over again. I was invested in making Flywheel a success.

Perhaps most importantly, I was finding my voice in the business world. I felt confident now that I had valuable skills to offer. David and Jay made it clear that my opinions mattered. It was a novel feeling, and I reveled in it.

A good thing, too: I would need that confidence and power during the trying times to come.

Lesson #10: Finding Your Investors: Believe in Yourself and They Will, Too

When starting Flywheel, we had to find a first round of investors who would have faith in our ability to create a successful company. The most common question our would-be investors always asked was how we could be so sure that spinning wasn't just a trend.

It's true that many exercise regimens are fads. However, I had a compelling argument. Spinning had started in the eighties and I had been developing my teaching methods for many years, always putting safety front and center. Since spinning is a low-impact exercise, I knew it could attract runners and older people interested in finding a way to stay fit without risking more wear and tear on their bodies.

In fact, many of our riders at SoulCycle were former runners who had to give up running due to their injuries; they were excited to discover that they could get a safe, satisfying, aerobic high on a stationary bicycle. People continued to spin well into their sixties, seventies, and even early eighties.

Given the huge number of aging Baby Boomers, I was convinced that spinning was here to stay. I made this argument again and again, whenever I met with potential investors.

During the first round, David and Jay each put some money into the business, but I didn't have that kind of capital. The three of us also approached our friends and family members. I went to people who I knew really believed in me, like a private client I used to train. She and I had a fifteen-year history of working out together. I knew that once she heard my dreams and goals she would believe in me enough to invest in Flywheel. She and others had seen what I'd accomplished at SoulCycle and elsewhere and trusted me to succeed again.

In addition, through my ten years of teaching spin before starting Flywheel, I had met many people who were real movers and shakers in New York. It was easy for me to approach them about investing in Flywheel because I wholeheartedly believed in what we were doing. If you're openly passionate and confident about your idea, then the odds are good that you can convince the right people to be passionate about your idea, too. I knew what spinning did for me mentally and physically, and I had seen what it had done for my riders. Since our culture was placing an increasing emphasis on health and wellness, I knew the timing was right for this kind of business as well.

Jay and David had a good record in private equity. They had picked successful businesses to invest in many times before, so they had a lot of credibility when they presented our business plan. Together, the three of us found it fairly easy to form our group of Series A investors, whom we referred to as our "friends and family" group. Once our Flatiron studio was starting to come together, we were able to invite people over, walk them through the space, and clearly explain our plans for the near future and our long-term goals. Based on our reputations in our respective fields, most people were impressed enough to sign on immediately. I imagine many who didn't are still kicking themselves today.

Once we got Flywheel off the ground, potential investors started approaching us. That was one of the ways we knew that we had a success on our hands. Our Series A investors would lend their opinions from time to time, and we certainly listened politely, but it wasn't until later, when our bigger investors—called Series B investors—came on board, that we gave them more time and say in the business.

If you need investors for your business idea, start by crafting a detailed business plan that outlines exactly what you are going to do, how much money you need, where it's going to go, and how the investors will earn their money back and make a profit, too.

One word of warning: your business plan should be as convincing and as well written as possible, but investors aren't going to buy into it unless they believe in *you*. The first thing you need to do is believe in yourself. Investors want to feel confident that you're the right person to run the business.

Where should you look for money? This depends on what kind of business you're starting up and how much money you need. For instance, a very small business endeavor might do well with Kickstarter or some other online crowdfunding tool, whereas a large business will need venture capital or bank financing.

A venture capital investment is perhaps the hardest source of funding to acquire. Venture capitalists focus on new products and new markets, ones where they can project increasing sales by huge multiples in a relatively short time. If you have to ask yourself whether your business qualifies as a venture capital opportunity, it probably doesn't. But you can always find names and addresses of venture capitalists online and explore the option. The worst that can happen is that you'll hear "no" for an answer.

Another avenue to pursue is a business loan through your bank or the Small Business Administration, using your home or other investments as equity. You can also search for investors through your local Small Business Development Center. These are usually found on college campuses or in business schools.

Or you can do what we did and turn to family and friends. Just be sure to inform them exactly what the risk is, and don't let them invest money they can't afford to lose. Your agreements should all be drawn up by professionals and signed by all parties with a legal witness.

Lesson #11: The Best Innovation Happens Organically

With Flywheel, I felt like Jay, David, and I had created a product that was the very best of its kind in the fitness field. The combination of our company's unique new technology, our talented and well-trained instructors, and the attention we paid to creating our playlists offered our riders the most enriching, effective mind-body exercise possible. Our innovations weren't being done for the sake of being novel or even marketable. We weren't creating our product out of thin air but as a result of listening closely to feedback from riders and employees, so that we could keep growing and enhancing what Flywheel delivered. Our bottom line was always consistent: we wanted to make a difference in people's lives. That's always the best motivation for true innovation.

8

The Joy of Competition

Competition is a good thing. It forces you to explore your own motivations, inspirations, and passions, pushing you to always strive harder and stay at the top of your game.

I tried to embrace this philosophy as I joined Jay and David in starting Flywheel, despite the many people who asked whether we really thought there was room for another indoor cycling product. Still, I had my own doubts during weaker moments.

For workout fanatics, the number of fitness class options was growing fast, including expanded varieties of barre classes, kickboxing, Pilates, yoga, boot camp types of classes, and Zumba. We were competing for clients with the many gyms and boutique studios popping up with increasing regularity now that the fitness boom was really starting to hit New York City. I had to hope that our strategy to be the first indoor cycling studio in the Flatiron district was a sound one.

There was no doubt that our primary competition was SoulCycle, which had developed a significant following, but we also competed against many other independent studios in the world of spinning. Whenever I started feeling nervous about all of the competition out there, I'd remind myself that there was a nearly limitless supply of riders. Spinning hadn't even reached most of the major cities in the United States at that time, much less gone international. People were just beginning to realize how efficient a spinning workout could be, with adults potentially burning at least six hundred calories during a single class.

Even where there *were* other spin studios, Flywheel had advantages. Not one of the others offered a high-tech bike combined with my unique method of spinning. I had always thought of spinning as not only a calorie burner but a mind-body exercise. When I first got hooked on spinning, staying fit was certainly one of my motives, but it was even more about the way spinning affected my mood and life perspective. Performing such an intensive exercise to motivating music, coupled with inspiring words and good choreography from a skilled instructor against the background sounds of fifty-some wheels spinning on a chain-driven bike, has the power to transport riders to another place in their minds. Every pedal stroke made people mentally and physically stronger.

Although the high-tech aspect of a Flywheel bike meant that most people wanted to track their workouts instead of just closing their eyes and pedaling, I believed it offered an even more mindful exercise in some ways, since riders were going to feel even more empowered by calibrating and quantifying their own journeys. In my most optimistic moments, I knew that if Flywheel could be innovative and different enough we'd find our following.

Elizabeth, Julie, and I had forged an original path with SoulCycle. Now, using the lessons I'd learned through that experience, I dared to hope that being second in the market might even be an advantage, allowing Flywheel to become successful more quickly.

All of my life, I've been a high-energy perfectionist, starting with my dance training. Now, I was determined to work even harder to make Flywheel a success in the face of what was, ironically, my first company. My girls were in college, so I was able to spend long days building the business. And when I went home at night, I couldn't wait to get back to Flywheel the next morning.

I sacrificed my social life and nearly every hour I wasn't sleeping to my new venture. I didn't care. I was having fun, and this was exactly what I wanted to be doing with my time.

When we discussed the Flywheel image, David, Jay, and I knew we wanted to create something that would differentiate Flywheel substantially from all of the other spinning studios out there. Even after we opened our first studio, we continued to carefully examine and evaluate the competition. Our primary goals were always to continue improving our product in ways that would maintain the integrity of our Flywheel business model and to develop a company in keeping with our own values.

We deliberately designed, branded, and marketed Flywheel as a club for everyone. We hired and trained our staff to be friendly and accepting to people of all ages, colors, shapes, sizes, and fitness levels. We expected our instructors to convey that same warm, open-door welcome; I trained them to make every rider feel included, safe, and valued. Our goal was to encourage riders and make them feel good about themselves, even if it was simply for walking through the door and actively making the decision to turn off their phones for forty-five minutes. No matter what their performance was like on a particular day, I wanted our riders to be congratulated just for signing up for class and taking that difficult step toward a more fitness-oriented lifestyle.

Conveying this attitude of warmth and acceptance at Flywheel was easy for me, largely because working with David and Jay provided me with such an ideal kind of partnership. They were confident, successful, generous men with integrity. I had also made a vow to at least *act* more confident when voicing my opinions, even if I didn't always feel that way.

If I could go back and give my younger self any business advice at all, first and foremost, that advice would be all about learning how to communicate effectively. I would tell my younger self not to act passive or defensive but to speak up and make my needs and opinions clear.

Fortunately, my Flywheel partners were willing to listen to my opinions and even encouraged me to speak up at times when I might not have done otherwise. For instance, after our first board meeting, David seemed frustrated by my minimal participation and said, "Ruth, you have a lot of knowledge about our business and need to speak up more."

Just as I valued their input on things like demographics, market analysis, and growth strategies, Jay and David made it clear that I brought a unique and essential professional expertise to Flywheel. My skills included a lot more than just the ability to spin my legs on a bike. I had honed what had become a popular teaching method, and I knew how to make personal connections with people from all walks of life. That went a long way toward building a client base, attracting investors, and making a business successful.

I also loved that both Jay and David were every bit as determined as I was to compete hard for a foothold in the spinning market. Their loyalty meant everything to me.

You can do all of the analysis in advance, have the best partners in the world, and work all day and night, yet still your idea might fail. I hoped that wouldn't be true of our Flatiron studio location, 39 West 21st Street.

Our studio was on a block of B-grade nightclubs. In the wee hours of Saturday morning, there would be black cars parked along the length of the entire block. But since the club hours wouldn't interfere with our class times, and since David knew the landlord and the price was right, we had decided this wouldn't be a problem.

To our advantage, the studio was on the street level of a large luxury apartment building that was one of the first to go up in this neighborhood. Another thing in our favor was that we had absolutely no competition from other fitness studios in the immediate area, with the exception of a small personal training gym across the street. We introduced ourselves to the gym's owner with the hope that we could refer business to each other, and we did.

Despite my initial fears about my following being rooted

on the Upper West Side, it soon became clear that our client base was going to be solid in the Flatiron studio. People started coming from the first moment we opened our doors.

As much as I had hoped that the majority of my Soul-Cycle riders would be loyal enough to ride with me at Flywheel, there was also something exciting about introducing our new take on indoor cycling to riders who had never tried spinning before. We quickly realized that once these riders became accustomed to the Flywheel bike with metrics we would probably never lose them to any studio where there were no metrics and therefore no accountability.

Meanwhile, Jay, David, and I focused on gathering the best possible group of employees and making it clear to them that, just as we respected each other, we valued whatever they brought to the business. We saw our teachers and studio staff as individuals with lives of their own—whether they were teaching, mopping floors, or working the front desk—and did all we could to keep staff morale high.

At one point, for example, Emilio, a member of our maintenance staff, told us that he was an artist. "I'd like to hand paint spin shoes," he said. "I think our customers would like to be able to personalize their shoes."

We could have easily said no, but we wanted to encourage Emilio to follow his passion, just as we were following ours. "We'll do whatever we can to help you," we said. "Show us what you mean."

Sure enough, he took a pair of shoes and transformed them, using a type of paint that could withstand sweat and wear and tear. They looked amazing. One of the riders saw the shoes and said, "I want a pair."

Another rider saw them and said, "I want eleven pairs."
Really!

Suddenly, Emilio had a side business that inspired him.
And, because he felt good about our collaboration and highly
valued as a person, he became more invested in making Flywheel a success.

We also continued to nurture our employees whenever they
were having a rough time. For instance, I knew from experience what it meant for an instructor to be truly fatigued.

I was sometimes left feeling as spent emotionally after a
class as I was physically tired, because my goal—as should be
the goal of any good instructor—was always to support my
riders by giving them not only practical instruction and choreography for the ride, but also any support I could for whatever
struggles they might choose to share with me. I was therefore
always careful not to place unrealistic scheduling expectations on any of our Flywheel instructors.

I was particularly supportive of the instructors who were
single parents, because I knew firsthand how difficult it was
for me to keep up the constant juggling act I had to do with
my twins, especially once they were in high school. As with
any teenagers, there were often late nights, school crises, and
relationship issues that needed—and deserved—my full attention.

Now, I vowed to support my own employees. Jay, David,
and I always did our best to honor any family issues and
scheduling demands. If employees needed assistance with
something, we'd reach a hand out to offer that help, too, even
loaning money for emergencies or household crises. For instance, one of our instructors was in her early forties and still

living with her parents. When we saw an opportunity for her to move to Chicago and become a lead instructor at our Gold Coast studio there, we paid for her moving costs and subsidized her living expenses.

We also believed in allowing people to make mistakes and gave them the benefit of the doubt. More than once, we granted employees second, and even third, chances to get things right. We wanted Flywheel to feel like a family, knowing that keeping our employees happy and feeling included in the business would pay out big dividends in the end. In turn, a positive attitude in the studio would keep our clients happy.

Even by doing all of that, would we be able to compete successfully with SoulCycle? Only time would tell.

As I continued refining my teaching techniques using the Flywheel bike, I developed an even greater appreciation for the workout it could provide riders. The technology allowed us to use metrics that made riders calibrate and account for their accomplishments. There was an actual, visible number on the computer screen that clearly tallied a rider's progress and goals met for each ride based on the torq and the rpms used during the ride.

For women, the eventual total score usually ranged between 220 and 300, and starting out, they might only reach 180 to 220. Men always shot for over 300; I considered numbers higher than 425 to be bordering on excessive and unnecessary, but riders would sometimes find a way to get a jump on points.

Certain people were also creative about designing their

own rides within the context of our classes. We included an upper-body portion during the ride, where the focus was less on achieving more points, but many riders would skip that part and do their own ride through the arms portion. There were also certain people—more men than women—who cranked up the resistance and pushed hard throughout the entire class to achieve a higher score. We didn't recommend this, but we didn't stop them from doing it, either, if we felt they were staying safe.

I trained our instructors to give balanced, well-thought-out, and effective rides that increased cardiovascular strength as well as overall muscle strength. We didn't teach a ride with a lot of heavy resistance, as many of the guys might have preferred, because our goal wasn't to bulk up the legs.

Women, especially, were wary of this happening; in fact, there was a whole myth that "spinning makes your thighs bigger." My response to this was that it depended on what you were doing on the bike. At Flywheel, our interval-based rides struck just the right balance between aerobic and anaerobic work, so that couldn't happen.

I also discouraged people from putting too much attention on their total numbers. I hated seeing people coming out of a class, drenched with sweat and fatigued from the work they had done, yet judging themselves only by their numbers. I made a point of reminding our riders—and the instructors—that everybody is different based on age, weight, and energy expended.

Our metrics-based formula was never meant to be an exact science. I primarily wanted to promote the idea of spinning as a healthy mind-body exercise that could help riders feel stronger and more confident, so they could succeed in all aspects of their lives.

We knew that the Upper West Side should be our next location, given my history and solid following there. Unfortunately, finding the right space was easier said than done. Leases were expensive and we weren't capitalized enough at that point to be able to afford any of the spaces we saw that looked suitable.

After searching every block for a new venue, we hit upon the idea of finding an existing space where we could embed a Flywheel studio. Partnering with the Jewish Community Center, where I'd taught for many years prior to starting SoulCycle, as well as during the interim between leaving SoulCycle and starting Flywheel, seemed like a logical choice.

I had a great relationship with the JCC team and asked for a meeting. We all hit it off and realized how this partnership could be beneficial for everyone. The facility already had an existing spin studio, which we could have used, but David insisted on demolishing it and creating a studio that would be identical to the Flywheel space in the Flatiron, albeit a bit smaller. Ultimately, this was a cost-efficient way of bringing our method and technology to the Upper West Side.

I worried at first that the smaller space wouldn't give the best impression of Flywheel's brand, but I needn't have. Many of our riders openly expressed their preference for the smaller size, saying they liked the homey feel. In fact, opening that studio felt like a homecoming for all of us, especially for the riders who lived on the Upper West Side who hadn't wanted to trek down to our Flatiron studio. It was wonderful to see so many of my old riders return to my classes.

Of course, the things you worry most about when you start a business aren't always the things that go wrong. At our JCC location, we had an incident that taught us that important lesson.

One of our maintenance employees was a young guy in his early twenties. Jason always showed up and did his work. He was amiable, soft-spoken, and liked by all. Then, one day, Jason didn't show up at the studio at the appointed time. This was unusual enough that we called his cell phone. When he didn't answer, we started to worry about him.

We had good reason to be worried, as it turned out: someone at the studio happened to see Jason's mug shot that day on the local news, linking him with the killing of a police officer in the Bronx. We were stunned. A group of nine detectives walked into our Flatiron studio the next morning, looking for any information we might have about his whereabouts.

Jason was just one of those good kids who got caught up in the wrong group and pulled along into trouble. He was young and impressionable, and eventually we learned that he had been involved with a gang. This gang had shot the policeman in the Bronx; Jason's friends had asked him to drive the getaway car, which he did.

Obviously, the lesson for us here was about the importance of doing rigorous background checks on all of our employees.

After having interviewed Jason, we thought we had a good reading of his personality. He was kind and enthusiastic about working for Flywheel. However, after Googling him, we realized we had clearly missed a lot of red flags, including a record for petty larceny.

The police officer survived and Jason went to jail. Moving forward from that day, we ran meticulous background checks on everyone we hired.

Succeeding in any entrepreneurial endeavor means that you must not only be prepared to offer a better product than your competition but also be ready to push beyond that to create and add products that are new and distinctive. The first year we opened the Flywheel studio in the Flatiron district, we had room enough to open a second studio in the same space, but didn't quite know what to do with it. We decided to expand Flywheel's unique brand by offering yoga classes and hired a group of instructors who came in and taught their own methods of yoga, whatever those happened to be.

After a while, it became clear that this wasn't the right fit. We needed to develop a more consistent product that would provide a better complement to Flywheel classes. Eventually, a friend of mine told us about Kate Bohner, a certified yoga instructor he knew in Florida. Kate had an interesting background. She was a serious athlete who had previously been co-captain of the University of Pennsylvania women's lacrosse team and a member of the World Cup team.

Kate was also a barre expert via Powerbarre in Delray Beach

and experienced at training other teachers in her method. In barre-based fitness classes, clients use the barre for balance as they perform isometric strength-training exercises designed to target and strengthen specific muscle groups while holding the rest of the body still. Prior to Kate's work in fitness, she'd had a career in finance, followed by a stint as a writer at *Forbes* magazine. Kate had even co-authored Donald Trump's book *The Art of the Comeback* in 1997.

Given my familiarity with the Lotte Berk method, from which so many other barre methods have been developed at different studios around the world, I was enthusiastic about meeting Kate. I had a hunch that offering a barre class might be exactly the right way to diversify Flywheel's offerings. After learning about her diverse experiences, I could see that Kate was clearly smart and must have a great work ethic. I thought she'd be a great fit for our new company.

Jay and I invited Kate to fly up to New York to meet with us. We liked her energy and enthusiasm immediately. When she taught a barre class for us, we saw for ourselves what an effective, inspiring teacher she was. We hired her to create a unique Flywheel barre class and develop the program with our input.

In the spirit of consistency, we wanted music to be an important part of what we later called the "Flybarre" experience. Typical barre classes always have background music, but we wanted movement that was choreographed to the music, just as we choreographed each spin class to the instructor's playlist.

Kate loved the idea. She set the program in motion, calling it "the sculpting boot camp for spinners," and really got it going by 2011. The fifty-five-minute, interval-based class included circuit training, yoga, Pilates, stretching, and strength building.

Interestingly, a lot of the Flybarre "pulsers," as we ended up calling them, came to Flybarre classes exclusively. However, many also loved the idea of combining Flybarre with Flywheel, and certain hard-core workout enthusiasts wanted the classes back-to-back. We began offering "Kate & Kate" classes—Kate Hickl's spin class, followed by Kate Bohner's barre class—for two-hour blasts that combined cardio and sculpting workouts.

After Kate Bohner left Flywheel, Kara Liotta took over the Flybarre classes and turned them into an even more compelling and popular program. Her poise and confidence are impressive, especially since she is only in her twenties. Kara is an inspiration to everyone.

Just as we were growing, SoulCycle was, too. By fall 2010, they had expanded to five locations.

We saw several press interviews with Julie and Elizabeth where they claimed they "never" viewed Flywheel as competition, but I suspected otherwise. I remembered how, when we had worked together in the early days of SoulCycle, Zone-Hampton had opened its first location on the Upper East Side after founding their flagship spin studio in East Hampton. Marion Roaman, who owned ZoneHampton (and would later change the name to Ride the Zone), had always struggled with her Manhattan location, so that studio was never a real threat to SoulCycle's rapidly growing business. Yet Julie would scour their online sign-ups on a daily basis to see how that studio was faring. With Flywheel enjoying success and offering SoulCycle their first real threat, I would have bet money that Julie knew our website like the back of her hand.

We examined SoulCycle and other spinning studios just as closely. I had once thought there was something nefarious in scrutinizing your competitors, but subsequently I have learned just how important it is to study and understand your competition. That knowledge will drive your own success.

Not long after turning the spin room at the Jewish Community Center on the Upper West Side into a signature Flywheel stadium, we started talking about developing a third Flywheel studio in the Hamptons to serve our clients there during the summer. This meant that SoulCycle, as one *New York Times* reporter put it, would now have "muscular competition in the form of Flywheel Sports."

I, along with all of the other Flywheel instructors, welcomed whoever came through our doors. We told SoulCycle riders they didn't have to whisper . . . it was okay that they rode at both studios. They were honoring their bodies and minds, and that was good enough for us, no matter where they did it.

I actually had one woman rider in my class approach me to say how much she loved Flywheel, but that her sister was a die-hard SoulCycle fan.

"It's great that there's something for everyone," I responded.

"Not really," she said with a sigh. "My sister and I don't speak anymore because of it."

That was disturbing, to say the least.

I've always encouraged riders and instructors to take classes at other studios, too. Being in another instructor's spin class, especially at a different studio, is a great way to enhance your own teaching through fresh inspiration and new music ideas.

Holly Rilinger, one of our superstar instructors at the time, experienced just that. It was the summer of 2013 and we were both teaching classes in the Hamptons. Holly had never taken a class at SoulCycle, yet she was very curious about what they were like.

I had remained friends with Stacey Griffith, SoulCycle's superstar. When I was still at SoulCycle, Stacey and I used to summer in the Hamptons, where we taught the majority of SoulCycle classes at the Bridgehampton barn.

Stacey has remained at SoulCycle, where she continues to inspire many and is a masterful motivational speaker with a real talent for knowing exactly what to say and when. Her classes are always sold out from the moment that the sign-up window opens. Riders who pay the premium price to be able to sign up in advance of everyone else would flock to her class while I was still there. From what I hear, this hasn't changed, as she continues to inspire riders and spread the word on the many benefits of spinning.

When Holly said she wanted to experience a class at Soul-Cycle, I called Stacey and asked if she could make that happen. Stacey was completely open to the idea.

Holly had come to Flywheel originally from Ride the

Zone. Since that was her only experience in the indoor cycling world, she was still finding her persona on the instructor bike. She was once a professional basketball player and pursued personal training after her basketball career. She was also chosen to be a Nike Master Trainer and led seminars and Master Classes all over the world. A true athlete with a body to prove it, she was incredibly strong, and it was motivational just to watch her ride.

Stacey's style of teaching was the antithesis of Holly's. For starters, Stacey rarely got on the bike. She always had someone from the class ride the bike for her. Holly's emphasis on the athletic ride was a strong contrast to Stacey's preference for highlighting the power of her motivational words.

When Holly took Stacey's class, she was most impressed by a certain lightness that Stacey brought to her ride. Being a professional athlete had added a certain hard-core seriousness to Holly's style of teaching; after watching Stacey, she realized that, by softening her approach, she might be able to enhance the motivational aspect of her classes even more. Simultaneously, she was doing a lot of yoga, and this practice also influenced her energy flow during spin classes.

For me, this served as a great example of how everyone can benefit when professionals share their knowledge and experience.

It didn't take long for us to recognize that Flywheel was going to become bigger than we had ever imagined. There were many signs along the way, like hearing Flywheel become the favored topic of conversation at a social event and having our classes consistently sell out. But probably the tipping point was when we opened our first Flywheel Hamptons location in Sag Harbor in the summer of 2010.

Jay and I were adamant about opening a studio there the summer after establishing Flywheel in Manhattan. We knew the kind of exposure the Hamptons could give us. David had never been a Hamptons fan and wasn't thrilled with the idea, but he capitulated when we came up with a space.

While we were searching for just the right location, my good friend Pam introduced me to Bruce Cotter, then the manager of the Sag Harbor Gym. It was a snowy, wintry day when David, Jay, and I decided to drive out to the Hamptons to meet with Bruce about possibly putting a Flywheel studio in his gym.

The snow worsened as we got closer to Sag Harbor. By the time we arrived, the snowdrifts were over five feet deep. We were pulled over by a local policeman at one point and told to get off the roads. Since we were close to the gym at that point, we kept driving and made it there in time for our meeting. We enjoyed working with Bruce and struck a deal.

That same day, we drove back to the city through the snow and went straight to the JCC to check on construction there. Crazy, yes, but we were on a roll and thriving on our relentless momentum.

Like the JCC, the Sag Harbor Gym also had an existing spin room. We treated it in the same way we had rehabbed the space on the Upper West Side, redoing everything to make it a Flywheel stadium. One stylistic difference was that the Hamptons space was mirrored on three sides, unlike our other studios, which created a massive look to the space. We built the stadium levels a bit steeper, so when the instructors were on the podium, they would feel like they were addressing a grand amphitheater full of riders.

Through the build-out process, we learned that working in a small town comes with its challenges. There were a lot of rules and different building codes, and the people in Sag Harbor let us know what they were every step of the way.

The night before our Memorial Day opening, for instance, the inspector came in and told us that our ceiling was not up to code and we would have to take it down. Every Flywheel employee who was on-site at the time worked through the night, taking down the ceiling and replacing it with metal paneling that was code-compliant. We finished the job scarcely an hour before our first class that morning.

That seat-of-the-pants strategy for opening new locations seemed to be our way of doing business in those early days of Flywheel. We used to joke about how, with each studio build-out, the place would literally look like a construction site mere hours before we were scheduled to open. Somehow, our devoted and passionate staff helped us do whatever it took to make it to the finish line on time, but Jay and I were sometimes at odds with David when it came to time and money. With each studio we opened, David always pushed to have it open as rapidly as possible, so that we could start classes and keep growing our clientele. As a result, a few of the studios struggled early on, and some failed that might have succeeded if only we had taken more time in opening them.

For instance, David had put us under a lot of pressure to open Flatiron. All three of us, plus our few employees, worked around the clock to get the studio ready for David's appointed opening date. Jay and I wanted to slow down so that we could spend a bit more time training everyone from the front desk staff to our instructors. In this rush to open, we forgot that, at the end of the day, the product we were really selling was the *method*. It was the most important thing we offered, yet our initial group of instructors had barely spent any time on a Flywheel bike with its proprietary technology.

As a result, there were definitely quite a few cringe-worthy moments in the first week at our Flatiron studio. While I had emphasized the importance of an eclectic ten-song playlist that included different genres and songs with lyrics, Matt, one of our instructors, decided to play four fifteen-minute songs of pure techno music with no lyrics at all. He had clearly missed the memo and that was how he had always taught spinning. Eventually, he understood what we were about and became a successful instructor for us, but it would have been far better for our early branding if he had fully understood our method from the beginning.

In another instance of poor planning, we had reached out to various big companies whose offices were in the Flatiron area. One was Polo, and the person who organized the group that was coming to ride with us was a fan of mine. We gave the class to another one of our instructors at the time and it was a complete disaster. This instructor basically taught how he wanted to ride. The class was super-fast, making it basically unattainable for many, and his playlist was terrible. He didn't last with us very long.

Unfortunately, though, he cost us an opportunity with a big company.

If we had taken more time to train our staff and finish the construction completely before opening each studio, we might have been better off. We certainly would have had a more refined product. We recovered quickly at Flatiron and it didn't take that much longer to really feel ready. But David, Jay, and I all certainly learned the importance of that first impression.

Despite our rush, however, the three of us were psyched with our Hamptons location right from the start. Our studio in the Sag Harbor Gym was located in the back of the building, which overlooked the pier on the bay. Walking around the gym to this rear entrance gave our riders an exhilarating view of the yachts docked there for the summer.

Jay's blue Jeep became the "company car" that summer, to the point where we sometimes referred to it as our "office." We had many meetings in that parked Jeep, sometimes with just the two of us sitting in the front seat, and other times with Shannon and Christy, who were managing and running things out there with us, seated in the back. We usually met in a parking lot, but occasionally we got a little more elaborate and parked by the beach, giving our mobile office an ocean view.

We rented a house and a car for instructors to share. While there was a little drama among the instructors as they managed their unique roommate situations and made do with one car, they all had a great time that summer and seemed to appreciate the opportunity to work in such beautiful surroundings.

Word of our Hamptons presence spread like wildfire, to the point where Jay, David, and I soon felt like celebrities

Our first Sag Harbor summer, "working" in our Flywheel office/Jeep

wherever we went. In addition to the riders we already had from the city, we were now attracting throngs of new people. People even came to the studio off their yachts to see what we were all about.

We began receiving regular invites onto people's yachts after class, and we were wined and dined by the abundant staff on each of them. This all happened so soon after starting Flywheel that we couldn't help but occasionally look at each other in disbelief. Sometimes it felt like a dream. It was difficult to believe that, not so long ago, as we set up a preliminary office a block away from our flagship studio, Jay had looked at me in the middle of our preparations and asked, "Is this business really going to work?"

"Uh-huh," I had responded. Despite my own doubts, I

always wanted to maintain a positive attitude. If we didn't believe in ourselves, who would?

Through our Hamptons studio, we met quite a cast of characters, from "Mr. D," who seemed to own most of Mexico City, to an extremely successful personal injury lawyer. When we joined the attorney on his yacht, I discovered that I had gone to high school with his wife and felt particularly proud owning my success in front of this woman I'd known back when I was a shy, academic dancer.

I suppose the first moment that really highlighted our success was a conversation during a pool party hosted by one of our riders. I met a couple there who showered me with praise about Flywheel, explaining what a big part it had played in their lives. They told me that after every weekend morning class their five-year-old son would ask, "What was your Torq score today, and whose score was higher?"

Clearly, in a very short time, we had invented a lexicon that people were using. Flywheel was becoming a household name.

Riders were so enthusiastic about Flywheel that David, Jay, and I were constantly approached about opening new studios in other parts of the country, or even abroad. "Mr. D" felt we would be massively successful in Mexico. We also got requests for studios everywhere from London to Dubai, and from New Delhi to Sydney.

We wanted to remain consistent with our strategy of getting ourselves out there as fast as we could. For that reason, our third and fourth Flywheel studios weren't anywhere exotic, but close to home.

When Marion Roaman approached us and said she wanted to sell both of her Ride the Zone studios to us, we were excited. The meetings that David, Jay, and I had with Marion were all very positive. We shared a vision and all got along well. We had to temper our excitement to some degree, however, because we knew Marion had also been talking with other spinning studios about selling the business to them.

In the end, Marion got extremely close to forging a deal with one of our rival studios, then pulled out at the eleventh hour, ultimately making a deal with us. The partnership proved to be a successful one. Gaining two more studios in prime locations gave us a great opportunity to firm up our following both in Manhattan and in the Hamptons, and we were pleased when Marion wanted to join Flywheel as an instructor.

We treated the Upper East Side space exactly as we had the JCC. It was on the third floor of a small building on a side street, and it had lovely sunlight, although our model called for riders to spin in a dimly lit room. We were able to capitalize on the light in our lobby and waiting area, however, which was a plus. To add to the appeal of this location, a private training gym, as well as various other small businesses, shared our building.

We opened our Upper East Side Flywheel studio in March 2011. The business grew quickly in that location, and that building has since become a fitness hub, with several studios all housed in one location.

Meanwhile, Flywheel copycats began popping up across the country. One new indoor cycling studio opening up in Southern California used our language and accurately duplicated the look of our website. Another opened in Pennsylvania that actually used our photos. There was an incident, too, at our Upper East Side studio, where a rider broke off our tech pack from the bike, clearly so he could figure out the inner workings of our metrics and mimic that in his own product.

If imitation really is the sincerest form of flattery, then we were being showered with compliments.

As our ridership grew, so did the number of celebrities who began championing the effects of Flywheel workouts. Our first was my dear friend Katie Couric.

Katie had been a superstar during her tenure at *The Today Show* but left NBC for CBS in 2006 to become the first woman to be a solo national news anchor—a risky move that definitely took Katie out of her comfort zone. I admired her intelligence, courage, generosity, and warmth enormously and counted myself lucky to have her as a friend.

From the moment we started Flywheel, Katie showed up to support us. One of our earliest and best press events came about as a result of her friendship and loyalty: when Katie was still hosting *Good Morning America*, she convinced the producers to offer Flywheel a spot on the show.

It was a really cold morning, and we were all bundled up in sweatshirts until it was time to do our piece. We had set up a number of bikes outdoors on the plaza in front of the General Motors building on Fifth Avenue, where we performed a mock class with me leading. We shed the sweatshirts when it was time to go on and froze our butts off!

Riding with Katie in support of Stand Up To Cancer

For me, there was an added problem: I was fifty-three years old and experiencing all kinds of menopausal symptoms. Here I was, a fitness leader and the face of the business, about to be on television with an extra ten pounds on my frame. Even if I hadn't wanted to admit that to myself, I was reminded of the fact when Jay and Jake Spitz, the head of our public relations department, approached me prior to the *Good Morning America* appearance with a pair of Spanx to wear under my leggings while I was on television.

Later, I found out that Jay and Jake had a conversation behind my back where they literally picked straws to see who was going to be the one to tell me I needed them. (Jake lost.) They brought me four different varieties to try, but the Spanx felt so awful under my leggings that I said, "Fuck it, I'm not wearing these!"

Of course, a couple of years after that, I happened to see the video of me on that show and thought, "Wow, I could have used those Spanx!" I looked terrible. To this day, though, I'd still rather wear clothes that don't require me to squeeze myself into something that feels like a sausage casing.

Other celebrities began supporting Flywheel early on as well. In the first year, a very well-known painter walked through our doors. It just so happened that she was in class the day a photographer came from *The New York Times* to photograph the Flywheel studio for an article that they were writing about us.

I hadn't recognized her. Nor did I have any idea at the time that she was a hugely successful artist whose paintings had been exhibited in galleries and museums around the world. After class, she approached us and was furious that she hadn't been warned about the photographer. She made it clear that she had no interest in having a picture of her, working out and sweaty, appearing in the *Times*.

I felt terrible. Not wanting to be photographed was a perfectly reasonable request on her part. Most people—not just celebrities—probably wouldn't want workout photos of them appearing in a publication. We were profusely apologetic and comped her class immediately. We also phoned the *Times* and asked them not to use any of the photographs without getting our approval first.

This painter and I became friendly as she continued taking my classes at Flywheel, and I'll never forget the excitement I felt when she first took me to see her studio and everything she was working on. Through her, and through other rider-artists at Flywheel, I've learned so much about our contemporary art scene.

I was especially touched when she told me that one of my classes had actually inspired her to create a particular painting she was exhibiting in a new show. When I went to see it, I was overwhelmed: it was a huge triptych and truly astounding. I'll never forget the incredible exhilaration I felt, knowing that I'd helped inspire her to create it, and that I'd had this kind of impact on someone.

Our celebrity ridership continued growing fast. World-renowned photographers and artists like Cindy Sherman and Clifford Ross became regular riders, as did many top athletes. From New York Mets baseball player David Wright to football player Shannon Sharpe, athletes seemed to be drawn to Flywheel because our model offered the potential for a more intensive workout.

For me, however, the most exciting celebrities to have in class were still the singers and songwriters, since music has been so important to me as I've navigated through life. I was beside myself when Patty Smyth came to class—who could forget "The Warrior" from the early eighties? It was a mainstay on my aerobic playlists from my Bjorkman and Martin days, and Patty is absolutely lovely. Later, Lady Gaga joined the ranks of Flywheel riders at our Chicago studio.

The biggest thrill for me was having Sting show up in my Flywheel class. He chose a front-row bike and was there for me to see during the entire ride. As an undying fan of The Police, as well as Sting's solo career, I was hardly calm and collected, but I did everything in my power to come across as unfazed.

Before class, though, I made one misstep: I decided to introduce myself to Sting as a co-founder of Flywheel. He had been a rider at SoulCycle after my departure. Based on the number of classes he had already taken at Flywheel, I assumed he was a fan and thought he might get a kick out of talking to me, once I identified myself as a founder.

That backfired. Sting was kind, but quiet, and he seemed a little uncomfortable. I wanted to kick myself. Why did I think that would impress him? Ugh!

I have to laugh at myself now. A year later, Sting continues to be a regular Flywheel rider, and he is truly wonderful— funny, smart, and with infinite talent. If he's in town, he typically comes in to ride every day, and if he's traveling to cities with Flywheel studios, he'll go to those as well.

When I read an article about Sting's daughter, Eliot Sumner, and her blossoming musical career, I started listening to her. I really loved Eliot's music as well and added it to my playlists. One day, I played her music in class when Sting was there. He beamed with pride.

Way back when, as I listened to "Roxanne" and "Message in a Bottle," I never would have believed that I would one day ride with Sting in a spin class, but here I was, and I was enjoying every moment.

Lesson #12: Why Waste Time Waiting for Something Bad to Happen?

When I look back on my life, I can easily come up with a pretty sizable list of downfalls, failures, and disappointments. With them all, I had a choice: I could wallow in the negative

Sting and his wife, Trudie, after class

aftermath and let each successive "bad" thing contribute to a downward spiral, ultimately landing me in a place of pessimism and bitterness, or I could use each failure as a lesson that could lead me to a better place.

Ultimately, I chose the latter course. I have discovered that every life event—whether it feels good, bad, or neutral—has something to teach me. Even the most disastrous mistakes can lead you to a better place if you use them to acquire new knowledge, strength, and skills. I'm living proof of that.

I don't think I could have seen the difference between having a negative attitude and a positive one demonstrated more clearly than through both of my parents. My mother lived in a constant state of envy. She suffered from massive insecurity, high stress levels, and minimal enjoyment in life as a result.

My father, on the other hand, lived for every day, embracing the fact that he had the honor of treating sick people and making them better. He relished the simplest things in life, like just sitting in his comfortable chair and enjoying a great book. I much preferred his infectious smile and laugh, or his attempts to whistle a tune, over my mother's pursed expression and pervasive negativity.

As I lay with my dying father during one of our last precious conversations, I expressed how much I didn't want to lose him.

"I'm ready to go," he said. "I've accomplished everything that I ever set out to do and have enjoyed my life fully."

I was overwhelmed by his sentiment and, even more, by his ability to express it. In that moment, as much as I couldn't help feeling my own sorrow, I was also inspired by his courage and his resolve.

After my father passed, my mother continued on the path she had always been on, one propelled by fear and anger and intensified now by the absence of my father. The thing is, Mom also had all of the trappings of a wonderful, comfortable life. She even had an old friend who was a widower and was always ready to take her out and entertain her. Yet all she did was complain.

"Hasn't my life been hard enough?" she'd ask. "What will be next?"

My mother was always waiting for the next blow. Living

with that negative perspective on life is a waste of time, and I decided that I would emulate my father's positive approach. Being able to find something positive in every challenge builds the strength we need to move forward to a happier place. There is always enough good in the world to balance the bad.

Lesson #13: Empathy Is Great, but Stay Alert

By the time we began Flywheel, I had learned a lot about business relationships. I felt like I was more adept at reading people and better at weeding out those I could trust and those I couldn't. I made every possible overture to support our employees and kept my empathy for them front and center, always letting them know they could trust me as their boss.

That being said, one of the most important lessons I've learned is that empathy is a slippery slope. Be generous and warm, yes, but stay on the alert, too. Not all business partners and employees will have your best interests at heart.

For instance, early on in the employment of one of our Flywheel instructors, issues started to occur. She seemed to have trouble getting along with her fellow instructors and frequently requested time off. I sympathized with this particular employee more than I should have, projecting my own situation onto her. Despite the fact that I sensed something off about her and wanted to let her go from the start, I couldn't bring myself to fire her. In retrospect, I can see that by relating to her emotional issues too closely I ultimately did the business a disservice.

We did eventually fire her. It's important to remember that no hiring practice is ever going to be 100 percent perfect. All businesses occasionally have employees who don't fulfill their responsibilities or who behave badly. While it's important to support your staff, it's equally important for company founders and managers to remain objective about performance and hold people accountable. When there is a red flag of any sort, it's also essential to keep close documentation of behavioral slip-ups, both so you can make clearer decisions about your staffing and so you will be covered if an employee ever decides to sue the company.

Lesson #14: Never Sacrifice Quality for Perceived Efficiency

We've all done it. We've all been in competition with others, or even with ourselves, to get tasks done as quickly as possible, and the result is that we too often sacrifice quality for what we perceive as efficiency.

The same is true in starting a new business. While it's exciting, and even exhilarating, to watch your new venture grow, it's essential to set a reasonable schedule not only for yourself, but for the goals you're trying to accomplish with your company. Set clear expectations of what "ready for business" means to you and your company. Then build more time into your schedule as a cushion, so you can anticipate, avoid, or quickly address any mishaps that might derail your company early on.

We didn't do that well enough in the first years of Flywheel. As a result, there were several times when we opened studios before we were adequately prepared to offer top-quality service to our customers. If I could have a "do-over" with Fly-wheel, that's definitely one of the aspects of the business that I would go back and change, especially when I think of the stress we could have avoided.

PART III

REWARDS

9

The Changing Face of a Business

I was expected to be the public face of the company at Flywheel. This was a role that came with a great deal of responsibility. Jay and David saw me as more than just "the talent"—they expected me to truly be an equal business partner.

Fully inhabiting my new role brought ups and downs. One of the biggest perks was that I experienced business travel for the first time. While these trips could be tiring, they were also fun.

Jake, our head of public relations at the time, often planned the trips around events he'd organized for us. I had originally met Jake in my classes at SoulCycle and Jay had gone to the University of Pennsylvania with him, so the three of us had an easy rapport.

In fact, Jake and I were so close, at times he felt like a brother. He is one of the funniest people on the planet, able to reduce me to the kind of uncontrollable laughter that sometimes ends in gasping and tears. The subjects of his quick one-liners and steady patter of jokes often left Jay and me shaking our heads and asking, "How, exactly, is that man's brain wired?"

Jay, David, and I agreed early on that one of our "rules" for business trips should be that we would only bring carry-on luggage to save time, but Jake wasn't having any of that. Even on two-day trips, he would invariably show up at the airport with a "valise," as we liked to call it, big enough for two weeks of travel. Jay and I would see him coming and roll our eyes. There were even times when we left him at the luggage carousel as we strolled off with our wheelies . . . always with a sense of humor.

Jake was a friend of TV reality star Bethenny Frankel, who is probably best known as a cast member of the Bravo show *The Real Housewives of New York City* and for her own spin-off, *Bethenny Ever After*. He had been a regular on both shows; because of that, Jake was often recognized in public. Jay and I shared in his enjoyment of being recognized and felt like celebrities by default.

One time, for instance, a rider started feeling sick during one of my classes in Sag Harbor and left the stadium before class ended to lie down. When she decided she needed to go to the Urgent Care near the studio, Jake and I volunteered to drive her. She was in so much pain that she could barely speak, but when she felt well enough, her first words were directed to Jake: "Did I see you on *Real Housewives*?" Naturally we all had to laugh.

Another highlight of having to travel for work was that it gave us opportunities to explore restaurants in different cities. The three of us would do our research and collectively choose a restaurant. One thing that always remained a constant was that we all worked hard and *loved* to eat. The more menu choices we could order for "the table," the happier we were.

After all, anything "for the table" has no calories, right? And Flywheel was always about working hard and playing hard—about enjoying life, not depriving yourself.

Often, after dinner we'd retreat to the hotel lobby and take advantage of whatever entertainment was on offer. In one Atlanta hotel, for instance, we always hoped to see the Michael McDonald impersonator headlining the two-man band that regularly appeared there. We had so much fun sometimes that we didn't want the evenings to end.

Despite our easy laughter and enthusiasm for new experiences, we were disciplined when it came to travel expenses. We always booked the cheapest flights available, and our only requirement for hotels was that they were clean and reputable.

There was one hotel that unfortunately didn't cut it for us. It was in Highland Park, outside of Chicago. Jake and I were exhausted when we arrived; the rooms were dismal at best, but I was so tired that I told Jake they would have to do.

I had a few hours of downtime, so I showered and fell asleep for a couple of hours. When I woke up, I connected with Jake, who told me he couldn't stay at this hotel another minute. He made up some crazy excuse to explain to the front desk why we had to leave, and out we went with our luggage to search for something a little better in Chicago. We often laugh, thinking back to this time when we basically arrived, I showered and slept, and then we *fled*.

As time went on and the company became more successful, we upgraded the hotel choices slightly, but not by much. We were still keen on pouring money back into the business whenever possible.

. . .

One of the earliest business trips I took was to Boca Raton, Florida, where we opened our first Flywheel studio outside of New York in April 2011. This was the third studio we had opened within the course of the first three months after founding the business, and I couldn't have been more excited. I loved the idea of opening studios in new cities, largely because it was kind of like birthing the company again on a smaller scale.

Our early model for expansion was to choose new sites based on the interest and recommendations of our riders. In this case, the inspiration came from Ann Kelman, a rider we had met in the Sag Harbor studio.

Ann summered in the Hamptons but lived in Boca Raton the rest of the year. She felt that the demographic there would be perfect, because Boca was an extremely fitness-oriented community.

David, Jay, and I were intrigued enough to fly down for a day of touring the area with Ann. She pointed out where the popular shopping centers were, as well as the exclusive private schools.

Before the trip, Jay, David, and I had heard about another boutique spin studio set to open in Boca. All we knew about it was that Angela Lutin, a local spin instructor with a strong following, was planning to open this studio with a single investor.

As we drove around the city to scout out potential spaces, we happened to stumble across this particular studio, Breathe.

It was under construction at the time; Jay and I had to laugh as we watched David waltz right into the space to look it over. Nobody was working, since it happened to be lunchtime, so he went directly to the plans set up on a table, put on his reading glasses, and helped himself to a look. Neither Jay nor I would have had the nerve to do this, but we appreciated David's bold nature.

It was a good thing we'd seen the space. Not long after our trip, Angela found my contact info and called me, expressing her concern about Flywheel putting her out of business and asking if we'd be interested in buying her out.

It was a tempting offer. We flew down to Boca again and asked Angela to teach a class for us. We were happy with the experience and bought Breathe in November 2010.

In renovating the studio, we had to rebuild the space so that it would be more in keeping with our signature Flywheel stadium. Joining forces with Angela allowed our opening to happen a lot more quickly; she taught classes for us and served as a charismatic draw in building our Boca business. It was a great coup for us to collaborate with her.

Our second out-of-state studio, in Millburn, New Jersey, opened on the heels of the Boca studio being finished, and was once again inspired by a loyal Flywheel rider. Sherri Shapiro lived in Millburn and knew it would provide a healthy ridership for Flywheel. We hadn't made a foray into the suburbs yet, but we decided to go for it.

We found a great space, smack in the middle of the main street running through the town center. This space was formerly inhabited by a Furrier retail establishment.

Soon after opening the studio, we experienced what we referred to as our first "Footloose" moment—in honor of the movie by that name, where a similar scene takes place as the young hero, played by Kevin Bacon, defends dance as a spiritual activity in front of a town board. We were forced to defend spinning in front of the Millburn Town Board when a local curmudgeon decided to protest our arrival, claiming that Flywheel had changed the space and was using it in ways that were not "appropriate" for Main Street, Millburn.

David and I were called to appear at the Town Hall meeting at seven o'clock in the evening and didn't make it out of there until nearly midnight. We both had to come up to the front of the room and answer questions posed to us by the board of selectmen. It was an exhausting evening, but we won and felt triumphant. Sherri helped round up riders in the community and got them through our doors in Millburn. The studio was soon a success.

The one extravagant business trip we made early on was to Los Angeles for a single lunch. That's right—we flew to LA from New York City to have lunch, then headed back to the airport when we were finished.

What prompted this impulse trip? A friend of Jay's had set up an opportunity for us to meet with celebrity fitness trainer Jillian Michaels, and we felt like we couldn't afford to pass this up despite the cost of the tickets. Jillian had been one of the original trainers on *The Biggest Loser* television show.

It was well worth the trip to California. We met Jillian at

SoHo House in Los Angeles, and I was immediately struck by her full-on, charismatic, television personality. I definitely didn't feel like I was on an even playing field with her. Nonetheless, once we began talking about Flywheel, I overcame my feelings of intimidation and enthusiastically explained how the Flywheel method had originated and what we thought was unique about our product. Jillian bought into the idea right away. By the time we were finished eating lunch, she had decided to invest with us.

Later, when we discovered that Jillian was going to be in Chicago at the same time we were opening that studio, we asked her to help me teach the inaugural class. We knew Jillian's star power would draw a big crowd of riders, as well as a lot of press. Originally, she and I were going to team-teach, but then Jillian's team got back to us and said she wanted to teach the class on her own. Part of me was relieved; I had been nervous about being on the instructor podium with a TV celebrity, especially one who seemed as take-charge as Jillian.

"We should ask Jillian to arrive at the studio an hour early, since she's never been on a Flywheel bike," I suggested to Jay. "I can at least show her how the bikes work before she starts teaching."

He agreed, but as it happened, Jillian arrived literally ten minutes before the class was scheduled to start. Jay and I rode in the class while Jillian was teaching. With every pedal stroke, Jillian called out various remarks to the riders, as if she were on an episode of *The Biggest Loser.*

While Jillian's coaching technique makes for good television, seeing the stark contrast between Jillian's teaching style and my own was a good reminder of how different the Flywheel philosophy is, in terms of being encouraging and supportive rather than using tough love to motivate people to exercise. While there is no question that the tougher "army boot camp" approach can be hugely motivating and effective for some, we eventually proved that a significant number of people respond better to a more nurturing and supportive method of training. Regardless, Jillian's presence was nothing less than thrilling for the riders who attended, and it was a great way to make our presence known in Chicago.

Jillian was one of the most recognized names in the world of fitness, and for the sake of the business we were happy and honored to align with her. At the end of the day, growing your business is often about photo opportunities, especially with celebrities, because social media will help your impressions go viral.

Less than two years after opening the doors of our first Flywheel studio, we got an added perk from our association with Jillian. She had become a co-host on *The Doctors* and invited us to appear on the show. This was a major press event for us, since so far we had never done anything on a national level other than *The Today Show*.

We got word from our PR team, and, with only a week's notice, I flew out to Los Angeles in December 2011 for the taping. I arrived on set first thing in the morning and went straight to hair and makeup (something I never tire of doing).

It was a challenge convincing the show's producer to allow me to wear a Flywheel shirt for the segment. We ended up

compromising: I wore a Flywheel shirt for part of the filming, then changed into a *Doctors* T-shirt they had made for all
of the twenty or so riders on set with me, a group made up of
volunteers from the TV audience.

The panel of experts on *The Doctors* was also riding
Flywheel bikes onstage, and they interviewed me as we
rode. I demonstrated different positions and took the team
through them. They were all huffing and puffing and laughing together.

During the interview, I mentioned that Flywheel "kept
me young," followed by "I'm fifty-three years old!"

There were literally so many gasps from the audience that
they decided to use that moment on the promo ad prior to the
show. "Can you believe this woman is fifty-three years old?"
were the words that ran across the bottom of the screen.

Not once in my life did I ever imagine publicizing my age
on national television, but there it was, and why not? I was
proud of the way I looked.

What I didn't realize going into that TV spot was how
long producers actually spend taping a single show to get it
right. What I also didn't predict was that I would have to ride
that bike *for the duration of the taping*.

Granted, I tried to ride at a fairly slow pace, with minimal
resistance, but by the time it was over, I had ridden the bike
for over three hours. It's amazing what you can do when operating on adrenaline.

Richard Simmons was also a guest on the show that day,
and I got to meet and chat with him as we were waiting to go
on. He was entertaining company and made me feel as if I
had known him my whole life. He is a truly warm, wonderful

Richard Simmons at the filming of *The Doctors*

person who has done so much to spread fitness to so many. I couldn't admire him more.

After we wrapped up, I changed at the studio, went straight to the airport, boarded the plane, and literally passed out for most of the flight back to New York. I'm not sure I was ever more tired, but I was proud of the way I'd represented the company on national television.

By 2012, Flywheel was jamming. We opened four more studios in five months. Our Buckhead studio opened in Atlanta in February and seemed like a perfect fit. We knew that there was a wealthy demographic in this city, which typically meant a larger percentage of residents who put "staying in shape" at the top of their lists, and therefore more riders.

In addition, we were lucky enough to attract TV presenter

Shannon Sharpe, a former National Football League hero, as a devout fan of Flywheel. Whenever a pro athlete becomes a Flywheel rider, that athlete helps validate the effectiveness and soundness of our workout. Shannon soon became addicted to spinning and was coming out with total scores of over seven hundred each class—almost three hundred points higher than anyone else who had ever ridden at Flywheel. I didn't know whether to be impressed or appalled.

If Shannon's score happened to be lower than he thought it should be on any given day, he would often call us, yelling and claiming that the bikes weren't calibrated correctly. Jay learned to brace himself whenever he heard that it was Shannon holding for him. I think there were times when he hid under the desk!

That being said, we love Shannon and ended up hiring his girlfriend at the time, Katy Kellner, to manage the Atlanta studio for us. She has been a true asset to our business and is now a major player at Flywheel. Katy decided to become an instructor and is as successful on the podium as she is behind it, unique in her ability to lead on both the creative and operations sides of the business.

We opened the Buckhead studio in a former Mercedes-Benz dealership. Located in a strip mall, there wasn't much else around us when we opened, but the space was beautiful, with floor-to-ceiling windows that made it feel airy and spacious. Thanks to being the first in the area, having a great location, Katy's hard work, and having a talented instructor team, Buckhead became one of our most successful studios. Katy saw to it that we had a great team of employees there and a core of enthusiastic riders. For the first time, Flywheel served as an anchor establishment, with juice bars and blow-dry bars quickly following us in the mall.

That spring, we opened a studio in Charlotte, North Carolina. Tom Montag, a loyal rider and a very good friend of mine, is the COO at Bank of America. He spent a lot of time in Charlotte, since their headquarters were there, and thought we would do well in that city. Before our March 2012 opening in Charlotte, we connected with Steve Justice, who owned a private training gym there and had heard about Flywheel. Steve became interested in teaching for us and we thought he would be a great fit, having been a pro football player for the Panthers and the Colts.

Since his prime days as a center, Steve had packed on weight and wanted to trim down. He was well on his way to doing that when we met him, and teaching at Flywheel helped him reach his target weight. He still teaches for us today and has always been a popular instructor.

Gina and Eric Hadley were instrumental in helping us open a studio in Seattle a month later. They both lived in Washington, but Gina had grown up in New York and was very connected with the fitness world. They wanted Flywheel to open a studio in Seattle for selfish reasons but also thought it would be another great market for us. The Hadleys joined in our expansion efforts by becoming Series B investors.

With their help, we found a great location next to a Whole Foods in South Lake Union, a neighborhood so named because it's on the southern tip of Lake Union. Architecturally, South Lake Union still remains my favorite studio. It's three stories tall and so spacious and airy that it has a loft-like feel, with a cool circular window at the top of the front wall.

This kind of space would have been too exorbitant for us to afford in New York City; it remains our largest studio to date. In designing the interior, we were able to perch a Flywheel bike on a shelf that extended out at a high spot on the wall. We also added a grand staircase leading up to the Flybarre studio.

Merely months later, in June 2012, we opened a Flywheel studio in Miami Beach. I call David a "visionary" for his decision to locate our studio on Purdy Avenue in the Sunset Harbor area. At the time we opened that studio, however, we definitely did not appreciate the choice. Flywheel was pretty much the only business in this newly developed area close to the bay side, with the exception of a yoga studio. This area was about ten minutes away from the center of South Beach and a far cry from bustling Collins Avenue. There was literally a dirt road leading to our studio that might as well have had tumbleweeds rolling across it.

I had the honor of meeting Venus Williams in our South Beach studio as we prepared to give the space a face-lift. Venus was doing interior design work then as well as a line of fitness clothing. When she came in to meet with us, I was blown away by how tall she was, and she couldn't have been nicer or kinder as I took her on a tour of the studio. We didn't ultimately use her as our studio designer, but we did partner with Venus in selling some of her activewear. She also supported Flywheel by making an appearance at our Upper West Side studio when she came to New York. We were thrilled to have another world-class athlete supporting our brand.

It was exciting to watch the Miami studio grow in popularity and to witness the growth of other businesses in the

With Venus Williams featuring her
activewear at Flywheel

neighborhood following Flywheel's arrival. That neighborhood became a true destination spot and hub for fitness businesses and healthy foods. Barry's Bootcamp joined the strip of stores, as did a Whole Foods–type market, Jugo Fresh juice bar, and a number of fancy clothing boutiques and coffee spots.

Our Highland Park studio in Dallas opened in October 2012. We chose this exclusive part of Dallas because the people there seemed focused on working out and had time and money to spare. It didn't hurt business that yet another famous football player, Troy Aikman, became an avid Flywheel rider and a fixture at our Highland Park studio.

The next month, we opened our official, stand-alone studio on the Upper West Side to replace our JCC studio. It was big and bright and probably our most beautiful Manhattan location at the time. Our clients were thrilled. So were we, though a bit breathless: in 2012 alone, we had opened a total of seven studios. Flywheel seemed to be experiencing an unstoppable momentum.

My visits to our other studios continued to be incredibly gratifying, even though I was initially nervous about branching out from my New York comfort zone. I didn't know how people in other regions would react to spinning or my teaching style. I emphasized a certain degree of mindfulness in every ride, and that didn't appeal to everyone. A lot of the younger spin instructors were focused on providing loud, high-energy classes to inspire riders.

My classes were quieter and more "Zen-like," and there were people who couldn't connect with that. This sometimes made me feel self-conscious about my age, but I fought against it. The truth is that it takes a certain number of years and an amount of life experience to understand the power in staying calm. You don't have to run people over like a steamroller to prove you're strong. My classes have always been about a never-ending evolution. I sometimes describe the "soothing power" riders can feel when they're on a Flywheel bike and journeying on a flat road.

To break through my own performance anxiety, I reminded myself that achieving any sort of "celebrity" status wasn't my goal. From the moment I started taking spin classes, it became a mainstay in my life. My purpose was to share the passion I felt about spinning and its benefits with others.

Ultimately, most studio openings were fun and proved to be confidence-building as well. This was especially true when we were the first indoor cycling business in the region; the novelty almost always sparked an excited curiosity among area residents. It was great to be able to introduce a new form of exercise, especially to those who had previously had difficulty getting themselves to work out in the first place. If they tried Flywheel out, most of them would get hooked, just as I had way back when.

During our opening weeks, we nearly always managed to land a spot on a local TV morning show to promote Flywheel. Seattle was one of those cities where we were the first to introduce spinning. With such a predominance of high-tech professionals living in the area, we were optimistic that our product would be a huge hit.

In Seattle, I was scheduled for an appearance to celebrate Flywheel's new studio during a show at nine o'clock in the morning. We brought two Flywheel bikes onto the set and had a live audience. The host of the show was named Margaret, and Jake had dared me to step onto the set (which was equipped with the requisite couch, side table, lamp, and interviewer's chair) and say "Hello, Margaret, and HELLO, SEATTLE!" I actually did it, much to the delight of everyone in the studio. Jake was crying with laughter.

It was far less funny when the producers said they would choose the audience member to ride the bike next to me for our piece. She was definitely not someone who was accustomed to working out. This rider seemed nervous from the get-go and by abruptly standing up and throwing her weight too far forward, she actually almost fell off the bike during my demonstration. Her shoes came unclipped from the bike pedals and she was understandably startled.

I rushed over to help her, and once I'd positioned her appropriately on the bike, I kept our ride at the lowest possible resistance and made sure she was riding in the saddle the entire time, rather than riding and standing in intervals the way we would in a typical class. My focus in teaching is always on keeping the rider comfortable and safe, and it is no different whether I am on television or in the studio.

As the Flywheel brand grew, my visits to our other studios became "events." There were celebratory announcements about my impending arrival, and once the reservations went live for my classes, they filled up immediately.

In addition to teaching classes for riders, I also taught classes for instructors, followed by a Q&A about anything from how I had developed my teaching method to my personal story. They seemed especially intrigued when I told them how I had first become involved in spinning, and how my personal journey had led me to found two national spin studios. My presence seemed to inject a renewed energy and inspiration into everyone's classes, as well as an appreciation for their own careers in such a great field.

Before and after class, I was often swamped by riders and instructors who wanted us to take pictures together. It was always an honor, and I was always surprised by it no matter how often it happened. I loved receiving framed pictures of me with various people, especially because these usually were accompanied by testimonies describing how the riders' lives had been enriched by their Flywheel experiences.

Despite how exhausting these events could be, I always came away feeling fulfilled and energized by the people I met. For instance, there was a family in Seattle who made riding together a weekly ritual. The mother had compiled an album of family photos: the whole family in Flywheel gear at the studio, on and off the bikes. There was also a long letter accompanying the album describing how Flywheel had impacted every family member.

I heard from other parents, too. These were often people who were struggling to maintain close relationships with their teenagers. They wrote to say that by making a steady plan to ride together at Flywheel, the classes provided a bonding experience that strengthened family relationships.

My initial visit to Los Angeles wasn't quite as rewarding as some of the others. From the start, we had found it difficult to gain ground in the LA area. By the time we opened our first studio there, SoulCycle had already established a footprint in Los Angeles, but we had heard that it had taken spinning studios a long time to succeed in this city. That was small comfort, especially when we saw that spinning in this area had taken on a very LA style: people always riding on the beat, often out of the saddle, using lots of extraneous movements and not a lot of resistance—hence, "dancing on a bike."

With Flywheel, we were introducing something that was quite different, more athletic and demanding. There was definitely some hesitancy among the riders in Los Angeles and among some of the LA instructors we brought on board as well. It was a "Why should we love you?" vibe, and we had to work a little harder at selling ourselves and proving the effectiveness of our workout.

I specifically remember teaching a class to these LA instructors and noticing that one in particular wasn't enjoying it at all. She had a certain "we know more than you" attitude written all over her face, and that was a bit hard to break through.

Other studios, too, sometimes posed challenges. Once, I taught a class to the instructors in Buckhead, the Atlanta studio, and was hurt and surprised when I heard afterward that one of their instructors had said, "I didn't think it was that good!"

Dealing with negativity is never easy, no matter how far you advance in your career. I talk about this a lot with my fellow instructors, and we all have the same experience. About 99 percent of each class can gush over your talent as an instructor and motivator, yet we tend to focus on the 1 percent that criticizes us. How pointless is that?

As we refined our early expansion strategy for Flywheel, we developed a cluster approach. Each studio was company owned; we would send a particular employee to the new region to scout out instructors and staff who could manage and operate the studio. Opening studios in clusters within given regions made sense, because that way the studios could share instructors, tech support, and other staff members as needed.

Still, even with this strategy, not every studio thrived. One example of this was our studio in Ballantyne, North Carolina, which we opened in July 2012 on the heels of our successful Charlotte studio in that state. One problem, in retrospect, was that we'd decided on this location for the wrong reasons: we were lured in by an inexpensive lease, and since our other suburban markets were doing well, we decided to jump on this opportunity. We were sticking to our "cluster" strategy, which allowed us the advantage of using our instructor team in both locations.

Ballantyne never took off, however. It turned out to be one of four studios in all that Flywheel opened and then ended up closing. No matter how many price adjustments we made, local residents never seemed to think spinning was worth the cost of classes and the place never attracted a steady ridership. We had to cut our losses and closed that location in February 2014.

Likewise, our Highland Park, Illinois, studio opened in April 2012 and closed within two years because there weren't enough people willing to support boutique fitness.

Another surprising disappointment was our Stamford, Connecticut, studio. Chelsea Piers, a brand-new, expansive sports complex offering athletic fields, an ice rink, and an aquatics center, had approached us to ask if we'd be interested in joining them in that prime location. With numerous activities there for children, we imagined parents could drop off their kids and then ride at Flywheel. We were also enthusiastic about the idea because we had no other studio in Connecticut. Jay was from Greenwich, and he had been hoping we could find affordable studio space there, but that proved to be impossible.

With the Chelsea Piers opportunity, we should have paid more attention to the fact that we were literally hidden in a back corner of the complex. I heard from so many people that they had no idea we were there. We also misjudged how far people were willing to travel to take a spin class, so this studio struggled as well.

For the most part, I loved being the face of Flywheel. When we first started opening new studios, I would typically arrive for the grand opening and teach several classes along with other instructors hired for the on-site team. I would teach preview classes as well as classes on opening day, sometimes staying for up to a week.

We filled the classes of each new studio ahead of time with people we considered area "influencers" and with any guests they might want to bring, calling them "Friends and Family" rides. These complimentary preview classes would usually run two or three days prior to our official opening, when we started charging for classes.

Often in newer markets, we would try to secure a spot on a local morning show so that we could introduce Flywheel to the area. During the evenings, we'd have lovely dinners with influencers in the market. Often these people became Flywheel fans and friends.

A few years into the business, I changed my schedule a bit and would purposely wait and head out to a new location a couple of weeks after the opening. By then the kinks were worked out and the opening excitement and free classes were over. It was a great time for me to arrive and reignite the energy for the staff and for the riders, too, giving them a reason to keep coming.

At times I'd be returning from a business trip wearing a Flywheel T-shirt and people would tap me on the shoulder and say how much they loved Flywheel, and how spinning had changed their lives. I had never fantasized about becoming a celebrity—being famous never appealed to me—but now I embraced my identity as one of the founders of Flywheel. The benefits of this type of exercise and the business model we'd created still inspired passion in me. I wanted to keep sharing my love of spinning with others.

For the first time in my life, I was not only happy in my work, but more financially secure, too. I reveled in this novel feeling and couldn't help reflecting on how, when I first moved to New York City as a new college graduate, I had to partially rely on my father's financial assistance as I tried to make it as a dancer. Once I married Jeff, I was still financially dependent. The amount of money I made teaching fitness classes barely made a dent in our lifestyle. Jeff's law practice paid the bills and afforded us a privileged life. I was grateful to him for that, and I'm still glad that he made it possible for me to stay home with the girls when they were small.

However, because Jeff and I shared a checkbook and the bank accounts, his assumption was that I would check in with him before making any purchases beyond groceries and general household expenses. Jeff paid all of the bills and kept our accounts. I never saw any of them, nor did I have much interest in knowing what was going on.

I had been raised to believe that finances should be strictly the husband's domain. It seemed natural for me to let Jeff be in charge, since he was providing for our family and that was the marriage model my own parents had demonstrated. I didn't grasp at the time how much this financial dependence hobbled my freedom—or my ability to advance my career. One of the reasons I never had the confidence to pursue much of a professional life beyond teaching classes at a fitness studio was because part of me believed I wasn't capable of ever having a "real" career or earning any "real" money.

After Jeff and I separated and divorced, I was able to make my own decisions about how to spend money. This was liberating, but it was also terrifying, because I had to be so careful in order to make ends meet.

Thanks to Flywheel, I was finally feeling solvent. I was able to buy almost anything I wanted, whenever I wanted, without asking anyone's permission. I've always been disciplined about shopping and spending. Now, however, every once in a while, I could spring for a luxury purchase without worrying about it. The empowerment and freedom this gave me was nothing less than thrilling. I could truly appreciate whatever I bought, because I had earned it myself.

Even more exciting was that I could better support my daughters and treat them to little luxuries, too. For example, after the divorce, Jeff had done all of the clothes shopping with the girls as they were growing up. During those days of alimony, child support, and my meager salary, I couldn't afford much beyond my monthly living expenses. Since clothes shopping with my own mother created some of my fondest childhood memories, being able to afford to shop with my daughters now fulfilled one of my dearest, long-held dreams.

Jeff had also been the one to take our children on vacations whenever he had them during a school break. Now it was my turn. When the girls graduated from college in June 2012, I decided to take them to Paris for their graduation gift. Kate and Rachel had traveled to Europe several times with Jeff, but never with me—I had never been able to afford to travel with them any farther than Florida. I was excited to experience Paris with them, especially since it would be their first time in that city as young adults.

We had the time of our lives. I was even able to book my own room, another first for me. The three of us created life-long memories from that trip. Since then, we have made it a yearly thing: every June, the three of us take a pretty extravagant vacation. We plan it in the beginning of the year and count the months down until we go. These shared experiences continue to be some of the greatest highlights of my life.

Despite my success with Flywheel, my mother made it clear at every opportunity that my achievements weren't enough to satisfy her. For example, she had raised us to think that it was of the utmost importance to mail her a birthday card every year. She did the same for us. After my divorce, I noticed that her cards to me were inscribed with a very consistent message: "Happy Birthday—Let's hope that this is a better year."

When I asked what she meant, Mom said, "I really want you to find someone." In other words, because I wasn't married, she still viewed me as a failure.

The year my father passed away, my mother moved from our home in Old Westbury to an apartment in the city; by the time Flywheel opened, she'd been living in the city for almost twenty

Boating around Capri with my girls

years. She was eighty-seven years old and nearly housebound, confined to her apartment most days due to a long history of spinal problems that ultimately impaired her walking.

Mom had an aide to help her. I came and visited at least once a week, but, at every opportunity, she made it clear that wasn't enough. In fact, she would often say this outright when I was sitting right next to her.

I would say, "But I'm sitting right here, right now. Can't we just enjoy the fact that I'm here?"

Apparently not.

My mother was well aware of everything that had transpired at SoulCycle and knew about all of the great things happening with Flywheel. Yet the strength that I had shown in getting to this point in my career didn't seem to count with her, since I didn't have a man to take care of me. I'm sure her attitude was partly generational, but to me it felt like a put-down, since she failed to recognize everything I *had* accomplished.

Whenever I talked about Flywheel, for instance, she'd say something like, "You know, SoulCycle is really a great name. Who thought of that?"

Or, Mom might mention that she'd seen an article about SoulCycle, adding, "They're doing really well, aren't they?"

She instilled an element of competition between all of us in the family, but she always had to be the winner by being the one who received the most attention. As far as my brother Paul was concerned, I was just in the way, hindering him from being her favorite. David, on the other hand, although conflicted, opted out by trying to spend as little time as possible with her. It took me a long time, but I eventually stopped playing the game because it was extremely stressful, and more importantly because I finally understood that her needs were insatiable. I tended to my mother as much as I could in her final years and was happy to pass on a lot of the responsibilities to Paul, who was willing to take them on.

My other brother, David, pretty much dropped the ball completely. He had written off my mother years ago and eventually cut himself off completely. It was ironic that, although he appeared to hate Mom, he mirrored her knack for distancing himself from everyone in the family. David didn't show up for Mom's funeral and I haven't heard from him since. Paul and I had our own period of estrangement.

Mom passed away in September 2012, a couple of months shy of her eighty-ninth birthday. Everything just started to give out and she was ready. She was surrounded by her granddaughters, Paul, and me when she died, and she said that she was ready to be with Dad. In true keeping with her personality and style, Mom made sure that Paul and I knew she wanted to be buried in her Giorgio Armani suit. We had to chuckle over that despite our grief. Her passing actually helped facilitate a rapprochement between Paul and me. While the timing was sad, it wasn't surprising.

The lack of support from Mom and my brothers as I finally created a life of my own pained me deeply. I suppose children always desire recognition and approval from their parents and family members. It took me many years—and a lot of spinning—to realize that it is *your own* approval that should matter the most.

Once you learn how to take pride in yourself and in your own achievements, you don't have to hope for "a better year." You can acknowledge that you're having a great year right now!

One of our longtime Flywheel riders, Josh Perlman, was always a delight to have in class. Josh knew the words to every song by Biggie, Jay-Z, and a whole host of other hip-hop artists. He would rap lyrics in a comically exaggerated way that could cause an entire group of riders to break up laughing.

Everyone was so entertained by Josh that they'd often ask which class he was signed up for on a given day, so they could take the same one. I loved seeing his name on my roster, too; if I knew Josh was coming, I would make sure to put songs on my playlist that he liked.

As it turned out, besides inspiring other riders and dem-

onstrating his friendship for so many of us at the studio, Josh
played a crucial role at Flywheel: he was the one responsible
for introducing the Frankfort family to our business.

In the fall of 2013, Alana Frankfort was the first member
of the family to accompany Josh to a Flywheel class. She is
the youngest daughter of Lew Frankfort, who joined the
Coach company in 1979 as a vice president and led the expansion of Coach stores and the brand's introduction into
international markets.

When Coach was acquired in 1985 by the Sara Lee Corporation, Lew became president, and in 1995 he was named
CEO and chairman. His track record in business is legendary; during his tenure, Lew spearheaded Coach's growth
from a modest $6 million company to a $5 *billion* company.

Alana absolutely loved the Flywheel class and told her
father about the experience. She had never approached Lew
about investing in any business, because she knew how many
people approached him about investing in their ventures, and
she knew how selective he was about choosing other business
pursuits. However, in this case, Alana felt so strongly about
Flywheel that she made an exception, imploring him to at least
check it out.

Lew was intrigued enough to ask us if he could bring the
entire Frankfort family to ride in a class and then meet with
us. Naturally, we were happy to invite Lew, his three children—
Alana, Sam, and Tamara—their spouses, and even his grandchildren (who could play in the Flybarre room during the
class and our meeting) to visit Flywheel.

We decided that I would teach a class for them. I made
sure to have a great playlist targeting all of the age groups.

The class was full and energized, and it felt good—that is, until Tamara, Lew's eldest daughter, had a mishap. When she attempted to rise out of her seat to perform a "standing run," Tamara's shoes came unclipped. She fell out of the pedals and straight down onto the metal bar below the seat.

Typically, the reason this happens to new riders is because, when they first attempt to stand up from the saddle, their tendency is to throw their weight forward, putting an abrupt pressure and force on the pedals that causes their shoes to come unclipped. It isn't usually a big deal. But, in this instance, when I was trying so hard to impress these potential investors, I was absolutely horrified.

I quickly dismounted my bike and rushed over to see if she was okay. I think Tamara was more embarrassed than anything else, and I was just glad she hadn't gotten hurt. I spent the rest of the class hoping and praying this incident wouldn't affect the Frankforts' positive feelings about Flywheel.

We all showered after class and met in our conference room. Lew asked us a slew of questions about every aspect of the business, including our numbers, our respective responsibilities, and what our evolution had been thus far. He was clearly very interested in all that we had done, and his enthusiasm sent us over the moon. It's one thing to see your numbers grow and catalog all of the other evidence that underlies your success. It's quite another thing entirely to have a titan in the business world like Lew Frankfort commend your work. I felt as if all of our strategies, creative ideas, and long hours were validated by his obvious approval.

This first meeting led to many more. Lew became increasingly enthusiastic about Flywheel, and eventually he made a strategic investment in the company so that we could rev up our expansion plans. We were thrilled not only to have this additional capital but also to have Lew as a mentor and father figure who could teach us a lot about how to grow our business.

With Lew's support, we felt certain we were about to take our company—and our dreams—to a whole new level.

In 2013, around the same time Lew made his first investment in Flywheel, Rob, a friend of Jay's, approached him to say that a man named John Foley was going to reach out to us. John had an extensive background in technology leadership and had last worked as the president of Barnesandnoble.com. He was familiar to most of us, since John and his wife often rode at Flywheel.

Rob explained that John was working on an idea he wanted to share with us. When Jay spoke with him, he was surprised and intrigued by John's idea for a "Flywheel at Home" concept. This "next-gen" home stationary bike would be equipped with an interactive interface, enabling people to take on-demand, online classes at home, as well as compete with others signed into the same site.

The impetus for his company, which John called Peloton, was simple: He and his wife both loved spinning, but between work schedules and having to find a babysitter, they had trouble fitting classes at the studio into their lives. Why not make it possible for busy people to take spin classes at home?

At our first meeting, it became immediately apparent that John was very keen to either merge with Flywheel or work with us in some capacity. He had already invested an enormous amount of capital into developing his tech platform, the physical tablet/iPad attached to the bike. John had basically taken our Flywheel concept and reapplied it to a home bike, which would be a natural extension for us down the road, and we recognized that the work he had done to date was solid. His new product would be worth something to Flywheel.

We nearly made a deal with John but ultimately walked. Lew was now involved in decisions about Flywheel's future, and decided that it was better to focus on building more studios for the moment. When the time came to design a Flywheel at-home bike, we would come up with something uniquely our own. As we had learned from going up against SoulCycle, being second in the market is not necessarily a disadvantage. We parted ways with John amicably, agreeing to treat each other with respect.

After Lew came on board with Flywheel, I made the most monumental and unexpected purchase of my life: a second home in Sag Harbor, Long Island.

This, too, was the fulfillment of a fantasy. I had been renting a house in Sag Harbor for several years, since I needed a place to live while teaching in the Hamptons each summer. The business provided me with the rental, and I fell in love with Sag Harbor's history, charm, and proximity to the water.

Between teaching classes, I would often take walks and admire the village houses that were hundreds of years old. I had never imagined owning one, not only because of the cost, but because I was on my own. How could I enjoy a second home without a partner to enjoy it with me on weekends and during vacations?

Then, one summer's day in 2013, I was taking one of my usual walks through the village when I noticed a "For Sale" sign in front of one of my favorite houses. Without any intention of buying, I decided to call the broker listed on the sign, simply because I was dying to get a look inside the house. We set up a time for the next day.

When I knocked on the door at the appointed time, the realtor showed me through the house, and it was love at first sight. The original honey-colored, wide wooden-plank floors and the beamed ceilings had me at "hello." Although the house was small and over two hundred years old, it had a beautiful flow of space and plenty of light. Even better, there were three working fireplaces, with one of them even in the master bedroom.

As I walked out of there, I thought, "*Now* what am I going to do?"

Within minutes, I was already in mourning at the thought of not owning this house. But buying it was impossible. Who did I think I was, even considering such an outlandish idea?

Still, I couldn't help myself: I called my friend Pam and asked her to come look at the house. Pam grew up summering in the Hamptons; she has always had good judgment and given me sound advice.

I walked through the house with Pam, and as we reached the kitchen with its cathedral ceiling, she whispered, "You need to put in an offer *right now, and give them the asking price!*"

Pam can be very dramatic, but I knew she was right: There was no turning back. I had to at least think hard about buying this house.

I became obsessed with the house and considered every aspect of owning it. Could I afford the mortgage? What if my financial picture suddenly changed, as it had in the past? Could I rent the house out to cover costs if that happened? Was it crazy to have a second house, if I didn't use it much in the winter? Was it too close to the main road? Would I be able to enjoy it without a partner?

I frantically crunched the numbers, figured out the down payment, and concluded that financially I could manage the purchase price. I went through the rest of the questions. I also reminded myself that, historically, I had always made smart real estate decisions: the three apartments and the Hamptons house that Jeff and I had purchased together had all earned significant profits when we sold them, and I was the one who had pushed to buy those particular properties.

Only one of the questions—whether I would enjoy this second home without a partner—held me up. But whenever I envisioned losing this house, I felt absolutely devastated. Something within me was pushing me to move forward—that inner strength and instinct I had too often underestimated or ignored.

Ultimately, I decided to follow my instincts instead of letting fear or a lack of confidence stand in the way of my going after what I really wanted. I was going to buy this house. That was my answer.

Once I made the decision, it couldn't have felt more right. Over four years later, I still walk around my Sag Harbor house and feel incredibly fortunate. It's a home filled with warmth and good karma, and everyone who steps foot inside says the same thing: "This place is so *you*."

Best of all, I get to enjoy the house with my girls. Rachel and Kate were pretty surprised when I told them I was planning on buying it. Once I did and it became real, however, they were not only excited for me but also proud of the role model I had become for them.

Previously, my children used to spend summer weekends only at their dad's house in Bridgehampton. Now they split their time between both of our houses, and I feel so fortunate to have a place we can call our own—a house I have earned. I've come a long way from that rental house with Julie and her family—which, interestingly, was only a block away.

It definitely changed the partnership when Lew joined Flywheel as an investor. He was a tall man with a commanding presence and always dressed tastefully, in the finest suede and cashmere in winter, and in fine linens and cottons in the summer.

As I soon discovered, Lew's personality was every bit as compelling as his physical presence. I quickly learned that Lew was aware of everything and everyone around him and was quick to take charge of every situation. It was easy to see why he was such a success in the business world.

With Lew's investment, we were able to expand Flywheel more rapidly. I was traveling a great deal and becoming ever more acutely aware of my role as the face of the business. One of my favorite aspects of this sometimes surreal new status was that I began participating in panel discussions, typically for women entrepreneurs and influencers.

The first one took place in the spring of 2013 for a group

called Diva Moms. During this event, I sat on a panel with five other successful women entrepreneurs in front of an audience of about a hundred women, all of them interested in starting their own careers or reentering the workplace.

I was nervous at first but quickly eased into the format and really enjoyed the experience. I was shocked but pleased when I saw a line of women waiting to ask me questions about my career path.

I started doing panels and lectures regularly after that. The icing on the cake was when my daughters asked if they could attend some of these events. I would see their faces in the audience, beaming with pride, and point them out during my speaking time, beaming right back at them. After the discussions ended, Rachel and Kate would quickly let me know what a great job I had done.

At one of these events, I shared the floor with one other female entrepreneur at Columbia Business School. Appearing in front of a room full of business students was truly mind-blowing for me. There I was, giving advice without any business degree at all—one more thing I never could have imagined for myself.

But there was a downside to being the public face of a successful business, too, as I discovered the following year, when I was accused of having an affair with a celebrity. It all began innocently, as so many scandals do: a well-known songwriter was a regular rider in one of my classes, and when I mentioned I was a huge fan of her husband's acting, she offered to bring him to class so I could meet him.

Over the next few months, her husband and I slowly became friends. Often we socialized together with his wife and with other people from Flywheel, too, especially once summer hit and we were all staying out in the Hamptons.

Back in the city that fall, her husband and I occasionally talked after class, mostly about films and different actors we both admired. I loved hearing his opinions and especially enjoyed introducing him to movies he had never seen before.

We met sporadically to have these kinds of conversations for quite a while. Then, one day, he took a class without his wife. When I came outside, I found him sitting on a bench near the studio and looking distraught.

I walked over to him and said, "Hey. Are you okay?"

That was all it took. "No, not really," he answered, and then it all came pouring out: his distress over his wife's substance abuse issues, which I had known nothing about, and the long-standing problems with their marriage. I listened for a while, not knowing quite what to say or how to comfort him. There were young children involved, and I felt terrible about the whole mess.

Then, as I started to feel like it was time to head back to my apartment, he suddenly looked me in the eye and said, "On top of all that, I have a huge crush on you."

I froze. I didn't know what to do. Clearly this man was in pain, but he was married. This was a mess I didn't want to be around. At the same time, we were friends and I knew the anguish of divorce firsthand. The last thing I wanted to do was hurt his feelings.

"Well, I really like you, too," I said, trying to keep things simple.

"What are we going to do about it?" he asked.

"Nothing!" I said. "You're married."

Things were awkward between us after that. He had revealed so much to me that our relationship was immediately transported to a different, more intimate emotional level. I fell right into my caretaker role—one of my instant fallback positions in the past. I was attracted to him, yes, but I was adamant about keeping the physical boundaries clear between us.

"I'm happy to be your friend, but we can't take it past that," I said.

"I totally understand," he agreed.

Over the next few weeks, however, he grew increasingly distressed and really leaned on me. I felt sympathetic but a little wary around him. I continued to see him now and then but kept to my promise and never let things get physically intimate between us.

Then, one evening, we met for an early dinner at a restaurant. We were seated at a quiet table. When he went to use the bathroom at one point, the maître d' asked his name and said there were photographers waiting for him outside.

He returned to the table and urged me to leave the restaurant alone, saying, "I'll wait for a while before I leave. Go ahead."

My heart was pounding hard enough for me to hear it over the other diners as I fled. The last thing I needed was a media scandal.

I was relieved to emerge from the restaurant without any camera flashes going off in my face. Maybe the whole thing had been someone's idea of a bad practical joke, I thought, breathing a little more easily as I took a cab back to my apartment.

The next morning, however, I woke up to find a story

about my friend's marital problems and his alleged "affair" with me plastered all over one of the big tabloid newspapers. The reporter had actually built it up to be a "love triangle." Another reporter for a different publication picked up on it and referred to me as "the divorced spin guru." Other media outlets got hold of the "story" over the next few weeks and ran various versions of this ugly rumor.

Needless to say, I was devastated by the publicity, ashamed primarily by the thought of my daughters reading this story and thinking it was true. Finally, the worst happened: Rachel did read it and came home crying. Even after I told her none of it was true, I could tell she was as horrified as I was to have the spotlight shining in our direction for something so sordid.

True or not, more magazines, newspapers, and online sites continued running this bogus story. I longed to defend myself publicly. I wanted to shout it from the rooftops that I was a mother and had a business to run and explain that I'd done nothing wrong. However, our PR team counseled me to keep quiet on the subject if any reporters approached me. As difficult as it was to maintain my silence, that's what I did. The last thing I needed was to be dragged into the public eye through the marital woes of a celebrity couple.

Fortunately, as with most of these dismal scenarios, the story lost steam in a matter of weeks. It quickly faded from everyone else's memories despite the wear and tear the rumor mill took on me.

Two years later, I found myself seated at a dinner party during Art Basel Week in Miami. As everyone went around the table introducing themselves, one of the women stated her name and mentioned that she wrote for one of the tabloids. I recognized her immediately as the reporter who had maligned me in the paper. It took all of my determination to stay silent, given how much I wanted to tell her exactly how I felt about her and her so-called "job." I managed it, though. The high road is always the best one to take when you're faced with a potential scandal.

Lesson #15: Handling Personal Criticism in the Public Eye

The negative side of being the face of any business is that you will be subject to intense scrutiny. There are people who will cheer just as hard when you fall as others cheer when you succeed.

When faced with a media scandal, ride out the storm. Keep your head high and don't engage. When I was accused of having an affair with a celebrity—who, worse luck, was married to another celebrity—my PR team advised me to remain silent while we waited for the story to snowball and then dissipate.

"Feeding the story by commenting or denying anything will only perpetuate the rumors," my team said. "Your best strategy is to do nothing."

Of course, when you're a high-energy person, doing "nothing" is exhausting and torturous. One strategy I've found for coping with bad publicity and interactions with unpleasant, vengeful people is to actually write letters or emails expressing my true feelings—then delete or tear them up instead of sending them. This allows me to work out my emotions while maintaining my dignity and protecting my company.

The other coping strategy is to remind yourself that you are a person with integrity. If you live according to your personal values, there is nothing more you need to do. Let the world think and say what it wants. You know what's actually true, as do the people in your life who truly matter.

Lesson #16: Accept That Things Will Change and Change with Them

One of my least favorite aspects of being the face of our new business was how closely my physical appearance was scrutinized by riders, instructors, potential investors, and the media.

About a year after starting Flywheel, I noticed that I was gaining weight and couldn't understand why. Jay, with whom I discussed pretty much everything, reminded me about the "French fries for the table" we often ordered for lunch when I expressed my anxiety, but I knew that wasn't the reason. I have always been body conscious. I had been a dancer before transitioning into a career in fitness, so I knew my body well enough to know when I was overeating.

With the exception of my college years, when I was striving to be as slim as possible and surviving on cigarettes, Melba toast, and diet soda, I had always maintained a stable weight. My goal has always been to be as fit, strong, and healthy as possible, while still enjoying my occasional indulgences, like a glass of wine or ice cream.

It took me a while to recognize that the onset of menopause was causing my body to undergo a serious transformation. I didn't like it. By the time we began Flywheel, I was fifty-two years old and the oldest instructor by far in our starting lineup. In fact, the instructor group seemed to be getting younger and younger. Between my age and the physical changes I was experiencing, I faced a sure recipe for feeling self-conscious and inadequate.

I tried to decrease my caloric intake to keep the weight off. This had always worked in the past, but it didn't seem to make any difference now. It felt like I had this extra layer of flesh that I couldn't shed no matter what I did.

To say I was frustrated would be a severe understatement. Flywheel instructors are exceptionally fit due to the effectiveness of our workout. That was part of our brand. Yet here I was, surrounded by beautifully toned and often "shredded" bodies, while my own body was being reshaped by factors I couldn't control. The worst part about it all was that as the years progressed I knew I would most likely be moving further and further away from the possibility of attaining anything near that Flywheel instructor "look."

Getting through this phase required me to learn how to evaluate my life, and my body, through a different lens. I had to accept that certain aspects of my physical appearance were out of my control—and always would be—because they were part of the natural female aging process.

As I tell my students, any discomfort or challenge we confront in life, however big or small, is temporary. We move through those challenges because there really is no alternative. We are often even better off for having survived them. It's just hard to believe that's true until we get there.

For women going through menopause, although you might

not always feel like lacing up your sneakers or putting on your Lululemons, maintaining a regular workout regime and eating healthy foods during this time are crucial for your body and your head. When I look back at pictures taken during my pre-menopausal symptoms, and even before that, I realize I've never felt better about my body than I do right now.

I eventually did manage to lose the weight I had gained. Still, my body is different than it was, and my skin is less elastic. What helps me accept those physical changes brought about by aging is the knowledge that I am more confident, mature, grounded, and appreciative of the time I have left.

My advice? Enjoy your life as much as possible, no matter where you are in it. I love to eat great food and drink good wine with it. At the same time, I know I'm going to work out the next day and will feel better after I've overindulged. In the scheme of things, having a taut, ripped body becomes much less important over time.

Accept that things will constantly change—your body, your relationships, the economy, whatever—and that sometimes you won't be able to do anything about it. What matters is staying healthy and embracing life's joys as much as we can.

Lesson #17: Always Follow Your Own Compass

While staying on at SoulCycle as an instructor was emotionally difficult, it was a way of following my own compass, because it allowed me to be loyal to my riders. That loyalty was rewarded when those riders then followed me to Flywheel.

At Flywheel, I also followed my own compass—something I have come to define as an amalgam of intuition and logical reasoning—by trusting my new partners, David and Jay, in starting the business, and by living my personal values of accepting and encouraging others while sharing my passion for spinning. I never let go of who I was. In fact, I doubled down on my vow to be trustworthy and honest with everyone—especially with myself.

How do you follow your own compass and stay true to yourself, especially when challenges present themselves that might sway you to act in ways that go against your own values?

As with any compass, the most important thing to do first is to stay still—in this case, within yourself—so you can discover where you really are before venturing another step. Look at and listen to the signs all around you. Is your mouth dry with fear? Is your heart racing? Do you have a hollow feeling in the pit of your stomach?

Those are probably all signs that you are headed in the wrong direction. Your body and mind sense a risk ahead and are urging caution.

If, on the other hand, your pounding heart is accompanied by a feeling of exhilaration or joy—as mine was, when David and Jay first proposed that I join them in forming a new kind of spinning experience—then chances are good that you are being true to yourself if you keep heading in that particular direction.

Yes, sometimes you must change your path to flow with the changes in your life, but be as still as you can, and make your decisions based not on other people's judgment but on your own. Remember, *you* are the one who will have to live with the choices you make.

And, finally, instead of asking what you want to *do*, ask yourself who you want to *be*.

Lesson #18: The Key to Success? Work Hard and Leave Your Ego at the Door

Throughout my career, I have encountered incredibly talented instructors who were either "homegrown" or already experienced in the fitness field. As both their followings and confidence levels grew, they often wanted more. "I want to be you," many said, explaining that they wanted to experience starting businesses in their own right.

Whenever instructors have expressed this goal to me, I have encouraged them to pursue their dreams, advising them to the best of my ability. I always emphasized the importance of choosing the right partners and understanding what is involved in starting any entrepreneurial endeavor, from the level of work intensity to the patience required to get a business off the ground.

In some cases, the less experienced, yet more popular instructors let their sold-out classes feed their egos, giving them the false impression that they were equipped to run a business. It took them time—and failures—to recognize that endurance, experience, and gravitas are required to succeed.

Experienced instructors often have the same unrealistic expectations of instant success. One very talented instructor with many years of overall fitness experience told me about her desire to leave Flywheel and become the creative director of an already established indoor cycling business that needed a boost of star power. She felt that this was a great opportunity for her, and that if she didn't try it, she would always regret it. She had been at Flywheel for many years and had a strong following. Leaving her role as one of our star instructors was difficult, but she wanted more.

Three months into the role with this new company, she threw in the towel and quit. She expressed many reasons for her departure, but one that stayed with me was when she confessed that she really only enjoyed teaching to sold-out classes. I don't judge this at all, as most of us enjoy sold-out classes more! As the instructor, you give so much, and in a sold-out class, you get that energy and exhilaration back from your students.

However, the truth is that starting a new business, or trying to put new life into a failing one, has to start from the ground up. You have to be willing to put in the work.

This leads me to highlight a key lesson: whatever your ultimate business goals, keep your ego in check. If you make your work about the riders, success is in the bag. They will feed off your enthusiasm and believe in what you do, no matter how many other people are in the room with them. Then they will tell their friends about you. When your class sizes start to increase, even incrementally, you'll know you're going in the right direction.

Recently, there was an article in *Bloomberg Businessweek* about the incredible success of Peloton, the first indoor cycling bike for home use. The article mentioned the founder, John Foley, and his "overnight success," and included crazy numbers indicating their huge ridership as well as income. I spoke to John to congratulate him, and he laughed as he pointed out that he didn't know that "five years of hard work" equated to an "overnight success."

I laughed, too, because I know exactly what he meant. If you're passionate about what you do, you'll love the hard work. You will wake up every morning raring to get in there and make things happen. That is a life well lived—and the definition of success by any measure.

10

Growing Pains

By the time Lew Frankfort made his first strategic investment with us in March 2012, Flywheel already had nine studios, with seven more under contract to open. There is no question that bringing Lew and his additional capital on board helped us extend our reach faster, satisfying our goal of opening studios in as many new cities as quickly as possible.

We were still second in the marketplace to SoulCycle in terms of studio locations and total ridership, but we were pleased to have created a product that was unique to us. We were also confident that we could catch up with them over time by providing riders with a better authentic experience. Feedback we received from riders demonstrated that if a rider's first exposure to spinning was at Flywheel with our metrics-driven bike, it would be very difficult for them to then switch to other spinning studios where there would be no way to track their workouts.

"It would be like trying to fly an airplane without instruments," as one Flywheel instructor said.

. . .

From the moment Flywheel started, the subject of our ongoing discussions was often expansion: how, why, when, and where to open new spaces. Then, if we opened a studio in a certain location and it struggled, we had to come to an agreement on how long to support that studio before cutting our losses and closing it down.

For David and Jay, the decision to close a struggling studio was nearly always made based solely on numbers. They became extremely frustrated whenever a new space wasn't an instant hit. I was generally the partner arguing for more time. I empathized with the local instructors and knew that sometimes classes ran small until word got around that Flywheel was in town. Given my own experiences in teaching and training instructors, I had learned that the strongest sell in this business was always the riders themselves, marketing by word-of-mouth. How long it took for a studio to ramp up depended on a variety of factors, including the initial excitement among the first riders, what was happening in that region economically, and how adept a particular studio's instructors were at managing social media.

In 2013, we opened studios in Los Angeles, Philadelphia, Boston, and Plano. Plano, a suburb of Dallas, Texas, seemed to all three of us like it would be an especially good choice for a new location. This city was home to a number of large companies, including J.C. Penney, the Dr Pepper Snapple Group, PepsiCo, Frito-Lay, Dell, Hewlett Packard Enterprise, and Cigna. Yet, it didn't offer as much competition for workout options as the other cities, which already had many other types of boutique fitness studios. We were certain Plano would therefore be a natural fit for Flywheel, given this gap in the fitness market and the high percentage of young professionals with disposable incomes living in the city.

Unfortunately, this turned out to be a false assumption. We opened the Plano studio in a shopping center. Very soon afterward, the local staff reported low class turnouts and a problem with the location. They thought the studio was struggling because it was too far from any major hub to offer enough exposure. Growth of ridership in Plano was disappointing. Jay and I used to refer to it as "Plano no bueno!" We could have a sense of humor about it because we knew the studio would ultimately succeed. Time and time again, one of my many roles in a partnership with two former private equity partners was to explain the concept of patience. When you have a great product and great instructors, success will follow. When you're brand-new to a market and people don't know who you are, let alone what you are, there has to be a ramping-up period.

The Plano studio ultimately thrived due to the charisma of one instructor in particular. By this time, we had a great staff in New York, and we started giving them opportunities to help us grow the business. As Flywheel began expanding across the country, we realized that many of our homegrown instructors who started with us in New York could be valuable assets in promoting Flywheel around the country. Many were young and without family ties, and they loved the opportunity to explore new cities.

One of these New York instructors, Aleah Stander, turned

out to be a dynamo. Jay and I had hired Aleah at the very beginning of Flywheel. At the time, she was an instructor at the Reebok Club and working as an assistant in a medical office, with plans to eventually go to medical school.

When we hired her, Aleah had the skills to teach a typical "gym spin" class. She went through a Flywheel training with me and adapted the changes in her method necessary to teach a Flywheel class. As Aleah gained confidence and experience, her classes started to pick up in popularity. She became one of our superstar instructors within a year of starting for us.

Training Aleah to be a Flywheel instructor was easy. However, her assertive, outspoken personality didn't always work once she began climbing the Flywheel career ladder and started managing other instructors. Several times, I had to take Aleah aside and counsel her on how to manage her emotions and talk to people more sensitively and professionally. She was always open to improvement and criticism, a quality I respected, because I thought it would take her far—and it did.

Being in the fitness field became Aleah's true passion. Her plans to become a doctor were derailed by her love of spinning, but her ambition to always push herself to be the best at whatever she did remained. Aleah agreed to move from New York to manage our Miami studio, and proved to be so successful there that in time we gave her more and more studios to add to her domain. She was instrumental in turning the Plano studio around for us when she agreed to take on that space as well. Not long ago, I was teaching a class in East Hampton when a rider mentioned that he had just ridden in our Plano studio. I was thrilled to hear that not only was his 5:30 a.m. class sold out, but the 6:30 class that day was packed as well, proving that we'd been right to be patient.

Aleah continued moving rapidly up the ranks at Flywheel to her current, very senior position as the regional creative lead in the Southeast, Texas, and Chicago.

Recently, I read an interview that made me so proud of her—and proud of the role I'd played in her development as a leader.

"It's been a wild ride," Aleah told the interviewer. "I am lucky enough to be mentored by Ruth Zukerman, founder of Flywheel, starting very early on in my career. Her leadership and guidance is phenomenal, and I am so grateful for her." Right back at ya, Aleah!

Another city that surprised us with a slow start was Los Angeles. We had heard about an existing studio in West Hollywood called Updog that offered spinning and yoga. This location felt like a natural fit for Flywheel, so we signed the lease to take over the space in December 2012 and opened our studio there the following April. We reconstructed the spin studio in Flywheel's trademark stadium design, as we had so many others, but kept their yoga program.

This proved to be a disastrous decision. The old Updog staff and clientele just didn't jive with the new, so we ended up phasing them out and bringing our Flybarre business into the yoga space. Even so, getting the West Hollywood studio to turn a profit was a steep uphill battle. I believe in karma around spaces, and there were reasons that Updog wasn't making it—reasons we probably should have paid more attention to from the beginning.

Probably the biggest barrier to success with this particular studio was that the space wasn't conducive to hanging out. Socializing is such an important part of the Flywheel experience because it helps people connect socially and form supportive relationships.

With time and experience, we discovered that the studios most likely to thrive were those that developed communities. Riders bonded through workouts, continued taking classes together, and even socialized outside of Flywheel once they discovered each other and a mutual love of spinning. Most of our studios had spaces where people could linger and chat before and after class, but not this one.

Los Angeles riders were also very accustomed to riding fast, with little resistance on the wheel. This was antithetical to the Flywheel ride. It was also much less effective, yet these riders did not adapt easily to our style of riding.

Our second studio location in Los Angeles was on Larchmont Avenue in Hancock Park. That proved to be more immediately successful. A broker talked us into opening there by pointing out that this was an affluent area with young families and professionals who worked mostly in the entertainment business. There was no competition for spinning in the neighborhood and we were well received from the start.

It was in Los Angeles that we began test marketing our "Flybeats" class through Victor Self, our West Coast creative lead. Victor had taught spin classes in this way before working for Flywheel. Since Los Angeles riders were used to this type of spinning, it made sense to try it out there first.

Our "signature" Flywheel classes were high-energy, motivating rides that incorporated interval training—riding on and off the beat, races and rhythm riding, an upper-body series, and real-time performance tracking with our tech-pack and optional TorqBoard participation. Now, the Flybeats class offered people the chance to ride on the beat the whole time. Flybeats fused the precision of rhythm riding with fun, athletic choreography and Flywheel technology. With rpm dictated by the rhythm of the music, the instructor might tell riders to turn up the resistance, but riders still held the beat. The class was such a hit in both of our LA locations that we began slowly adding it to other regions so riders could choose between signature Flywheel classes or Flybeat classes.

In February 2013, we celebrated our Philadelphia opening. Since Jay, David, and Jake were all alumni of the University of Pennsylvania, they were especially excited about this location for Flywheel. We even toured the campus and I got to hear their old college stories.

Our Philadelphia Flywheel studio was located in a basement beneath a great delicatessen called Schlesinger's in a prime Philly location. As we soon discovered, the advantage of opening in a basement space is that sound from the music being played in the studio wasn't an issue; this was a definite plus, since noise complaints weren't uncommon in some of our other spaces, especially if they were located near apartments. Another perk was the deli itself. Schlesinger's even created a (somewhat) healthy sandwich—it had avocado—and named it after Flywheel.

The Philadelphia studio took off quickly. Since this was another city where we were the first spinning studio to appear, it wasn't long before we felt confident enough to open a second space in that area. Flywheel opened its Bryn Mawr studio in May 2013 to accommodate riders who worked in the city but lived in the suburbs.

By October 2013, we were ready to tackle Boston. This turned out to be our favorite scenario: the sort of location where people were eagerly awaiting our arrival so they could sign up for Flywheel classes. We had enough studios in the Northeast by then that many Bostonites had already experienced us elsewhere. Now they eagerly embraced Flywheel in their hometown, and that studio was booming right from the start.

To my delight, this phenomenon was happening more frequently. I was still teaching at all of the new studio openings; before I started the first class, I always asked if anyone in the room had ever taken a Flywheel class before. A larger percentage of people raised their hands with each new opening. It was incredibly gratifying to watch this happen— especially in Boston, where Flywheel occupied a beautiful studio space in an upscale shopping mall beneath the famous Prudential building. Having the actress Jennifer Lawrence find us in Boston didn't hurt business, either.

Despite our success in other Northeastern cities like Boston and Philadelphia, business was sluggish at the studio we opened near the train station in Scarsdale, New York. Once again, we had to ask ourselves whether people in the suburbs would want to pay for classes at Flywheel, especially since we'd finally raised the price of each class. Sometimes, as in Scarsdale, the riders eventually adapted to the new prices and the business grew, but one must always expect casualties along the way whenever there is a rise in prices.

At the same time that we were rolling out new studios around the country, we began testing Flywheel abroad. One of our riders split her time between New York City and Dubai; she felt so strongly about Flywheel's potential success there that we decided to explore the option. We formed a partnership with this rider and her family, and they put together a team to handle the day-to-day working of a studio in Dubai. Flywheel was so successful in that city after opening in 2012 that we added a second Dubai studio two years later.

Toward the end of 2012, we also partnered with Steiner Leisure, a large, innovative spa company that controlled most of the spa and fitness enterprises in the cruise ship industry. This allowed us to build "Flywheel at Sea" studios on several ships, including a Celebrity and two Norwegian new builds (best-of-class) cruise programs. For us, this was a low-impact enterprise from an operational perspective. We supplied the instructors; with a steady inflow of playlists contributed by our New York instructors, we were able to inject a little of our New York vibe on board the cruise ships. We were also responsible for training instructors and controlling the quality of the bikes, which we managed from our Miami studio.

Our last international location was in England through Soho House UK, which specializes in private clubs of all kinds. After several meetings, we eventually struck a deal to open a Flywheel studio in Shoreditch House. I was excited about the opportunity to bring Flywheel to London and jazzed to spend time there in general. Danielle Devine, one of our lead New York instructors and now our creative lead for the Northeast region, assumed the responsibility of recruiting and training instructors over there, and we sent our tech team to London regularly to make sure the equipment was up to par and well maintained.

No doubt about it: things were growing and changing fast at Flywheel. The amount of energy that David, Jay, and I had generated and sustained with our employees during the first four years of the business was vibrant and palpable. The three of us were often exhausted, but our enthusiasm never waned. In fact, the more successful we became, the more energized we felt.

Our staff expressed the same positive attitude and passion for Flywheel that we felt. Despite our rapid growth, we had successfully maintained a cohesive feeling at the company. Jay, David, and I had established a level of comfort and trust that caused nearly everyone we hired to feel valued and empowered.

For many of us, work was the highlight of each day, above and beyond anything else in our lives. Our energy and passion led us to successfully create a company that we knew could eventually have huge potential, culturally and globally.

Then, in 2013, everything changed.

Flywheel's transition from a small, personable business to a major corporation began when we were approached by an athletic footwear company based in the Midwest. The company wanted to buy Flywheel outright. Jay, David, and I were excited about the possibility. We had been working nonstop to get the business off the ground and the thought of finally making some real money was definitely appealing.

We began holding regular meetings with the company to negotiate a deal. Lew was experienced enough in business to know that many of these prospective deals fail to materialize. We were a little jaded, too. By this point, we had started receiving regular inquiries by various companies interested in acquiring Flywheel, though none of those offers had panned out so far.

But this particular company made us a firm and generous offer we were poised to accept, and at that point, Lew stepped in and said, "If anyone is going to buy Flywheel, I am."

Under Lew's helm, we quickly opened seventeen more studios, bringing our grand total to forty. There were other, internal changes as well—so many, and so fast, that at times I had trouble keeping up. Flywheel was officially no longer a start-up business.

For starters, there was a huge uptick in data analysis. Our finance department, which had been based in Florida, was transferred to New York. Our head of human resources also worked out of the Florida office, and with the growth in the number of employees, and therefore potential employee issues, we now needed someone who could physically be in our New York office.

Another enormous change was the way in which we now approached selecting locations for new Flywheel studios. Previously, we had relied heavily on our riders and intuition in considering new locations. This was definitely a trial-and-error approach to expansion.

When we first teamed up with Lew, we were consulting with outside real estate experts; now Lew persuaded us to hire a realtor to work in-house and create her own team. In addition, Lew felt strongly that we should limit our expansion to heavily populated urban areas within the United States, since there was still so much untapped territory right here in our own country. We were going to have to both rein in our expansion efforts abroad and be choosier about our domestic locations. Lew was willing to make an exception to this strategy only if we were absolutely certain that a location beyond those parameters would be a guaranteed success.

One new site we had to work hard to convince Lew about was Sunnyvale, California, near San Francisco. The lease had already been signed before Lew became our majority investor, which influenced our decision to go ahead with the opening despite his objections.

David had chosen the Sunnyvale location based on the attractiveness of the deal on the space, and on his certainty that this area was destined to become a busy corporate hub. He based this prediction on the fact that Sunnyvale was part of Silicon Valley, which was undergoing rapid population growth in response to the explosion in tech companies.

SoulCycle had opened its first Bay Area studio in 2013. Choosing to build a studio in Sunnyvale was our first foray into the California market. Sunnyvale wasn't in a major city, but David thought that people commuting between work in San Francisco and their homes in Sunnyvale could become loyal Flywheel riders.

Lew, on the other hand, felt that because the Sunnyvale location was an hour's drive from San Francisco even with light traffic, it was too remote. He was also worried that it would be difficult to find instructors (this would in fact prove frustrating for the creative team).

In this instance, I agreed with Lew. Having visited Sunnyvale quite a few times, I was puzzled that David championed this location so adamantly. The block where the studio would be located literally had no other retail businesses on it. There was a vacant apartment complex across the street and that was about it. Sunnyvale felt like a ghost town.

Lew's fears were well founded. Kate Hickl, who was leading our instructor recruitment efforts at that time, struggled to find talent in this area, since spinning didn't have much of a foothold there yet. That studio eventually grew and thrived. Once again, however, we had learned a valuable lesson: our experience in Sunnyvale taught us how important it was to ask our instructor recruiters to weigh in on the feasibility of studios succeeding in more remote locations.

Thankfully, other new Flywheel locations were quicker to gain traction. The studio we opened on Dupont Circle in Washington, DC, was an instant success from the moment the doors opened in March 2015. A year later, we opened in City Center, a fairly newly built area in the city, and that studio thrived as well.

"Scaling" was now the operative word at Flywheel. I quickly learned what this meant: once a company has developed a sales model that can be successfully replicated, the next logical step is to accelerate (or "scale") the growth of your business. To accomplish this, we needed a whole new team with a set of skills in place that would enable further growth. Essentially, that meant hiring people with a formal business education.

The Flywheel team that Jay, David, and I had built through our early years operated by our instincts and trial and error (or even trial by fire). Most of the time, we got things right. But Lew was experienced enough to know that this model wasn't going to move us forward and allow the business to catch up to the level of the brand we had built, much less move beyond it to make an even greater impact. He began to make enormous changes in company staffing to accelerate our forward momentum.

When we first began the company, for instance, we were always stretched thin financially, so we hired generalists—people who could do a lot of different things. Jay and I often chose employees based on what we saw as their intrinsic potential skills rather than on the basis of their resumes. Most of these early Flywheel staffers learned on the job. We gave them a wide berth to make decisions (and mistakes) as they grew into various roles at the company according to their interests and talents.

Even after we had built a structure around the organization, prior to Lew joining us we were still drawn to people more for their general leadership abilities than for specific skill sets. We had hired many employees who had started their careers with Flywheel when we were a small, personable company. Now, however, we were becoming a large company with many organizational layers, and the people who worked for us needed different skill sets.

Lew recognized all of this and made a very clear choice to hire people based on their previous work history. These employees had performed specific roles before, even if they had been in another industry.

Our annual holiday party served as a clear indication of the changes occurring within the company. Up until this point, these parties had been pretty scrappy affairs. We'd choose a downtown bar, provide a buffet dinner and lots of alcohol, and the Flywheel family would let loose. We all worked so hard every year that this evening was always about showing the love and throwing caution to the wind. We were all simply thrilled by the prospect of getting to dress up for each other, since otherwise we only saw each other in workout clothes.

We even had a sacred tradition: each year, David, Jay, and I would give a short speech. David's was always the same. He would ask, "How many people have been with us for one year?" There would be a small show of raised hands.

"How many for two years?" he'd ask then. More hands would rise.

By the time he reached the most years possible, the majority of hands in the room would be raised. This was a tried-and-true display of our "Flyfam" and sense of belonging.

After Lew took over, however, we could no longer do this. The number of employees had grown exponentially. Many of us who remained from the early days barely knew the newcomers. We were now a large, diversified company. That boded well for Flywheel's future, but I missed the smaller, more familiar work environment.

I admit it: I struggled during this early phase of working with Lew at the helm. The first big change was that David left Flywheel right away. He sat in on some of the board meetings and was still an investor, but that was it, and I missed him.

A year later, Jay was gone, too, other than as an investor in the company. That left an even bigger hole, not only in my work life, but in my heart. Jay had always been extremely protective of me. Whenever something had come up at Flywheel that made me feel unsure of my own opinion, or if I faced a particular challenge with clients or employees, Jay always had my back. His emotional support had given me strength and confidence through the years. Because I had been raised by a family that showed little loyalty to me, Jay's place in my life was particularly powerful.

Now I was operating without that safety net of having Jay and David beside me. This wasn't easy, given Lew's ongoing encouragement about my expanded role. He believed that I should take on a certain set of responsibilities at Flywheel. In his view, Jay, especially, had been *overly* protective of me. There was some truth to that.

Lew now expected me to be involved in every aspect of the company. He offered to mentor me from the very beginning of his partnership with us.

"Oh, that would be great," I told him, and meant it.

As time passed, however, I realized that Lew wanted me to take on certain responsibilities that didn't feel like the right fit for me. He definitely wanted me to be more analytical, for example, when that wasn't really part of my skill set, at least in business. Whenever I resisted doing organizational charts and spreadsheets, for instance, I had to wonder whether I was backing away from these responsibilities because I didn't like them or because I was afraid I couldn't learn how to perform them.

Was Lew right? Was I allowing my own lack of confidence, or disinterest, in these areas to hinder my growth as a manager? Was I holding myself back in my career by not developing these new skills that Lew seemed to think I needed?

Another issue I faced was that my presence was expected at all of the meetings. I had always chosen to work in fields where I could be active—dance, aerobics, spinning. Now, as I was forced to sit at a conference table for hours on end with other executives at Flywheel, I remembered with horrifying clarity that dingy basement where I'd worked for a caterer so many years ago. True, I wasn't in a basement now—these were pretty swanky conference rooms—but I might as well have been. I felt trapped and claustrophobic.

It took time, but upon closer reflection, I recognized that I wasn't avoiding these new responsibilities because I *couldn't* learn how to do the things Lew was asking me to do. The real truth was that Lew was asking me to weigh in on matters that didn't much interest me. Halfway through many of the meetings, I discovered that my biggest challenge was actually keeping my eyes open.

Without David and Jay to bounce ideas around with and back me up, I felt adrift and bereft. Flywheel had been my family for years. Now I was mourning the fact that Flywheel, as I had known it, had grown up, just as my daughters had grown up and left home. With no close partners at work, and no partner or children at home, I felt alone and anxious. A life where I could feel safe and secure suddenly seemed precarious, even out of reach.

As I was living through these growing pains, I reflected on how much happier I had always been when I was doing work that focused on what I loved. I guess you could say that I preferred going narrow and deep. Jay, David, and I had been a team, but we had always worked autonomously. We were three partners who did different things. My former partners hadn't expected me to crunch numbers any more than I'd expected them to be creative when it came to arranging music, training instructors, or developing the choreography we used in teaching spin classes. (Jay did once attempt to make a playlist for our "Mother's Day Ride," and it was a disaster—we still laugh about it today.)

At one point, I remember feeling particularly distressed because nothing I was doing felt organic to me or true to who I am.

The following week, I traveled to Miami to teach their instructors how to run a Flybeats class. As I worked with the Florida instructors, I saw how excited they were about mastering new teaching skills. As they talked to me about how Flywheel had changed their lives and how thankful they were that I had started the company, my confidence came flooding back. *This* was why I had started the business and what I loved about my career: to bring my passion for spinning into the lives of others. I vowed to hang on to that.

I also continued to learn a great deal from Lew. For instance, in the very beginning of Lew's days as chairman of

Flywheel, we were affiliated with another private equity firm. As I sat in on meetings with executives from that firm and members of Lew's team, I remember being asked various detailed questions about how we planned to scale the Flywheel model so the company could expand and turn a profit in return for that firm's investment. Whenever I got stuck on questions like that, Lew took over and made it clear that he and his team had the experience Jay and I lacked. They could grow Flywheel quickly and efficiently in ways we couldn't have done alone.

Lew also made me see that Jay and I had adopted a somewhat haphazard approach to managing the instructors that could never work in a larger company. Jay and I had always treated each instructor individually; we often made concessions based on an instructor's personality and immediate needs. Now, Lew taught me the importance of having more consistency and structure when it came to what we expected of our employees. It was less about the individual and more about setting equitable company policies that were followed across the board.

While I resisted this idea at first, I soon realized that Flywheel needed these rules in place so we could successfully scale the business. Without them, it would be hard to grow the company to that next level. Here's a good example: We had one instructor who had been with us for a while. He had earned a real name in the New York/LA indoor cycling world and I had nothing but respect for him. Long before Lew took over, Jay and I knew this instructor wasn't fulfilling his class load, but we let it slide because of his reputation.

Understandably, Lew was not happy with the situation.

One day, he and I took a walk in Central Park and had one of the "check-in" talks we so often had in the beginning days of the takeover. Lew specifically asked me during that conversation if I had been in touch with this instructor, and whether I had been firm with him about the number of classes we expected him to teach.

I had to admit that not only had I been lenient, but I'd let the issue slide because of my usual hesitancy to confront people and instigate a conversation that might lead to conflict. In addition, since I had always been an instructor at heart as well as in practice, my tendency was to empathize too much with the instructor group in general. That wasn't helpful when it came time to enforce certain expectations. Having Lew mentor me clarified the fact that my management style needed to improve.

It wasn't always easy for me to have these conversations with Lew. Jay, David, and I had been equals. Within a year of Lew purchasing the business, I was left working with him in a very different way.

My new challenge was to develop a relationship with a chairman who had a management style that was vastly different from my own. Lew wanted to be involved in every aspect of the company. That wasn't my style. I also found myself grappling with trying to understand and navigate a new business culture, one with different expectations and even a whole new lexicon of business terms and acronyms. I was drowning in org charts, spreadsheets, decks, and slides.

The only slides I knew were the ones I'd been shown on an overhead projector back in late '70s high school. During one particular meeting, Flywheel's new CEO at that time asked me to submit a list of my "strategic operative initiatives." I had to lean over to one of my co-workers from the old guard and whisper, "What is that?"

"It means 'What's your plan,'" he translated.

I never understood why we couldn't just *say* that.

As time went on, these kinds of meetings and the detailed paperwork involved became less and less gratifying to me. I began to notice that my enthusiasm for work was flagging. For the first time since beginning Flywheel five years earlier, I found myself dragging my feet about going to work. I was experiencing a pervasive sense of dread that was beginning to permeate the rest of my life. What was I going to do?

I thought about leaving the company, as Jay and David had done, but the reality was that I still needed a salary and had equity to vest. If the company continued growing, I'd receive a bigger payout if I remained.

More importantly, I didn't *want* to leave. I wasn't ready to abandon Flywheel and my peeps. I knew the creative leads and instructors were struggling with the transition in leadership and the company's growing pains, just as I was. They were really relying on me and I felt protective of them.

No, I had to find a way to stay, but that meant doing something scary: I was going to have to step up and make my voice heard, loud and clear, as I designed my own future at Flywheel.

Lesson #19: Embrace Your True Self

In an odd way, starting Flywheel and then having to let go of full control when Lew became our major investor helped me rediscover my true self. We had started the company to offer riders an authentic athletic experience with a mind-body component that could help empower them to transform their lives. Our company values at Flywheel—based on inclusion and passion—were integral to the company's success. These values were also integral to who I was as a person, which is what made me so passionate about the business—and no doubt contributed to our success.

One of the most difficult things for us to do in life is to recognize who we really are—our true selves—when confronted with others who are confidently telling us that we're doing things wrong and should change. Maybe those other voices telling you what to do belong to your colleagues. Or maybe the voices are emerging from your partners, your so-called friends, or even your parents. Whatever their origins, ignore these voices if they are contrary to your own values. You will be happy—and successful—only if you drown them out and embrace your own authenticity. Examine your life and ask yourself if you are being true to yourself, not over a year or even during a given month, but moment to moment, too.

What does this mean, exactly?

- Accept who you are—strengths, talents, flaws, and everything in between.
- Ask yourself, "What do I want?" Then go after it.
- Live by your own values and nobody else's.

- Be honest with yourself and sincere with others.
- Take risks, make mistakes, and learn from them.
- Remember that nobody can tell you how to be true to yourself but *you*.

Lesson #20: The Importance of Alone Time

Throughout my life, I had a habit of repeating certain patterns in both my personal and professional relationships. In my love life, two requirements were of paramount importance to me. The first was that my partner had to be extremely intelligent and at the top of his game in whatever field he chose. The second was that he had to be financially well-off, because for a long time I couldn't let go of the idea that I needed a man to take care of me.

The common thread running through all of my most intimate relationships was that the men in my life were controlling, perhaps because I felt on some level that I "needed" to be controlled. In exchange, I made it my responsibility to please the other person and make him happy. Since I typically chose intense and often depressed men, this was quite a formidable task, but I wouldn't let myself be deterred from trying.

My resentment would kick in when it became clear that I couldn't make my partner happy. That's when I would start to realize just how unhappy I was in that particular relationship. I would try to communicate what I was feeling, and the whole initial "contract" would blow up, because I was changing the rules. That would be my cue to exit—only to find the next boyfriend and start the same exhausting pattern all over again.

It wasn't much different with my women friends. I was

drawn to women who were bossy and controlling, because in my mind, that meant they must know better than I did about nearly everything. I deferred to them for advice, never believing that I actually had good intuition and the ability to logically solve problems myself. Ultimately, I would land in a place where I no longer felt wanted or needed, my own voice would start growing louder, and these friends and I would experience a falling out.

Yet, despite my quest to constantly take the backseat in relationships and let everyone else drive, my inner strength would surprise me by emerging when the going got really rough. Leaving my marriage was probably the most monumental example of this, but that core resolve showed up again and again in every subsequent relationship that I left before making a permanent commitment or being destroyed emotionally.

Going through the failure of my SoulCycle partnership was another wake-up call that things would have to change radically in my life. That experience demonstrated, among other things, that I had a lot of inner work to do if I was going to alter my go-to relationship dynamic in my love life, my friendships, and my career. First, I had to examine my decision-making process, until eventually I was able to start slamming on the brakes when something didn't feel right. This meant I had to focus acutely on one relationship in particular: the one I had with myself.

Once Flywheel started getting under way, I became consumed with building the business, and that pretty much replaced any need—or opportunity—to form relationships outside of work. I was incredibly lonely. Navigating through a weekend with no plans, vacationing alone, and going through entire days without so much as a text message or phone call were excruciating at times. With both of my parents gone, two estranged brothers at the time, and a social circle almost exclusively made up of couples, things got very rough.

For a time, my knee-jerk reaction was to reach out to ex-boyfriends. They were always there when I needed them. Eventually, however, I realized those relationships were leading me in circles and might even impede me from being open to someone who was actually right for me—the "new" me. Clearing that "shelf," as a therapist once called it, was a challenging process, but I did it.

I felt more alone than ever afterward. However, by then I had realized that change and growth could come only when I accepted the fact that I just had to sit with those feelings and not "do" anything. These were the moments when I truly started to work on my relationship with myself. I learned to use this time to do things that made me feel good, whether that meant going to a museum, taking a course, or having a bath. The choices we make often have significance down the road. Who knew that, when I decided to take a writing course years ago, I would choose a class in memoir writing? And now here I am, writing a book about my life.

You cultivate strength and confidence when you carve out some alone time. Sometimes being alone can even help you get to a place where you can be more open to hearing the truth from others. I'll never forget talking to Jay one day at the office, a couple of years into Flywheel, at a time when we were starting to feel successful. I had just seen a press piece about SoulCycle and I was reflecting on that partnership and how it had ended.

Jay listened as he always did, then made a suggestion: "Why don't you turn things around, and think about the fact that you started not only one successful business, but two?"

He was right. And, once I was able to own that idea, I felt incredibly empowered and started to build my self-esteem. As I continued to see Flywheel becoming more successful, I became better at feeling good about my accomplishments. It almost felt like a process of getting to know a different "me"— a woman who actually does have a lot of opinions, a wealth of knowledge, and an inner strength. When I look back on my past relationships, I can't imagine going back to any of them, and that feels really good. I'm where I'm supposed to be.

11

The Future of Flywheel

It took me over two years to arrive at a comfortable place in the "new" Flywheel. Gradually phasing out my participation in corporate meetings and top-level decision making was a tough process. I began by initiating several discussions with the "SLT," the Senior Leadership Team, through which I began the painful process of negotiating my new role at the company.

Why was this process such a struggle? Partly because it's always tempting to think you're being "weak" if other people seem to think you don't want to learn something new, or aren't learning fast enough. I second-guessed myself many times whenever people in this new, corporate iteration of Flywheel asked me to take on new company responsibilities that I didn't want to shoulder.

Gradually, however, I realized that just because my new colleagues at Flywheel—Lew, in particular—wanted to alter and add on to my role at the company, that didn't necessarily make it the right career path for me. While I certainly appreciated Lew's confidence in me and his desire to expand my skill set, I had reached an age where I knew myself well. I'd had various experiences that had tested my courage and my integrity, and I had passed those tests. I was strong and knew what made me happy. I had a solid understanding of my own strengths and the sort of work I enjoyed. I also knew what sorts of things made me miserable.

This wasn't a question of me not "wanting" to take on responsibilities. Rather, it was a deliberate choice I made about my career and my future role at the company. After initially agreeing to participate in so many meetings, I discovered that all of the time I was spending in conference rooms was taking me away from where I could make the biggest impact: in the Flywheel stadiums around the country, promoting the business. All I had to do was articulate these things with confidence.

The bottom line was that Flywheel still felt like *my* company. I had helped build it, and I wanted to stay and help Flywheel grow—but on my own terms.

During each of my meetings with the SLT, I was asked to answer various questions as they tried to decide what to do with me: "What will make you happy, Ruth? What do you want your job to be? Where do you belong?"

Together, we worked through this phase, assessing and refining my role. I felt nervous talking about my own strengths and what role I wanted to play. I certainly didn't want to say anything that might jeopardize my future at Flywheel. Nor did I want to set myself up for responsibilities I would later regret assuming.

However, as I grew more comfortable with this new team and began articulating my needs clearly, I discovered that I could advocate for myself. I knew exactly what responsibilities I wanted to keep and which ones I wanted to jettison.

Through this process, I was startled to discover how much more assertive I had become about expressing my opinions without equivocating or doubting myself. One day, for example, our head of human resources asked me to meet with her and an instructor we needed to terminate. Going into the meeting, I had thought I would let her handle things. That had always been my typical mindset in the past, a product of my nonconfrontational personality and laid-back managerial style. This time, however, I found that I didn't want to let HR handle things completely. I wanted—no, I *needed*—to speak my mind about this instructor's inappropriate behavior, and I did.

In another instance, I brought forth a suggestion that I knew was counter to Lew's plans for Flywheel's growth. He had made a blanket statement about our expansion strategy, deciding that new Flywheel studios should be located only in major urban locations because some of our suburban studios had struggled in the past. For the most part, I thought this strategy made sense and agreed with him.

However, every summer I received many requests from people who rode with us in the Hamptons to open a Flywheel studio on Long Island, specifically in the Roslyn–Great Neck area where I'd spent my childhood. Many of these riders lived in that area the rest of the year. I knew there was plenty of opportunity there for us.

I went straight to Lew and proposed the idea. "I would so appreciate you rethinking the suburban model when it comes to Roslyn," I said. "I think a studio would do really well there, and really believe it should be an exception to our expansion rule." I started listing all of the reasons a studio would be profitable in that area.

Lew listened closely, then nodded. "Okay," he said. "Let's look into that." We notified our real estate department of our new goal, and while it has been a challenge finding the right space, we are hopeful that we'll have a presence there eventually.

Ultimately, I have found my place in this newer, more corporate version of Flywheel by continuing to do the things I really love. My main focus has turned away from boardroom meetings and is once again on teaching seven or eight classes every week, training instructors, and traveling to teach in studios we've opened in other regions of the country. I also continue to assume the responsibilities that go along with being the face of the business and am proud to do so.

The Flywheel instructor team has continued to grow exponentially. We now have over four hundred instructors with five creative leads overseeing them in forty studios across the country. I'm responsible for working with the vice president of creative, who oversees the creative leads around the country. I also work with the creative leads here in New York and the other leads on-site in their regions. Whatever goes on within the "Flywheel Method" creatively still falls under my domain as creative director.

This means that I'm traveling about twice a month to different parts of the country. Every trip leaves me feeling exhausted. Yet whenever I visit a different studio and work on-site with Flywheel instructors and employees, I feel completely happy. I'm always gratified and reinvigorated by the positive impact Flywheel is making on people's lives.

As the face of the business, it is also a given that I am available for all press and PR opportunities. This role has increased over time as more and more companies promote their products by associating them with a certain lifestyle. It is particularly popular to link a product to a "Flywheel" kind of lifestyle: one that embraces life to the fullest and maintains health and wellness.

My first big press opportunity was with Sony during a digital ad campaign they created around "passion." Sony approached me because my passion for music and indoor cycling was so strong that it had led me to start two businesses. In addition, Sony is known for designing products for music lovers, and music plays an essential part in the Flywheel experience, as well as in my own life.

Filming for the Sony campaign took place in a generous loft space in downtown Manhattan. When I arrived, the production crew and director asked me to sit on a stool in the middle of a big room, where they interviewed me about my passion for indoor cycling and how I used music in my profession.

During the interview, I was surrounded by two dozen people and a lot of equipment. Although I felt pressured to give Sony what they wanted, I also experienced a certain level of comfort because of the years I've spent performing as a dancer and spin instructor. I've had a lot of audiences through the years.

Probably the most surreal moment of this campaign occurred when I was traveling uptown by bus and passed the imposing Sony building, with its floor-to-ceiling windows on Madison Avenue, and saw a poster of me that was about twenty feet tall. I probably texted a million people, saying, "Whoa, you won't believe what I just saw!"

Next, Porsche asked me to appear in their own passion-infused digital ad campaign. This time I flew to Chicago, where the filming took place in a stunning penthouse apartment in a luxury high-rise building. As I answered the interviewer's questions about how passion led me to start Flywheel, I found myself choking up as I spoke openly about my divorce and the struggles that had led me to discover indoor cycling and its therapeutic qualities. This company was part of me, no doubt about it.

Despite the fact that I'd gotten what I wanted, giving up control of Flywheel was difficult. I'm definitely a Type A personality who loves a challenge. Eventually, I talked to a person I truly respected, an established business professional, who gave me some sound advice that really helped my perspective.

"You've worked hard, Ruth," he said. "Try and relish the fact that you can sit back now and let other people do the heavy lifting."

Recently, I was strolling around Little Italy on a beautiful fall Saturday in New York. I was supposed to be teaching in Sag Harbor, but I had decided I needed a weekend off from traveling to recover from my various business trips. It was a perfect Saturday: nothing on the schedule, nowhere to be. A real rarity in my life.

As I window-shopped and watched the people streaming by me on the sidewalk, I was thinking about how days like this often reminded me of why I love New York City. Suddenly, I noticed a woman walking past me who personified "downtown hipster" by combining an "I don't care how I look" attitude with what I was sure were fabulously expensive clothes. She was extremely thin, with a shaggy blonde haircut, and looked too young to have a ten-year-old son riding on his skateboard alongside her.

Then I did a double take: that boy was wearing a hooded sweatshirt with the big SoulCycle wheel logo emblazoned across his back. My immediate gut reaction was regret that perhaps Flywheel just wasn't "cool" enough. Both the cool-looking mother and her son outfitted in SoulCycle gear caused a momentary flare-up of self-doubt. Had we taken Flywheel in the right direction? Should we have gone for a hipper vibe? Did we make a mistake?

Fortunately, I was able to quickly sweep that negative reaction away by focusing on Flywheel and what the brand means to me and the thousands of people who love the accountability provided by the metrics and the company's integrity. These people benefit from riding with us every day.

I continued walking. When I reached the C train on Spring Street, I descended to the uptown platform behind a young, happy-looking couple holding hands. Lo and behold, the guy was wearing a navy blue baseball cap backward, with the word "Fly" above the peak. Both he and his girlfriend were incredibly fit and personified all that is Flywheel: athleticism, authenticity, and a positive outlook. I smiled and headed home, feeling happily at peace.

. . .

When I reflect on how we branded SoulCycle early on, I realize that Julie did an amazing job with the SoulCycle brand right from the get-go. She always stayed on top of trends, from the camouflage pattern on SoulCycle's very first T-shirt to the skull and crossbones flanking everything from sweatpants to bandannas. She created a culture with this look, and people aspiring to join that community flocked to buy the gear.

It took us a long time at Flywheel to settle on our overall brand and visual ID. When we first started the business and people asked us to define our brand, we didn't have a ready answer. We figured it out along the way, and it all came together organically. What we landed on eventually was the result of a family of riders who loved simply exercising and sweating together, whether they were competing with each other or their personal bests, or simply closing their eyes while riding to an amazing playlist. We strive now to keep our identity as a fitness brand consistent.

There is room in the world for variety in every market, and it's no different in the world of boutique fitness. Over fifty-four million people in this country alone paid some sort of gym membership fee in 2014, a jump of nearly 19 percent since 2008. That's great news.

However, according to the Centers for Disease Control, over 70 percent of adults are overweight despite our new passion for fitness. I'm proud of Flywheel's ongoing efforts to promote health and wellness.

Not long ago, I flew to Los Angeles to film Flywheel's newest branding video with a company we had hired to head up our "at home" bike project. This company felt like they could significantly improve upon the video we were currently using.

When I arrived at our Woodland Hills studio for the filming, I was astounded to see how many people and how much equipment had been brought into the space. The filming was going to take place in the stadium and people were waiting for hair and makeup while the equipment was being set up. Others were filling out paperwork to be extras in the video, while wardrobe consultants decided what we would all wear. I stood there for a minute, marveling at the chaos, until someone greeted me.

From then on I was handled like a star. It all felt a bit surreal. Much of our Los Angeles staff from the other studios participated in the filming, and I realized there were many I hadn't met until that moment. Still, there was a feeling of warmth, as there always is whenever I meet Flywheel people across the country, with hugs beating out handshakes at every introduction. Much like our riders, Flywheel's employees shower me with gratitude for creating a company that has offered them the opportunity to love what they do every day.

Victor, our West Coast lead creative, arrived with me at 8:30 a.m., but it was clear that most people had come earlier. Within an hour, we were ready to start shooting. I got up on the instructor bike and the room filled with riders.

"So, Ruth, I want you to start as you would any class, with music and getting everyone motivated and energized through your words and riding," the director said. "Once you begin, we'll open the door, move closer in with the camera, and stop right in front of you. Right before the stop, I want you to bring the riders up out of the saddle, and tell them that you are all 'taking it to the next level.'"

That sounded easy enough, I thought, since that wasn't much different from what happens in a real class—minus the camera, of course. Still, I was nervous and self-conscious. I was acutely aware that I was not only a stranger here, but also a good deal older than most of the other riders being filmed.

Despite my professional success, when faced with an unfamiliar group, I always get hit by this familiar feeling of needing to prove myself—especially since I know people might have high expectations of me as an instructor, given that I started the company. I'm not sure I'll ever get over feeling anxious about appearing in front of a new audience. But maybe that's a good thing, because once the adrenaline kicks in, the fear typically disappears and I'm in my element.

There was just one problem on this particular day: filming required seventeen takes, and inspiring the group seventeen different times was no easy feat.

On top of that, halfway through the takes, the director eliminated the music, since they'd be inserting their own soundtrack into the video. Spinning without music isn't nearly as much fun; in fact, it can feel downright torturous. With every subsequent take, that much more energy was required from me to accomplish what the director wanted. I delivered what he asked, but the whole ordeal lasted two hours and I was sapped by the end of it.

A couple of guys from the production company told me I

was "probably" done but said I should stick around for a bit in case they needed anything else from me. I changed out of my sweat-drenched clothes and sat outside the studio, soaking up the California warmth and feeling like I'd accomplished something despite the fatigue.

We all broke for lunch. Filming resumed an hour later. Afterward, one of the directors informed me that they needed me to do one more take. So, at six o'clock, after everyone else had gone home, I climbed back on the bike and powered through another session of teaching and riding until they were happy with what they'd captured on film.

I went back to the hotel, showered, and dressed to meet friends for dinner. I could barely stay awake through the meal. Thinking about the fact that I was going to have to wake up the next morning and teach in our newest studio in Playa Vista almost brought me to tears. But I made it through dinner and crashed on the hotel bed after setting my alarm.

Thank God I was still on New York time. I woke early, edited my playlist, and arrived at the Playa Vista studio. This was my first trip to that studio and I was blown away. The recent improvements in Flywheel's studio design, sound system, tech offerings, and overall visual feel were readily apparent here, and it really hit me how far Flywheel had come as I walked through those studio doors.

With the company takeover and increased capital, we were able to institute some exciting changes along with our expansion plans. We were able to upgrade our studios, from the tech on the bikes and the sound systems to the actual studio design. We were able to hire a renowned branding agency to help us revisit and freshen our overall look, tweak our logo, and determine where we should make changes in the actual finishing touches inside the studio.

To accomplish this, we had numerous meetings with the branding team, during which they really dove deeply into determining the essence of Flywheel's core values. The team conducted interviews with me as well as with other employees representing different facets of the business.

One of the things we discussed was how, when David, Jay, and I initially opened the first Flywheel studio in the Flatiron district, we had created a look that was consistent with the Flatiron/industrial feel: steel beams above and darker finishes. After Lew came on board, our branding meetings ultimately led to a much cleaner look, more polished finishes, and a brighter and lighter feel for Flywheel's visuals. What we ended up with was much more welcoming and a bit less masculine—which made sense, given that our demographic was predominantly female.

The infusion of capital also allowed us to upgrade our sound systems, much to the delight of our instructors; this top-quality sound was made possible by using a more sophisticated system with an increased number of speakers. Volume is always an ongoing challenge in spin studios. Instructors typically err on the side of the music being too loud, while staying within safe noise levels so as not to upset our neighbors or endanger our hearing. With a more sophisticated sound system, we could now enjoy a fuller sound without having to play the music at an increased volume.

We were also able to make improvements on the tech side of the bike. We could actually program the bikes to greet riders in each class; their names appear on the tech packs, along with a countdown of minutes to the start of class. This sounds simple, but this feature really goes a long way, because our riders absolutely loved it.

In addition, we added features to the screen located next to the instructor bike that made it easier to operate. Our race feature, one of the most popular moments in the class, now had a countdown clock on the big screens in the front of the room. Alternating colors on the screen made it more visually exciting.

I took in all of these changes at the Playa Vista studio and reveled in the marvelous look and feel of everything. Even better, the staff greeted me with so much excitement that I felt energized all over again. Then the riders started filing into the studio and introducing themselves. They were equally enthusiastic, saying, "When we heard the founder of Flywheel was coming, we made sure we wouldn't miss it. We're so excited to take your class!"

People requested pictures before and after class. It was gratifying, once again, to hear everyone talk about how much pleasure Flywheel had brought to their lives. The energy in that studio was through the roof, and seeing the smiles on everyone's faces meant my job once again didn't feel at all like work—and that's the best kind of job to have.

One woman's story in particular stayed with me afterward. She was in her late fifties, a former soccer and basketball player who stopped working out after giving up her athletic career. She hated going to the gym and couldn't seem to motivate herself to exercise. Then she found Flywheel.

"It's the first form of exercise that has hooked me since my days as an athlete," she said.

She told me that, after she had committed to a regular schedule of Flywheel classes, one night her husband had looked at her and said, "You're alive again!"

The woman had tears in her eyes as she shared this, and so did I.

From the moment Julie, Elizabeth, and I made the decision to start SoulCycle, people questioned the longevity of indoor cycling. Even more baffling to me are the number of people out there who are still asking this same question.

The fitness workout "trend line" is definitely cyclical, moving over time from "hard-core" to "Zen/mind-body" and back again, but the one modality that seems like it covers both and will always be popular is indoor cycling. After spinning came on the scene, it experienced a bit of a lull in the early 2000s, but it wasn't long before people began migrating back to this form of exercise.

I personally never doubted its value. I always believed spinning was here for good. Most people with busy, stressful schedules appreciate the efficiency of the workout, as well as the mind-body aspect of this particular form of exercise, as soon as they try it.

Another important, enduring selling point is the safety of a spinning workout. According to the Administration on Aging, people ages sixty-five and older currently represent about one out of every seven people in the United States. By 2060, there will be about ninety-eight million people over sixty-five, more than twice the number in 2014. Among this rapidly aging population are runners and other athletes who can continue to stay fit through spinning, even if their knees or hips are compromised by years of impact. Even people who have never exercised can start spinning at any age because it's a safe workout.

Spinning has always been an equal-opportunity brand of fitness, too. It's a popular workout for men and women of all ages. Another reason we're confident that Flywheel and other top-quality boutique fitness brands will continue to thrive is because our customer acquisition strategy is less about taking customers from each other and more about exposing people to the benefits of boutique fitness and the communities that thrive within the sector.

What's more, the community that forms around each spinning studio, seemingly a byproduct of the classes, becomes almost as important as the exercise itself, if not more. People of all generations enjoy participating together and spinning is a great bonding activity for families. It doesn't really require any experience or much coordination, and riders can pace themselves according to their own needs.

The concept of "community" that comes so naturally to Flywheel and SoulCycle is incredibly powerful. That's very hard to achieve if you don't have a brand and a business that truly stands for something. "Real"—which I define as honest and authentic—is an overused word these days, but in environments that feel "real" to consumers there is a tremendous brand loyalty. Too many new fitness brands that have come on the scene in the last few years have ridden a wave of popularity but have ultimately failed because they didn't have anything "real" to offer. When Flywheel came on the scene, we were able to differentiate ourselves easily with our tech pack and its impact on results, making the Flywheel brand recognizable for its athleticism and authenticity. With different types of spinning studios, the world of indoor cyclists now offers a variety of choices. Rather than one brand "winning" over others, people have become drawn and loyal to the method they prefer.

At Flywheel, we are continuing to expand our product development and offer an array of classes that will invite variation, but the core method will always remain the same. Currently we're focusing our expansion efforts on two fronts: adding new studios within the country and creating an at-home product.

Finally, I have to add that I am especially proud of the preponderance of women who have become so prevalent in the fitness industry, either as founders or senior leaders.

Boutique fitness is always on the "trend curve," and women are generally the first movers and the innovators. If you look at all of the top boutique businesses, the vast majority of them were founded by women: Payal Kadakia, the founder and artistic director of the Sa Dance Company, is also the founder and CEO of ClassPass, the successful fitness membership start-up; Vanessa Packer is the co-founder of modelFIT, a company offering nutrition and fitness classes and one-on-one personal training sessions; Michelle Davidson has made a success of Pure Barre; Jennifer Maanavi and Tanya Becker have created another very successful barre method concept with Physique 57; and Leanne Shear is the co-founder of the women-only Uplift studio brand. I could go on, but the point is that women have laid the foundation for the boutique fitness industry and will continue to be leaders and innovators in the field, not just with the workouts, but with clothing, editorial websites, apps, and many other essential aspects of the fitness business.

Lesson #21: Learn to Delegate So You Can Do More of What You Love

When you're building a business, probably one of the most difficult—but important—tasks ahead of you is carving out enough free time for yourself so that you can refresh, reset, and be that much more productive when you get back to work. If you own the business, you become habituated to the 24/7 lifestyle. You probably have too few employees for you to delegate much of the work, so you become accustomed to having a hand in every aspect of the business. You hit the ground running every morning, work through lunch, and fall asleep with your mind still reeling as you consider the next day's to-do list.

As you expand your team, it's essential to delegate responsibilities and trust that others can successfully handle them. This keeps you from burning out *and* helps build your business. As I did with Flywheel, you need to decide where your strengths lie, what skills you want to learn or keep honing, and which responsibilities frankly make you yawn. Make lists of these things and put them in three categories: things you definitely want to do, things you can do if nobody else is around, and the things you absolutely don't want to tackle. Then hire or train your employees according to those lists.

When we get stuck thinking that we are the only ones who can "do it right," we limit not only ourselves, but our entrepreneurial endeavors. Put your ego aside. Allow yourself to recognize that other people have strengths you lack and trust them to fill in the gaps as you scale your business model.

12

Karma Comes to Those Who Wait

From the moment I started to teach spin classes, it has been a growth process. For me, teaching is like dancing: I never arrive at an endpoint because I'm always learning something new.

Now that I have celebrated my sixtieth birthday, I'm a much more confident instructor, especially when it comes to the things I say in class. I put more time and emphasis on the messages and emotions I convey to my riders, and I think that because I'm older people are more apt to listen.

Most of my messaging is centered on helping people learn how to be patient and forgiving, especially with themselves. I know from experience that it's a tough world out there. We all face challenges. I love knowing that within the short span of forty-five minutes, I can often transform a rider's mood by giving her a different perspective on life, as well as empowering her with the physical and mental strength to overcome whatever hurdles she's currently facing.

No matter how much my teaching methods have changed

throughout the years, my ultimate goal—and hope—has always remained the same: that as people ride with me, they will discover how important it is to learn how to make themselves happy, rather than rely on others to do it for them. This is a message that comes from my heart because this is where my own path has led me.

As Flywheel grows, my corporate role might continue to evolve, but my integrity and belief in this exercise as a passionate mind-body workout that can help people transform their own lives will remain constant. I'm reminded of that often, no matter where I am, whether I'm teaching riders or training instructors.

One of these unforgettable exchanges happened this past year, when a woman I'd never met approached me after I finished teaching a class on the Upper West Side. This woman proceeded to tell me that it was her fiftieth birthday. She then shared why it was such a significant birthday for her: both of her parents died in their fifties, and she was never confident that she would make it this far in her life.

As if that weren't enough, "I got the highest total score ever today!" the woman added joyfully.

Aside from being so moved by what that particular rider shared with me, on that day I had yet more proof that Flywheel—a ride with metrics—gives people the power to change their lives. Being able to constantly monitor her stats meant this woman had been inspired to keep pushing toward accomplishing this wonderful and meaningful achievement, to keep fighting to achieve her own personal best.

Perhaps less dramatic, but equally impressive, was an encounter I had with a woman who was leaving our Flywheel studio at Lincoln Square. When she saw me leaving at the same time, this woman said, "Ruthie, Ruthie, Ruthie!"

I had never met her, but I stopped to greet her, immediately drawn in by the woman's obvious warmth and the humor sparkling in her eyes.

"Today is my birthday, and I have always hated my birthday," the woman said, "but starting the day with your class just made me love my birthday for the first time. You turned things around for me. It's the first time I'm actually excited about this day."

I immediately gave the woman a hug and felt so happy for her, because I know how difficult birthdays can be for all of us. Even as adults, we have echoes of the same expectations we had as children—hoping to receive presents, cakes, and endless adoration on our birthdays. We're always bound to be disappointed unless we take it upon ourselves to make our birthdays special. If I can help someone do that, my job is well done. This particular woman did it for herself just by showing up for class.

More recently, I was teaching on the day after Thanksgiving and thinking about someone I knew who had just lost one of her oldest, closest friends to a rare form of cancer at age forty. It was the time of year we were all supposed to be reflecting on what we're grateful for, and I knew she was simply trying to wrap her head around the fact that this life, this precious person, was taken away from us far too soon. What could I do to help her?

As we rode, I began talking to everyone in that class about all of the things that happen in life that don't seem to make sense. I pointed out that, at the end of the day, all we can do is keep going. This means we must constantly strengthen ourselves so that we can handle the hardships that come our way when we least expect them.

Afterward, a woman came up to me and told me how much my class had helped her that day. "It's not even about the workout and how it affects my body," she said. "It's about what it does for my head and my feelings about myself. I feel like a different person at the end of the ride. It's my therapy."

I smiled at her. "I know exactly what you mean."

Despite my ongoing connection to Flywheel instructors and riders and my continued passion for spinning, sometimes I walk into my office and still feel like I'm dreaming.

When Jay, David, and I started Flywheel, we economized as much as possible. We were scrappy entrepreneurs whose office was an old electrical closet. Now, in keeping with Flywheel's status as a major company, Lew has built new offices on 23rd Street between Fifth and Sixth Avenues. The offices were completed in 2016 and occupy the length of a city block. They're so vast, in fact, that the first time John Wellman, our national director of training, visited, he laughed and said, "Is this Verizon?"

I still don't feel completely at home here in this corporate atmosphere. I miss our old gritty atmosphere and the excitement of not knowing what will happen next. Instead of working with my Flywheel family, I am always acutely aware of how many complex moving pieces—and people—it takes to run a company this size.

At the same time, whenever I walk into my corner office,

with its comfortable black leather couch creating a separate seating area, I marvel at how far I have come. I know how lucky I am, since a recent survey by Catalyst, a nonprofit that tracks gender parity in the workplace, revealed that women still occupy only about 4 percent of corner offices at S&P 500 companies and hold only 25 percent of executive or senior-level jobs in those same firms. My new Flywheel office serves as a daily symbol of my professional success.

So do my continued opportunities to represent the company. Recently, for instance, I had another spectacular opportunity to promote Flywheel. I took on this opportunity despite having to travel in the summer.

While traveling to Flywheel's different studios across the country is an important part of what I do, I generally use the summers to recoup and to be available as an instructor in the Hamptons. I covet this block of time when I don't have to get on an airplane or train, and cherish the time I spend on the eastern end of Long Island. The farmland meets the ocean here, and neither the views nor the lighting ever get old. I love to teach spinning against that incredible backdrop to people who come to the Hamptons from all over the world. Because everyone there is in vacation mode—typically on break from high-powered lives—they want to take care of themselves and kick back. This brings a great energy to the classes. There is a lot of hooting and hollering, and it's just *fun*.

However, as the summer of 2016 was coming to an end, I received a call from Jake with an offer I couldn't refuse. Pantene was in the process of launching their new line of ProV shampoos. The premise behind this product was that it was important to "fuel" your hair rather than just shampoo it.

When "fueling," you are actually replacing nutrients in the hair to build strength and shine, while "shampooing" implied stripping away dirt and oils without replacing the good stuff.

With this concept in mind, the Pantene executives realized what a great idea it would be to partner with Flywheel, since ours is a fitness company that centers on fueling the body and mind, thereby building strength and confidence. When the Pantene representatives asked if I'd be willing to participate and be one of the faces in their national ad campaign, I loved their concept and jumped at the opportunity.

When I told everyone what I was going to do, their first question was always the same: "Are you going to flip your hair around like those models do on the commercials?"

Apparently I was. A few days after getting the call from Pantene, I was on a plane to Los Angeles, where I had to wake up at five o'clock in the morning the next day and spend seven straight hours shooting the commercial on the Hollywood movie set where they had just filmed *Star Wars*. There was so much happening, with so little notice, that it was hard for me to prepare for this, or to even process it all in real time.

Let's start with the fact that I had my makeup done by Beyoncé's makeup artist, and my hair done by Cher's stylist. Cher had some really good hair days, and with her stylist's expertise, my hair never looked better. I also had a handler who stayed with me every step of the way. When I went to wardrobe, I was able to choose my outfit from an entire rack of beautiful designer clothes.

On the set, I had to repeat the same lines over and over

Preparing for the Pantene shoot

again, so that they would have enough to choose from. For the second half of the shoot I had to dump my head in a bucket of cold water and make a big splash as I whipped my head up from the bucket, spraying water everywhere. Can you imagine the absurdity of that? Two hours of work, resulting in perfect hair, only to have me dump my head in a *bucket*?

When it was all over, I had to rush to catch my plane, where I eventually fell fast asleep despite my wet head of hair. It was all worth it, though: the ad aired five months later, and I got more social media hits than I've ever received.

To date, my highest honor has been my invitation to participate in a new series on both PBS and the BBC entitled *Breaking Big*. This twelve-episode series from the digital publisher Ozy explores how some of the world's most influential artists, innovators, athletes, and leaders have gotten their big breaks.

I was delighted to be interviewed for the series by Carlos Watson, who has interviewed a wide variety of luminaries, including Barack Obama. A crew came out to my Sag Harbor house to speak with me there, and our conversation continued on camera during a walk along the Bay and on the beach. Part two of my interview was filmed in a Flywheel studio in New York City to highlight how teaching spin has been such an integral part of my personal and professional story.

The series will air nationally and internationally. This is yet one more experience that I never could have imagined being a part of my life; once again, I had to pinch myself to make sure I was fully awake.

As fun and exciting as it is to have a wonderful office, to continue doing the teaching and training I love, and to represent Flywheel to the world, there is still nothing else in my life that serves as a better symbol of success to me than my house in Sag Harbor.

No matter how far I've come from my days with Julie and Elizabeth, my Sag Harbor house is located in such close proximity to that house on High Street where Julie, her family, and I lived together during SoulCycle's first summer in the Hamptons in 2007 that I can't help thinking about them occasionally. Havens Beach, a quiet beach on the Bay, is walking distance from my house, and the road I follow to get there passes our old rental.

For years, I walked by that place on the way to the beach. Each summer, the rental house grew more dismal and dilapidated looking, until it literally seemed to be sinking into itself. The paint faded and chipped off the clapboards. The unkempt hedges bordering the front lawn grew bigger and more gnarly in shape with each passing year. Seeing it that way used to make me feel sad.

Gradually, however, more time passed, during which I was striving to make Flywheel a success. Finally, this past summer, I strolled by that old rental again, and was shocked to see that it had been demolished. A new house was going up in its place. This transition seems symbolic of my own transformation and reinvention, and I was happy to see it.

Recently, we celebrated my daughter Kate's wedding. She is deeply in love and I couldn't be happier for her. What makes me even prouder is that I have raised both Kate and Rachel to believe that no matter how much you love someone, the most important person you need to be able to rely on is yourself. That self-reliance can come only from the trial and error of putting yourself out in the world, taking risks, failing, and learning how to be resilient.

Though I struggled financially at times, ultimately I'm glad to serve as a personal and career role model for my daughters, as well as for the many young women I've mentored throughout my career. Because I have experienced great success in business, I hope to demonstrate to my daughters and other young women that they can be professionally successful, too, if they so choose.

When I think about my own goals for the future, one of my final frontiers is to find the right person with whom I can move forward and share my life experiences. I am satisfied with my professional accomplishments. I enjoy my career and socializing with friends. However, while I have been, and will always continue to be, a mother first, my girls are older and living more independently. I am freer than I have been in decades and it would be nice to share life experiences with someone special.

I have had a long career journey that certainly had its challenges as well as its wonderful moments. In addition, I have worked on my emotional life through therapy, a painful process of peeling away the layers and developing a keener self-awareness over the course of many, many years. Part of my own personal journey involved leaving my marriage so that I could get to know myself more fully. Now, at long last, I feel ready to be an equal in a loving personal relationship, just as I have learned how to hold my own in professional partnerships.

It has been a long road, one pitted with the shards of various relationships that splintered and failed. Those failed relationships were painful. However, as with my experiences in business, they helped me learn how to recognize my patterns and what I truly need from a partner. Probably the most important lesson I've learned so far is that now that I have finally found my voice, I will never again be with someone who only hears his own.

A couple of summers ago, for instance, I met a man at a party and became involved with him. It didn't take long for me to realize that he fully fit the description of my usual go-to choice in men: narcissistic, controlling, and capable of demonstrating only fleeting moments of empathy for others. In the past, I stayed in relationships with men like that because they provided the perfect vehicle for me to defer my own needs or even subsume them entirely. I'm happy to say that I recognized the pattern and ended the relationship quickly, rather than trying to "fix" things or engage in the frustrating process of "making" him happy for years.

This pattern isn't one I have followed only with men in the past, but with female friends as well. I have sought out opinionated, aggressive women as my companions, looking to them for advice through the years. Now that I've gotten to know myself better, I have reached a point where I feel comfortable speaking out whenever I need to express my differences with someone, so that these friendships—which historically would have ended in a falling-out, or even a traumatic breakup—can often withstand our differences.

With time, I have learned to develop relationships with wonderful friends who know how to listen to others, and who celebrate me because I can celebrate myself. If there are times I don't agree with them, I say so, and if I don't want to go along with a plan, I don't. It has been incredibly liberating.

Something has shifted in me. I no longer thrive on being needed. Nor do I have to feed my own self-confidence by knowing that someone else—whether that person is a man in my life or a woman friend—has put me on a pedestal.

Recently, someone asked if I would like to be set up on a date. The word on this guy was that he was successful, very nice, and a gentleman, so I thought, "Why not?"

"Nice" wasn't always a word I typically used to describe past boyfriends, so I thought I should give "that" a try. Here is what I learned: there is something really *nice* about "nice." There's also something really nice about being treated as an equal.

The best thing of all? This person didn't seem to "need" me to be happy. He respected everything about who I was and not only admired my independence, but encouraged it. Just as important to me was that I respected this man and his independence in return.

I knew that, if I hadn't heard from this man within a certain time frame, he was busy. In fact, I was no longer even aware of a time frame! On the flip side, if we made a plan and I had to be late, or even had to cancel the plan because of some unforeseen complication, this guy always seemed to understand and told me it was okay.

After we had been seeing each other for a while, I invited my new companion to a big party where he wasn't going to know anyone. He happily accepted and, completely unsolicited, assured me that I wouldn't have to worry about him not knowing anyone, and that he would be fine on his own at any point. Wow.

Could a relationship really be this easy?

Maybe so. A girlfriend once told me that when you meet a good match, you will know it, because relationships don't always have to be difficult. I am finally beginning to understand—and accept—the truth of this. It's incredibly freeing and gratifying to share experiences with a companion without also feeling the tension of wanting to constantly please that person.

I have no idea what will happen with this particular relationship, but in many ways it doesn't even matter. I am able to appreciate and enjoy him in the present because of my own new and hard-won independence. It certainly took a lot of time and work to build it, but boy, was it worth it. These days, I no longer feel that I *have* to be with a partner. I simply *want* to be—but only if it's the right person. I no longer need someone to make me feel validated because I can do that for myself. I am finally owning my accomplishments and fully embracing my life and all of the opportunities that come my way because of my entrepreneurship.

Some of these opportunities still amaze me, like my recent invitation to the White House Christmas party. Years ago, I might have earned this invite through one of my former boyfriends who gave sizable contributions to the Democratic Party. Or I might have been invited through Philippe, thanks to his extremely close ties to the Clintons.

No, I was invited to the White House because of the work *I* have done. I created my own opportunity through my business associations.

Years ago, we hired Moki Media, a PR team based in Washington, DC, to help us with our two Flywheel studios there. Moki maintains a significant presence in DC and I had participated in some of the events they had organized to promote our company.

This past fall, I traveled to DC and had lunch at Moki, during which they told me about their annual invites to the White House Christmas parties. This year, they promised to land me an invite as well.

"Really?" I asked, thinking I shouldn't get too worked up about the possibility, since this didn't sound like an easy promise to keep.

I forgot about the conversation until the day I received a call from Dania Hakki, Moki's co-founder. "Are you sitting down?" she asked.

"Yes," I replied.

"We want to formally invite you to the last Christmas party under the Obama administration," she said, adding, "It's next Friday."

I think I might have actually let out a scream, followed by a practical question: "What should I wear?"

The experience of attending that party was thrilling, if a little surreal, starting with having to go through the intense security process as we approached the White House. From the first step I took into the East Wing, I was awed by the grandeur. On our way inside, we were greeted by two nearly twelve-foot-tall stuffed replicas of Bo and Sunny, the Obamas' dogs, as we were serenaded by a choir singing Christmas carols. Framed photographs of the Obamas hung on the walls, depicting a family that was real and that we can all relate to, yet that also deserved to be honored as royalty. The Christmas decorations were so gorgeous that I couldn't help but wonder how many people it had taken to install them all.

Once we were inside the White House, I could actually roam around and see all of the rooms at my own leisure. I felt like I was dreaming as I wandered past portraits of former presidents and first ladies in a long corridor, then toured the Library and the Green Room. Decorated Christmas trees ornamented every room.

Eventually people began gathering by the podium where President Obama was scheduled to appear for a brief speech. I deliberately went early to secure a spot near the president, who descended from the residence upstairs and was as personable and charming as could be. I even got to say hello and shake hands with him.

I will always remember the honor of being invited to this party. One of my favorite souvenirs of that night was a picture I took, posed in front of the largest, most beautiful Christmas tree in the White House. I posted it proudly on Instagram and that photograph definitely ranks as one of my most popular pics.

The last White House Christmas party under the
Obama administration

Recently, a pair of eager young entrepreneurs asked me for advice about their fledgling business. Hearing this young couple's dreams for the future caused me to reflect on my own journey. I never in a million years pictured myself arriving at a point in my life where I would be a successful entrepreneur with the confidence and ability to help others.

Yet here I am, in a position to reach out to others not only one-on-one, but through public appearances. In addition to commercials for various products, I have appeared on *Fox Business News* to talk about the current trends in boutique fitness and on panels of business experts at various events.

Today, as the proud founding partner of two national fitness brands, I can offer this important message: it is possible to follow your heart to success. It hasn't always been an easy ride for me. In this book, I have shared my journey's low points as well as what incredible joy comes from achieving and then surpassing your professional goals, especially when it comes on the heels of thinking you've been outgunned by your rivals.

From branding to customer service, from protecting yourself legally to speaking confidently in boardrooms, from training employees to handling media nightmares, I have earned a hands-on business education in the trenches. Now I've passed these lessons on to you.

Lesson #22: You're Stronger Than You Know

People often comment on how "strong" I am. This used to surprise me. I have always been strong physically, thanks to my early career in dance and my passion later for aerobics and spinning, but the truth is that I had very little confidence as a girl and a young woman. If you had asked me if I was "strong," I would have said no.

In retrospect, I understand that I was stronger than I realized. In dance class, you are always striving, trying to perfect your technique enough to move on to the next level. My years of dance training not only taught me to work hard, but also gave me practice in being persistent and resilient—essential skills both in business and in life.

My choice to start psychotherapy when my father was dying, rather than medicate myself with alcohol, pills, overzealous exercise, or some other unhealthy alternative, took a great deal of strength. Leaving my marriage took moral courage. So did reinventing myself over and over again: when one career move didn't work out, when I left SoulCycle, when I created Flywheel, and when I had to decide what role I wanted to play at Flywheel when the leadership and direction of the company changed drastically.

As I reflect on the path I've taken, I realize it was my inner strength that got me here. That knowledge has translated into a new and remarkable sense of power.

Like me, you've probably had life experiences that have given you valuable skills. Take a few minutes to list them. Maybe even write them down. Say, "I am strong because." That will help you feel more confident.

Finally, remember that no one else feels totally confident, either. We all have those voices of doubt inside us, those people who told us we'd never make it. The difference between successful people and everyone else is that successful people, at some point, tune those voices out and just take the leap. So figure out when you're ready to take yours. Look at everything you have accomplished, tap into your own power, and use it to your advantage. You are already strong—the next experience, whatever it is, will only make you stronger.

Conclusion

Before publishing this book, I showed the manuscript to several people. Due to the open and authentic voice I used in telling my story—the only voice I know how to use— one advance reader expressed discomfort with my willingness to openly share so many moments of vulnerability. This person also reminded me of all of the people who look up to me, and insinuated that my reputation would be affected negatively if those people read this book. He asked if I really wanted to take that risk, and even suggested at one point that I might want to rework the book to make it "all positive."

I thought about this. In fact, there was a part of me that actually reconsidered whether I should publish this book at all. What if I rock the boat and make people unhappy?

But the truth is that I relish having arrived at a place where I have so much to share. And who would want to read a book that's all happy anyway? That's not a book about real life.

I reminded myself of what it seems like I was put on this earth to do: to inspire others by sharing all of the lessons I have learned through times of both crippling pain and exhilaration. My story is one about starting from a place of extreme vulnerability and low self-esteem, and taking an unexpected path to victory in so many ways.

In fact, being able to tell a story *without* being embarrassed about sharing the weaker times in my life is one of the most significant examples of the kind of strength I have today. I put a lot of effort into not judging myself or others. This isn't always easy. We all have our own ways of navigating through life, and we all make mistakes along the way.

For all of you out there who don't yet have the strength to be vulnerable or to face your own truths, whatever they may be, I am trying to do it for you, or to at least open the door, whether it's through my story or while I'm on the bike. The gratification I get from being a source of inspiration for the riders and now, hopefully, for readers, will always be immeasurable.

Maybe you have a fresh, exciting business idea that keeps you up nights, but you lack the confidence to pursue it. Or maybe you're already a seasoned entrepreneur, but right now you're struggling with failure or financial challenges.

Perhaps you're not interested in owning a business at all, but simply looking for ways to move forward after a difficult personal challenge, like a divorce or the death of a loved one, or you're stalled in your profession and don't know how to find a new passion and reinvent yourself.

To all of you, I want to say this: I succeeded. You can, too.

Even without a traditional business background, an MBA, or a boardroom skill set, you can find success doing work you love. And even when others don't believe in you, if you believe in yourself and keep moving forward, you will turn your dreams into reality, one pedal stroke at a time.